# To Benin and Back

**Front cover photo:** My neighbors hanging out at their family housing compound preparing palm nuts to make red palm oil used for cooking.

# To Benin and Back

*Short Stories, Essays, and Reflections About Life in Benin as a Peace Corps Volunteer and the Subsequent Readjustment Process.*

## Chris Starace

iUniverse, Inc.
Bloomington

**To Benin and Back**
**Short Stories, Essays, and Reflections About Life in Benin as a Peace Corps Volunteer and the Subsequent Readjustment Process.**

*iUniverse books may be ordered through booksellers or by contacting:*

*iUniverse*
*1663 Liberty Drive*
*Bloomington, IN 47403*
*www.iuniverse.com*
*1-800-Authors (1-800-288-4677)*

*Because of the dynamic nature of the Internet, any web addresses or links contained in this book may have changed since publication and may no longer be valid. The views expressed in this work are solely those of the author and do not necessarily reflect the views of the publisher, and the publisher hereby disclaims any responsibility for them.*

*ISBN: 978-1-4620-4621-8 (sc)*
*ISBN: 978-1-4620-4622-5 (hc)*
*ISBN: 978-1-4620-4623-2 (ebk)*

*Printed in the United States of America*

*iUniverse rev. date: 10/26/2011*

# CONTENTS

**4. The Bush Taxi Ride from Hell** ...............................................................106

When you do not have your own car in Benin, bush taxis are usually your only option for long trips. They are always adventure filled experiences to say the least. I recount my harrowing trip from Djougou to Allada.

**5. A Visit to Melissa** ...............................................................126

# PREFACE:

I served in Benin, West Africa, located between Togo and Nigeria, as a Peace Corps Volunteer from 1995-1997. As many volunteers do, I began my adventure a few months after graduating from college at the age of 22. While in Benin I lived in a town named Allada as a small business development trainer and consultant. Allada is a small town of about 10,000 people, located on the main north-south paved road about 35 miles north of Cotonou, the economic capital of Benin. It was an incredible adventure living there for over two years at the same economic level as the people I was there to serve. I made many Beninese friends and I saw other Americans at least every few weeks. Nonetheless, I felt very isolated due to the vast cultural differences between the Beninese and myself.

I was in Benin from 1995-1997, and this collection of stories and essays is based on my experiences during those years, aside from the last chapter, "Seven Years Later," which was set in 2004 when I returned with my wife for a two week visit. I organized the chapters more or less by chronological order. It has taken me fourteen years to write and publish this book, as I've only had time to work on it in fits and starts. I had many distractions, such as readjusting to life in the U.S., getting a master's degree, establishing a career as a high school French and Spanish teacher, getting married, buying an old house, fixing it up, and having two children. In those fourteen years, many things have changed in Benin. Today there are more paved roads, technology and media available. There are more TV stations, radio stations, and newspapers. Cell phone usage has exploded, and even the poorest Beninese people use them since they use prepaid phones. Today, internet cafés are in every city, as well as most large towns in Benin. Due to these many changes the Benin I describe based on my experiences from 1995-1997 and 2004 is not exactly the same Benin as today.

## My Source of Inspiration:

While I was in Benin, my best friend was my journal. I wrote over 2,000 pages during my two plus years there, during my readjustment period after returning to the United States, and finally during my trip back to Benin after having been back in the U.S. for seven years. This book is a collection of my most interesting stories, anecdotes, reflections, essays, excerpts from my journal and cultural observations. When it comes to West Africa, I believe truth is unequivocally more entertaining than fiction.

I felt compelled to write this memoir because I had such a unique experience that relatively few others have ever had. Many people have little understanding of what it is like to live in a very poor West African country on $6 a day, in a village, for two years. I try to paint a picture of what it is like, and I show how it is possible to adapt to a culture that is very different than one's own. I hope it will make you see your own culture from a different perspective, and I hope it leads you to question certain cultural practices and beliefs you take for granted, just as I did when I returned home from Benin.

Most people have a very negative image of Africa, as they know little about it aside from the overwhelmingly depressing stories they hear about in the news. When covering Africa, the media usually reports on things such as poverty, epidemics, war, natural disasters, and famine, so we are naturally biased and think that Africa is inferior, undesirable, backwards, and violent. On the other side of the spectrum, for many reasons, we as Americans often hear that our country is the best place in the world. As an American, I agree that we have much to be proud of, but obviously not every aspect of life in the United States is the best. It may seem ironic, but we have a lot to learn from this small, little known, impoverished country, and I hope you will find examples of this.

Despite my many frustrations, ordeals, and suffering while there, overall my experience in Benin was very positive, and I maintain a very favorable opinion of the country as a whole. I included many details about how it was difficult living in Benin, as Peace Corps Volunteers endure many hardships and frustrations. I also included positive aspects of living there, but it wasn't until after I returned to the U.S. that I became fully aware of the many positive aspects I had overlooked previously. I explore many of the positive aspects of life in Benin in the last two chapters: "A

Stranger in my Old Life" and "Seven Years Later." After reading this book, I hope you will have a greater appreciation and respect for Benin and the Beninese people despite its many shortcomings.

Lastly, I hope "To Benin and Back" will inspire you to step out of your comfort zone and explore other cultures that are very different from your own. You cannot do this by staying in all-inclusive resorts, going on cruises or beach vacations, or by taking bus tours to popular tourist destinations. Your experience doesn't have to be as extreme as spending two years as a Peace Corps Volunteer in a developing country living on a shoestring budget, but it should include a lot of interaction with local people who do not make a living off of tourism. Making at least some effort to speak to the people in their language and experiencing an authentic cultural event are also crucial. Of course, you must travel with an open mind and be able to suspend judgment. It is amazing how much you can learn and grow when you challenge yourself to truly understand another culture.

Keep in mind, that I spent most of my time in a small town and in remote villages so my generalizations are based mostly on those environments. There is a very small Beninese middle class and most of them are government employees as the private sector is still very underdeveloped. There is also an even smaller, educated, westernized upper class in Benin that lives for the most part in Benin's larger cities. Most generalizations I make do not refer to the upper and middle classes as they are much more westernized than the rest of the Beninese.

## How Technology Has Changed the Peace Corps Experience Today:

An important aspect of my experience as a Peace Corps Volunteer was being relatively isolated from the United States, which forced me to immerse myself in the Beninese culture. I saw my postmate, the other Peace Corps Volunteer (PCV) posted in my town, usually once a week, and occasionally I would travel to see other PCV's who were posted in other parts of Benin. I received one prearranged phone call from my parents on a monthly basis at a Beninese friend's house who had a phone. Every few months when I was in Cotonou, I would see other volunteers. Sometimes while there, I went to the American Recreation Center that was tied to the American Embassy. There, I hung out with other American expats, usually embassy employees, ate hamburgers, and watched American TV via satellite on a big screen TV in an air conditioned room. Other than that, my only other connections to the U.S. were letters which I cherished, an occasional care package, and my short-wave radio. All PCV's also had a subscription to "Newsweek" magazine provided by Peace Corps. The magazine wasn't mailed to Allada, so I received multiple back issues only every 4-6 weeks when I went to Cotonou. The isolation from the U.S. was difficult, but ultimately I was grateful for it because it forced me to delve into the local culture instead of escaping from it.

Today's Peace Corps Volunteers have a different experience than I did from 1995-1997 due to the availability of the internet and cell phones in Benin. Current Peace Corps Volunteers have informed me that almost every volunteer today has a cell phone that they use at their posts on a regular basis. They use them to text other PCV's and they even text and receive texts from the Peace Corps administration. Many PCV's receive calls from and make calls to the U.S. several times a month. Some volunteers even have internet enabled cell phones!

Because volunteers only receive a $6 a day living allowance, they have to make very short calls or they have to use money from the U.S. help afford the expense. PVC's also use cell phones to communicate with people they work with and their Beninese friends. Today, in 2011, many villagers use cell phones if they have family members who have moved to a town or city. They can charge their phones as the volunteers do: they can find someone who has a generator nearby, they can charge them when they go to a town that has electricity, or use a solar cell charger.

Almost all of Benin now has cell phone coverage so only the volunteers who are posted in the most remote areas do not have coverage. It is amazing considering that most Beninese people who don't live along a main road or in a big town or city, don't even have electricity!

The internet is usually not available in rural areas, but most large towns and cities with electricity have cyber cafés so most volunteers can get to them relatively easily. The internet is very slow so they often write letters on laptops they brought from home and then upload them from a flash drive at the cyber café. Now volunteers can communicate with loved ones back in the U.S. much more quickly and as a result, many do not write letters very often. Most PCV's update blogs and Facebook to keep friends and family up to date with their activities and receive news from home. They also get news from the internet and do not have to rely solely on short wave radio and "Newsweek" magazine. As a result, they do not feel the same level of isolation PCV's did when I served.

In one way, I envy Benin volunteers today, as I am sure having cell phones makes their lives much easier. They can call people they are working with to prearrange meetings, and can also call each other if they need to cancel. I lost countless mornings and afternoons due to the lack of communication when I was not able to get a message to someone I was working with, or the people I was working with were not able to get a message to me. I would have killed for a phone had they existed when I was a volunteer because it would have allowed me to be much more efficient, and as a result, I would have been more effective as a volunteer. I am also sure that an easier connection to home would have made the lowest of lows that every volunteer experiences much more bearable.

On the other hand, PCV's today are able to use these means of communication to escape from Benin and not feel that same sense of isolation that forced me to integrate more into the culture. I'm sure the more frequent communication makes friends and family back in the U.S. worried since they hear so many details of problems and hardships. As a result, Peace Corps administration has had to make some changes to deal with more frequent communication with concerned loved ones of PCV's.

I'm sure Benin PCV's today don't go to the post office with the same sense of anticipation as I did. In fact, mail, besides my one monthly phone call from my parents, was my only connection to friends and family in the U.S. You can only imagine how elated I was when I received a letter, and how disappointed I was when I went more than a week without one. When I was a PCV, the internet was only available at a few internet cafés in Cotonou, the de facto capital city in Benin, and I never used it while I was there since none of my friends and family were using it then.

Beninese culture has been greatly influenced by a lack of communication for thousands of years until recently. The result is Benin, a country the size of Pennsylvania, speaks 50 indigenous languages! Now that rapid communication is possible due to cell phones and there is more access to TV and radio, it is precipitating rapid westernization and change in Benin.

## The Trilogy:

"To Benin and Back" is part three of a trilogy: part one is the website I created, "Fon is Fun," (www.Fon-is-Fun.org) that teaches people *Fon*, the language of Southern Benin. Part two is the documentary video, "Discovering Benin" (available on www.Fon-is-Fun.org). Please also go to the "Fon is Fun" site to see more photos of Benin that I did not have space to include here.

**One final note:** A majority the chapters of this book are direct excerpts from my journal or stories that I wrote while I was in Benin. Those chapters are written in the present tense. The other chapters: "Working in Benin," "Stories from Benin," "Interesting Cultural Differences," "A Stranger in My Old Life," and "Seven Years Later," I wrote after I returned and are written in the past tense.

## Dedication:

I'd like to dedicate "To Benin and Back" to the Adjacomenule. Adjacome is the name of the small "neighborhood," an extended family of about 40-50 people, who were my neighbors. "Adjacomenule" means the people of Adjacome in Fon. They were my friends for the two years I was in Benin and they still are. I have been back to visit them twice since I left in 1997: once in 2004 and again in 2009, and I still keep in touch with them. To this day I correspond with my friend Nestor via e-mail, and I send money for gifts and school supplies for the children in his family every year. While living there they supported me emotionally, and they were always there for me when I had questions or problems, or when I simply needed company. They were always very patient, kind and forgiving of my odd American ways. They were a very important part of my experience in Benin. I also dedicate "To Benin and Back" to Nestor Djossou, my best friend in Benin.

## Acknowledgements:

I'd like to thank my reliable editors Mike Perry and Ronnie Viggiano for all their hard work. A special thanks goes to my contributing editors:

Stephen Arbogast, Cara Viggiano Starace, and Michel Dognon. My appreciation goes to recently returned and current Benin PCV's for updates on technology in Benin: Catherine North Hounfodji, Jessica Bruce, Veronica Swank, and Natasha Thompson. I'm grateful to my wife Cara for being so adventurous and accompanying me on my first return trip to Benin. Finally, I would like to thank Peace Corps for giving me the opportunity to serve in Benin.

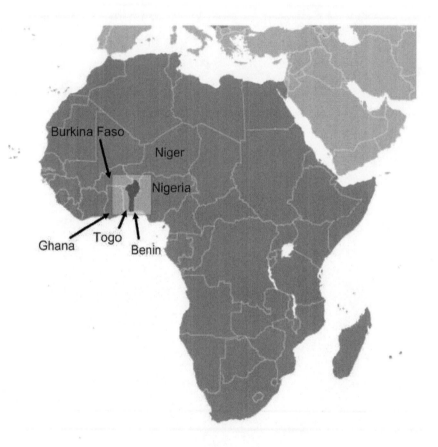

Map of Africa

From CIA.gov's World Factbook

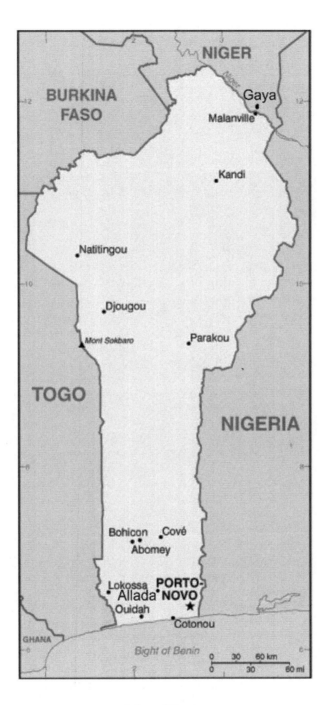

Map of Benin

From CIA.gov's World Factbook

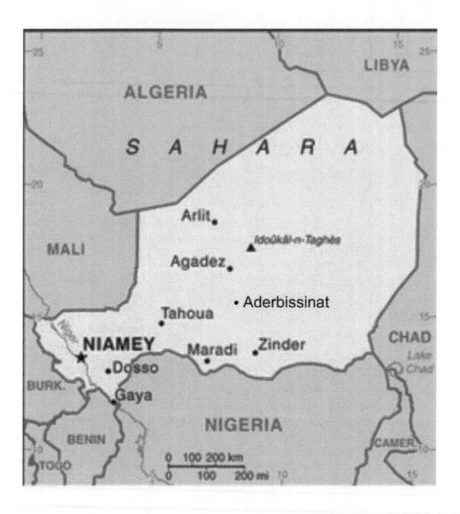

Map of Niger

From CIA.gov's World Factbook

# Glossary

These are mostly French and Fon terms commonly used in southern Benin as well as a few English words that have different meanings in West Africa.

3 S's
: The most common topic among Peace Corps Volunteers: Shit, Sex and Sustenance. Note they appear in order of importance.

Akassa
: Fermented cornstarch gelatin that is served in a ball and is wrapped in teak tree leaves. You dip chunks of it in a spicy sauce before eating it with your hand.

Allada
: My post during my two years of services as a Peace Corps Volunteer. It is a small town of about 10,000 people located around 30 miles north of Cotonou. Because it is on the main paved road in Benin, there is electricity, phone service, a post office, a high school and local government offices. I lived on the outskirts of town in a rural village setting.

Benin
: There are two Benin's in Africa: The "Republic of Benin," or the country of Benin, and "Benin City," a city in southern Nigeria. Benin City is now the capital of the Edo State of Nigeria. It was once the capital of the famous Kingdom of Benin that is famous for its bronze art. This book describes the Benin Republic and not Benin City in Nigeria.

Bush
: Literally it means thick vegetation but in West Africa it means remote and undeveloped areas.

Bush taxi

An informal taxi that runs from town to town or city to city. It is usually poorly maintained and runs on no schedule. The driver will usually wait at the taxi station to fill up the car before leaving. To keep costs low, four people sit in the back that is made for three people. Two people sit in the front seat that is made for one. Since there are no prescribed stops, it stops wherever the passengers want to get out. The driver then stops wherever another passenger waves him down so he can fill any empty spots in the car.

Buvette

An outdoor bar / restaurant. They usually also sell snacks and dry goods.

CARDER

The rural extension agency that I was assigned to work with. The agents were responsible for training and assisting rural farmers with things such as improving farming techniques, improving the organization of cooperatives, teaching healthcare techniques such as nutrition and STD prevention. There was also a veterinarian who helped maintain livestock which were usually chickens, goats and pigs. There was a fisheries expert who helped villagers that had fish ponds.

CFA

The West African currency that is backed by the French government and is universal in most all former French West African colonies. It stands for "Communauté Financaire Africaine" (African Financial Community)

Cotonou

The de facto capital or economic capital city of Benin. The population is approximately 700,000 and is the major port city in Benin. It is a very crowded, dirty and polluted city.

Fah              Fah is a form of geomantic divination. The Fah priest uses a chain containing seed pods to reveal the unknown with the help of divine intervention. The Fah priest throws the chain of seed pods on the ground and the eight seed pods either fall up or down, allowing for 256 possible different symbols. The Fah priest interprets the symbols for his client and uses the information to tell his or her future and to answer questions about the unknown.

Fishbowl effect    Peace Corps Volunteers are constantly stared at, talked about and noticed because we are so different. We are the fish and cannot escape from the constant scrutiny so it feels like we are trapped in a fishbowl.

Fon             The indigenous African language of Southern Benin. It is not at all related to French, however some French and English words are used in Fon today. It is primarily a spoken language as few people know how to read and write it and it is not taught in schools. Only educated people speak French well because it is the language taught at school.

Fou             French for "crazy." "Un fou" is a crazy person. There is no such thing as political correctness in Benin so anyone with a mental illness is a "fou."

Gandaho      My Fon nickname which means "big chief."

Gari            Cassava or manioc flour. They sprinkle it on rice and beans or eat it straight with water.

Gendarme     The national police.

Guinea worm    It is a parasite that people contract by drinking contaminated water. They ingest the larvae eggs in the water. The eggs usually plant themselves in the lower parts of people's legs and a worm grows under the skin. When the worm matures, it breaks through the skin and lays more eggs when the person steps in water completing the cycle. It has to be removed slowly by wrapping it around a matchstick over several weeks. It is painful and infections often develop.

Lokossa    A small city in south western Benin. It is close to Togo and is where I lived with the other seven trainees in my group for our three month pre-service training.

Medevac    To be medically evacuated. If Peace Corps Volunteers gets sick, the embassy medical staff treats them. If it is a serious injury or sickness or one that the staff cannot treat, volunteers are sent back to Washington D.C. for treatment until they are medically cleared. If they are not medically cleared, they are "Medsepped" or medically separated from Peace Corps.

NGO    Nongovernmental organizations that provide aid to Benin.

Nigerian    Someone from Nigeria.

Nigerien    Someone from Niger. Notice there is only one letter difference.

| | |
|---|---|
| Paillote | A straw gazebo where people sit outside shaded from the sun. People spend a lot of time outside because it is hot and dark in their huts. When they sit outside, they need shade from the intense equatorial sun. |
| Pâte | A corn flour paste served with different types of spicy sauces and eaten with one's right hand. It is pronounced like "pot" so many Americans think people are talking about marijuana when they hear the word the first time. |
| PCV | Peace Corps Volunteer |
| Porto-Novo | The political capital of Benin. It is in the south east, next to the Nigerian border. |
| Postmate | A Peace Corps Volunteer posted in the same place as another volunteer. Not every volunteer has a postmate. |
| Sodabi | A Locally made, very strong clear whiskey. It is made from distilled palm wine. Palm wine is fermented palm tree sap. |
| Street food | In towns, and cities you can buy many types of inexpensive home cooked food at informal stands on the side of the road. What you can find depends on the time of day. You can commonly find omelets, corn porridge, rice and beans, pâte, akassa, fried cassava, and beignets. Meat and fish are usually cooked in sauces. Dairy products of any kind are rare. |

Village
A group of people who live in a remote location. Because it is remote, most villages do not have electricity, or many government services. Most villages have elementary schools but not middle or high schools. For this reason most villagers are uneducated, illiterate, and do not speak French very well. This is especially true for the village elders.

Vodun= Voodoo
The Voodoo most Westerners have heard of is from Haiti. Voodoo in Haiti came from slaves. Most slaves sent to Haiti came from Benin. In Fon, "Voodoo" is pronounced "Vodun."

WAWA
"West Africa Wins Again" American expats have coined this expression to show their combined feeling of frustration and helplessness at the many inefficiencies and inconveniences of living in West Africa.

Yovo
"Whitey" in Fon. The Beninese call anyone who is light skinned "Yovo" including other Beninese. They don't believe in political correctness so it is a term I heard constantly, probably dozens of times a day. Adults as well as children called me Yovo and it got old fast.

Yovo song
"Yovo Yovo bon soir, ça va bien? Merci." (Whitey, whitey, good afternoon. How are you? Thanks). The children sang this song repetitively every time they saw me (or any Yovo) and it drove me nuts!

Zemidjan, Zemi or Zem
A motorcycle taxi. They are everywhere in Benin because they are cheap and fast. "Zemidjan" in Fon means "take me quick." They will carry you and unbelievable amounts of baggage short distances for less than a dollar.

# TEN DAYS IN DAGLETA

**November, 4ᵗʰ 1995 (Saturday)** Mathieu, our Peace Corps chauffeur, turns off the paved road and onto a narrow dirt path that twists and turns past many groups of small mud huts and people are staring at us with intense curiosity as we pass by. We follow the path for about a kilometer, and then turn onto an even narrower sandy path. It is so narrow in fact that the brush on both sides is almost rubbing the sides of the Toyota SUV we are in. We continue down the dusty and bumpy trail through dense brush for another kilometer. As we near the center of the village, a group of small children runs behind our car in excitement. Moments later we pull up in front of a group of mud huts, and I step out into another world. I am immediately surrounded by dozens of children and adults, all of whom are curious to see me, the *Yovo* (Whitey). The children are very excited and burst out signing repetitively, "*Yovo Yovo bon soir, ça va bien? Merci?*" ("Whitey, Whitey, Good Afternoon, How are you? Thanks" in French). The song is a combination of derision and innocent fun, but we Yovos feel it's more derision than anything else. The Beninese children serenade us Yovos with this song constantly wherever we go. I have been in Benin only one month and I have heard it countless times. It's not very often that a *Yovo* comes to Dagleta, and the children make the most of it, as I am the first Yovo to have lived in their village since many years ago.

My host Felix shows me to my room, which is in a mud hut that is located in his family compound. The roof is tin and the walls and floors are mud with a crumbling layer of cement over them. There is no electricity or running water and there is only one window, so it is very hot inside. I knew that it wouldn't be comfortable, but it doesn't matter to me. I am intrigued by the adventure of living in an African village, the likes of which I have only seen on National Geographic documentaries. Already I feel like I am living that exotic experience in a far away land.

My room is not ready, so Felix has some of his children quickly sweep it out. Mathieu leaves me with a mattress, a mosquito net, a case of bottled

19

water, and sheets to sleep on to assure that I have a bare minimum of comfort. Before I know it, the vehicle is gone, and I am left alone, surrounded by dozens of men, women, and children all staring at me intently, trying to get a look at the Yovo. Up to this point I have only experienced cities and small towns in Benin such as Cotonou (the de facto Capital city, population approximately 700,000, and the major port city in Benin), Porto-Novo (the political capital), and Lokossa. I have a feeling that living in a Beninese village will be as much of a new experience as arriving in Benin for the first time. I am quite a spectacle in the cities I have been to in Benin, but I can see that effect is magnified ten times here in the village. I draw so much attention that I feel my white skin is glowing compared to the almost black skin of the Beninese.

Shortly after I arrive, the adults disperse, but the children follow me everywhere I go and mark my every move. About 30 of them squeeze into my small room, and many peer into the door just to watch me unpack. I cannot close the door because it would be too dark and hot if I did. Hours later they are still here, and they watch me as I am trying to read. I cannot concentrate, so I play the harmonica for them and give them some balloons. They play with them gleefully, hooting and hollering, and fight over them as if I had given them something precious and novel. Perhaps they have never had their own balloons to play with before, or at least not ones from *Yovotome* (the land of the white people).

The hut where I lived for my ten days in Dagleta. My Peace Corps issued mountain bike is out front.

This was a typical scene in any village that I visited: gleeful children having fun and following me everywhere I went. Having their picture taken was always very exciting for them.

My group of eight Peace Corps small business development trainees has been in Benin for our initial pre-service training for only a month now. The goal of our training is to acclimate us to the Beninese culture over a three-month period, before we swear in and are sent to our posts in the villages, towns or cities where we will be stationed for our two years of service. At that time we will be expected to fend for ourselves and we will be completely on our own. We will have a medical kit to self treat any minor ailments because healthcare is either non-existent in Benin or scary at best. They actually give us hypodermic needles and syringes in the medical kit in case we have an emergency and can't get to Cotonou in time. This is because "hospitals" in Benin have been known for reusing needles and syringes. If a major ailment arises, we have to high tail it to the American Embassy medical center in Cotonou by bush taxi, a usually a very dilapidated car that operates as a bus with no schedule and the driver packs so many people and goods in that people are practically hugging one another for hours on end. In case of emergency we can pay considerably more and rent the entire vehicle, which would assure we arrive faster. Luckily, I'm in the south and only one and a half hours from Cotonou. The volunteers who live 12+ hours away up north will have to rely on the American Embassy to get a plane to pick them up and bring them back to Cotonou for any major illnesses or accidents. That actually happened when a volunteer had appendicitis not long ago.

Before we arrived in Benin, we had three days of orientation in Philadelphia. Today I came from the École Normale training center in Lokossa (a small city in southern Benin) where we are spending three months for our pre-service training. Pre-service training is designed to gradually introduce us to the Beninese way of life, so they coddle and shelter us most of the time (except for this week). If they just dropped us off at our posts without proper training and time to acclimate, most of us probably would not survive and if we did, we would certainly be less effective as volunteers. At the École Normale we are living in a dormitory and have a very structured schedule of classes with Beninese instructors six days a week. We have cooks to prepare our meals, and drivers to transport us to training activities. They even organize weekend cultural getaways. However, the next ten days here in Dagleta will be a completely different story.

The eight Peace Corps newbies or *stagiaires* (trainees, as they call us in French) are living at our posts, which are located in far-flung areas around

Benin, for the next ten days. Our posts, where we will serve our two years after training, are varied. Some of us will be sent to small villages, some will go to medium sized towns, and some will be placed in cities. In the past month of in-country-training, we already learned a lot about health issues in Benin, Beninese culture, speaking French, bicycle repair, how to get around in Benin, how to buy things in the market, and about our jobs as small business advisors. When we first arrived, we lived with a current Peace Corps Volunteer for a week, which was very interesting as we saw what our lives will really be like once training is over. In Lokossa (where we are doing our training) we spend a few nights a week away from our training site to live with local Beninese families. It is more or less a sleep over, as we ride our bikes from the training center in Lokossa to our host families in the evening. We eat dinner with them, and the next morning we ride back to the training center for our classes.

Up to this point we have had some exposure to Benin outside of what the Peace Corps has structured for us, but living on our own at our future posts for ten days is a test to make sure we can survive without their help. Everyone in my training group is relieved to finally find out where we are going to be posted. We are all very excited to get to know the place where we will live for the next two years when our training is over two months from now. The eight of us will be spread all over Benin from north to south, so each of us will surely have a very different experience.

Today we were escorted to our sites by either current Peace Corps Volunteers, or by Peace Corps trainers. I had the luxury of going in an air-conditioned Peace Corps vehicle. My future post, Allada, is a small town of about 10,000 people located approximately 30 miles north of Cotonou. Although I will be posted there for my two years of service, I am staying in a small village called "Dagleta," which is about 2KM south of Allada. *Dagleta* means "in the field" in Fon. Although it is only about a kilometer from the paved highway, like most villages, it is indeed in the woods.

Getting out of the car, the first thing I notice is how poor the village is compared to the city of Lokossa. There is no pavement, no cement, no grass, or landscaping to be seen, but instead there is dirt everywhere. The roads are dirt. The huts are made of dirt, the floors in the huts are dirt, the areas surrounding the huts are dirt, and of course everything is covered in dirt. The people are very poor and have few possessions, but they greet me very warmly with smiles, handshakes, laughter and much curiosity. It is very hot and humid and some people are scantily dressed. Most of the children are wearing only shorts or underwear, and many older women and teenage girls are bare breasted, a vivid reminder of how different this culture is compared to the United States. Most of the men are wearing pants and a T-shirt, or the traditional African *bomba* (a loose shirt and pants that resemble pajamas made of thin and brightly colored cloth), while most of the women are wearing simple pieces of brightly colored cloth wrapped around their waists and torsos.

Felix is the head of the union of farming cooperatives in the area, and his union agreed to pay my rent over the two years while I live and work in Allada. In return, I offer the member cooperatives my services of teaching them small business management skills. Although the Peace Corps can easily pay my rent of less than $20 a month, this arrangement is conceived to give people in the community a vested interest in working with me.

Felix comes to my door while I'm unpacking and introduces me to his two wives who live in adjacent huts and to some of his many children. Although he is Christian, he has two wives. Go figure! He tells me that he belongs to a Beninese Christian sect called *Crétianisme Céleste* that actually permits polygamy! I have heard about the mixing of Christian and traditional African beliefs, but I doubt the Vatican would approve of this. Felix speaks French well so I have no problem communicating with him. Some of the children who go to school also speak French, so they are the only people that I can communicate with easily. I feel somewhat lost, as most everyone else only speaks Fon. I find a few children who speak pretty good French, so I have them interpret for me when I need to communicate with someone.

When I ask Felix where I should go to the bathroom, he informs me that there are no latrines in Dagleta. The Peace Corps said that we should all have latrines where we are staying for these ten days, but they dropped the ball on me. Felix shows me a pile of bricks behind the hut and explains that he doesn't have enough money to finish it yet. He said I should pee in the shower, and he shows me where to defecate. He leads me out of the housing compound and down a bush path to a secluded patch of teak trees where he says I should go. I ask if he has a shovel so I can bury it. He says, "No, don't bother burying it because the pigs and dogs will dig it up anyway." I tell Felix that this is very unsanitary, as the pigs, dogs, and flies can feast on the human waste, then bring back parasites and bacteria to the village. They land on their food completing the "oral fecal vector."

He just nods and shrugs. He says that many Beninese are unwilling to use latrines because they are afraid that the floor will collapse beneath them. I don't doubt that this has ever happened, but I'm sure it is rare. I hope that when they are built, they reinforce the floor with metal bars but you never know for sure.

On the way to the "bathroom" we pass a Vodun fetish, an altar and dwelling place of a Vodun god, called "Legba" that is there to protect the housing compound from evil spirits. It looks like a short round person with no legs. It has two eyes, nose, mouth, horns and a large penis that represents its virility and power. Felix tells me that the fetish has been there since the origin of the village hundreds of years ago. When they created it, they made a human sacrifice, whose corpse is buried beneath the fetish! He assured me that they no longer make human sacrifices, and I am relieved. Hopefully Legba will protect me if I have to come here in the middle of the night, I think to myself. We return to my hut, and he shows me the "shower." He points to a flat stone on the ground by the side of my hut surrounded by bamboo walls put up for privacy. It reeks of urine. He says that when I want to shower, he will have one of his children bring me a bucket of water. I will have to stand on the stone and pour the water over me with another small container. I have taken bucket showers before at the École Normale when the running water stopped working a few times so this is old hat for me now. Going to the bathroom in the woods is another story. I am not looking forward to that. At this point I am only getting used to using latrines, not squatting in the woods!

I go back to my hut to rest a little, and it rains for about an hour. The sound of heavy rain on a tin roof is deafening because there is no ceiling or insulation. Outside my hut a huge puddle forms so I have to walk through a mud bog to get in and out until it dries up the next day. I notice that there is a constant chug, chug, chug of what sounds like a steam engine coming from a shack near my hut. I later discover that it is a one-cylinder diesel engine that powers a corn mill. It runs all day and all evening. A constant stream of people arrives with bowls and basins full of dried corn kernels, and they leave shortly after with corn flour to make *pâte (a* corn flour paste served with different types of spicy sauces and eaten with one's right hand), which is the Beninese staple food.

I have some children show me around the village. They take me to the village school, and I am aghast at how primitive it is. It is only a tin roof with no walls. There is a chalkboard and basic wooden benches and tables, and that is it. I am sure that when it is raining they have to cancel class because any student except the ones sitting in the center would get wet from the driving rain. After what I experienced in my hut, I am sure that the rain on the tin roof is so noisy that the students cannot hear the teacher. They started building a new school next to it out of cement blocks, but it is only half completed and it seems as if work stopped some time ago. I wonder if they ran out of money, or if for some reason local politics halted construction.

The village elementary school of Dagleta.

Later, Felix brings me to Allada for a late lunch at a local outdoor restaurant on the back of his motor scooter. When I get back at night, I am exhausted from such a long hot day. My skin is caked with salt that the sweat left behind, as well as the dirt that stuck to it, as dirt and dust in Benin is ubiquitous. Felix has one of his children bring me a kerosene lamp to use at night. I have *pâte* for dinner, although I am not yet used to it because at the Peace Corps training center they make an effort to provide some Western style meals for us. I have no choice but to get used to it, and it is difficult considering it is only corn flour paste with a slimy gumbo sauce. It must be possible, however, as many Beninese eat it every day for more than one meal. I do not yet know how they do it, but I am guessing they do it out of necessity and habit.

By 9 PM the children return to their parents and are finishing their evening chores and getting ready to go to bed. I'm sitting in my tiny mud hut with dirt floors and I am writing in my journal on a rickety table covered in dust, using a kerosene lamp as my only light source. Writing in my journal is a way for me to process everything that happened in the day, as there aren't any other westerners around to share them with. It is 85 degrees and muggy even at 9:00 PM, so the heat from the lamp only adds to my discomfort, not to mention the bugs that it attracts. I hear all sorts of strange noises such as the corn mill outside my window, as well as thousands of insects buzzing, pots and pans clanging, babies crying, animals bleating, and various people walking by my door speaking Fon. I don't speak Fon yet but I hope to learn. It is the traditional African language spoken in southern Benin and is not related to any European colonial language. Where am I!?, I think. Everything seems so foreign and bewildering to me . . . I have to remind myself where I am and how I got here.

The night is very peaceful and relatively cool and I hear the diesel corn mill outside my window is still chug, chug, chugging away until 10 PM or so. I walk around the village with my flashlight a little to explore more, as I am very curious to explore my new surroundings and to see what people are doing at different times of day. Everyone in the village uses kerosene lamps to light the area around them. Because they put off so little light, there is almost no light pollution, and the stars are amazingly bright. Having lived in light polluted areas all my life, I have never seen the Milky Way, but here it is an amazing bright stripe of milky white emblazoned across the sky. I go back to my hut and find a bucket of water waiting for me. The cold bucket shower feels very refreshing after sweating all day, and it is nice to wash outside under the stars. Unfortunately I drop my soap, and it lands in the sand. I try to pick out the sand with my fingernail, but I can't get it all out. When I continue washing, I scratch my skin in a few places from the embedded sand! Arrrgh!

When I go back into my hut, I notice something moving on the walls. After closer inspection, I realize that there are cockroaches crawling out of the cracks in the wall! There are at least a dozen of them, and they are huge, probably three to four inches long! I don't want to deal with them so I crawl under my mosquito net, and go to bed on my mattress that is laid on the floor. As I am getting into bed I notice that a large spider is camped out above my bed above my mosquito net. As I tuck the mosquito net under all sides of my mattress to keep the monster roaches, spiders and mosquitoes out, and I realize how lucky I am to have it. Without it I would literally "bug out." Despite all my hardships, I am loving this experience as I am learning so much and experiencing so many new things that I have never dreamed of before. I am also testing myself and stretching my limits of comfort that I have been brought up with all my life having lived in a middle class family in suburban Connecticut. I feel satisfied because I know I am living in the same conditions as a Beninese villager. Few Westerners have had a experience like this and it will certainly make me a better person.

**November 5th, 1995 (Sunday)** This morning I am awoken at about 6AM by many new sounds. I hear roosters crowing, goats bleating, pots clanging, babies crying and people talking in Fon. I hear the corn mill start up and the sound of the women sweeping their huts and the dirt outside. It is particularly noisy because my hut shares a roof with Felix's wives so when they talk, the sound travels over the dividing wall. I smell smoke from a wood fire on which the women started to cook breakfast. This all happened before 7AM, so it isn't easy trying to sleep late. Everyone gets up early because there is no electricity in the village, and everyone goes to sleep by about 10 PM. Today is Sunday, so I have the day to get acclimated to living in the village, explore my new surroundings more and rest up a little. During the coming week I will have a busy schedule of meeting people from CARDER, the government rural extension agency that I will be working with. I am told someone from CARDER will take me to visit village cooperatives that I will work with after I am sent to my post.

While exploring the village I talk to the people and the children as best I can. I find that very few people speak French, and I only know a few words of Fon that I learned in the two or three lessons I had in training. I meet Felix's parents and they start talking to me in Fon. I'm lost. There are no children around to interpret for me so I just smile and try to figure out what they are saying. The old woman is smiling and takes my hand and says,

-*Kwabo Yovo. A do gangi a?*

I just smile and shrug my shoulders. Then she points to me and says,

-*We o, viche* and points to herself and says,

-*Nye we, notowe* she points to her husband and says,
-*Totowe.*

Again I have no idea what she's saying so I just shrug my shoulders and smile. I can tell she's determined to get her point across and she repeats herself again. I still don't get it and she repeats herself again. Then she starts looking for someone to interpret in French for me, but no one is around. I can tell she is saying something friendly and eventually she gives up. It wasn't until months later that I learned enough Fon to figure out what she was saying. It turned out that she was welcoming me by saying that I am her son, she is my mother and her husband is my father.

As I'm struggling to understand her, I decide I must do my best to learn Fon well because it will help me to communicate with anyone who isn't educated, and there are many, especially here in the villages. I find that the village is separated into housing compounds. Each family has its own compound that consists of a series of huts located next to each other. The grandmother, grandfather, all their sons, their wives, and all their children live there. The daughters don't live there once they are married, because they go to live with their husbands' families. It provides a strong social net, especially for the elderly. There is always someone around to help take care of them as there are no assisted living facilities in Benin, nor could anyone afford to pay for them. Living so close to one another, I am sure that they have very close-knit families, but I imagine they must have many disputes as well. Everything here seems so strange to me, and I feel like a helpless puppy exploring his new environment. There are children everywhere, and there are goats, chickens, and pigs roaming all over. The population of the village is about 1,000 people: 400 adults and 600 children. Although I have seen birth control pills for sale in the Allada market, they obviously don't use them much!

For breakfast, lunch, and dinner, they bring me a selection of pâte, rice, beans, and fruit. I have pineapple often as Felix grows them for a living. They are huge and incredibly delicious! By night time, my stomach is starting to feel funny, and I am a little worried about what is brewing down there. Felix's wives have been cooking for me, and I have been eating with their utensils so who knows what microbes or parasites I may have already ingested. Luckily, Peace Corps left me with a case of bottled water to drink, and that is all I have been drinking. Here they drink water from a cistern (a large open cement tank that collects rain water from the gutters of houses).

As usual, it is very hot as soon as the sun comes up, and by 1 PM it is a scorching, humid 90 plus degrees. The entire village and I take siestas every day to escape the heat and recover from the fatigue it inflicts upon us. I have to keep my front door open because it is so hot but there is no screen door. My room only has one window, so I will cook if I close the door. When I wake up from my siesta, I am sweating, and I see a goat staring me in the face. Apparently, it wandered in looking for something to eat. Luckily I put my snacks in a closed box so he doesn't find them. I soon find out that on a daily basis, I have chickens, goats, and children wander in my hut. Later a baby, who is not wearing a diaper, wanders into my room. He pees and craps on the floor as I am sitting there listening to the radio. Luckily another child comes in right away to clean up the mess and she takes the baby away. I'm amazed at how very young children, probably five years old and up, help take care of the toddlers in their family, and I'm sure this gives the parents much relief from childcare duties. I have even seen very young girls carrying infants on their backs as their mothers do. It's surprising to me to see how much young children are given adult responsibilities.

I call this girl a "baby, babysitter" because often very young girls are asked to help take care of their younger siblings.

Earlier Felix showed me where he sleeps, and he has his own hut separate from his wives. I guess he invites his wives over for a "visit" when he feels like it. I notice that he is never around, as he is always off doing something away from the village. I am not sure what though. The women cook outside in a *paillote* (a straw gazebo). They use firewood and support a pot on three stones above the fire. The smoke filters through the thatched roof, so there is no need for a chimney. I cannot believe the paillotes don't burn down due to errant sparks.

This is one of Felix's wives heating oil over a wood fire in her "kitchen" to make a sauce that will be eaten with pâte.

So far I have met so many people here in Felix's family that I cannot keep everyone straight in my head. Everyone in the village seems to be related to Felix somehow, so I imagine he is someone important. As a matter of protocol, Felix takes me to see the village chief, as the village chief is supposed to be apprised of all that happens in the village. Upon meeting him, I notice that he looks and dresses like anyone else in the village. He invites us into his hut, offers us some soft drinks, and we chat for a while.

**November 6ᵗʰ 1995 (Monday)** Felix takes me to the CARDER office in Allada. I meet many people there who are all very friendly and helpful. The person that I am assigned to work with during my two years is named Clément, and he takes me on his motorcycle to the important places in town and to meet a few government officials. Clément takes me to the town hall, the social center and to the *buvette* (an outdoor bar that also serves food) for lunch. That afternoon I spend some time exploring Allada on my own, since that is where I will be living once my training is over in two months.

I have the opportunity to meet the other Peace Corps Volunteers (PCV's) who live in and near Allada at the *buvette*. Marcus lives in Allada and Kate and Kirsten live in neighboring villages several miles away. Since I will only have my Peace Corps issued Trek mountain bike to get around, I will probably only be seeing Marcus on a regular basis. We knock back a few *Grande Beninoise* beers, and chat. They all seem nice, albeit a bit jaded from being in Benin, as they know what it is really like here. At this point I can only guess. It's reassuring knowing they won't be far away because I'm sure I will need other Americans to lean on when the times get tough. From what I have seen already, living here will not be easy. Having spent only two days in the village, I realize how much I crave being with people who I can relate to and communicate with easily. In the village I never feel alone because there are always people around, but I do feel very isolated due to communication gaps caused by cultural differences and language barriers. Hanging out with Americans I feel I can let my hair down and be myself. It is very cathartic. After hanging out with my new postmates for a few hours, I take a *zemidjan* (motorcycle taxi) back to Dagleta.

Every night I listen to my short wave radio to keep up on world events. It is odd for me because I feel as if I am in the depths of Africa, far from civilization (even though I would consider Allada more or less civilized, and it is only 2KM away from Dagleta). On short wave radio I listen to the Voice of America, the BBC, and Radio France. They speak in depth of events going on in the U.S. and the world. They speak of President Clinton, and I even hear a story about Connecticut. It is odd because it makes me feel like I am not so far away after all.

One nice thing about being in this village is that I feel as if I have room service. The children bring my food to me, and they sweep my room every day. It gets dirty fast from my shoes since outside my door is all dirt. It is November and it is what's known as the "little rainy season," so it rains every day for at least a half-hour. The children also get me water every night for my bucket shower. I eat dinner alone in my hut, but I don't mind because it is one of the few times during the day when I get peace and quiet. Felix comes and eats dinner with me every few days. I think it's odd that the women eat together around a small table, the children eat together, and the men eat together, but I never see them all eat together as a group unless there is a party.

**November 7th 1995 (Tuesday)** My fears of gastrointestinal woes from the gurgling going on in my stomach and my intestines are confirmed this morning in the teak forest at the edge of the village. I start feeling weak, and I have a full-fledged case of diarrhea. I feel horrible! As volunteers affectionately say, I am "brewing butt custard" and "blowing mud." The old motto is "American Express—Don't leave home without it." My new motto is, "Toilet paper—don't leave home without it." I have been here only a month, and this is not the first time I have had diarrhea, but this time it is much worse. Many of my fellow trainees have gone through it already since we arrived in Benin. It happens to PCV's quite frequently, especially early on, before our bodies get used to the microbes. So we learn to not be shy about it; hence the colorful terminology we use to describe it.

That night I realize that I probably have giardia (an intestinal parasite) because I am having sulfur burps, intestinal cramping, and I am running to the teak forest several times an hour. I find myself in the woods at 2AM with only my little Maglight flashlight to see, squatting in the pitch black in a place that I am getting to know quite well. Before I am done doing my business, I hear rustling in the leaves not far behind me. The sound is getting closer as if it is coming towards me! I have no idea what it is, and my imagination takes over. I fear I am about to be attacked by a wild animal or person since I can't see anything. I yell, "*c'est qui!?*" (Who is it?), but there is no answer. I yell again, "*c'est qui!?*," and again there is no answer. The sound is getting closer and closer and I'm getting really afraid. I then hear the grunt of a pig and I am very relieved. It is coming to the village bathroom for a midnight snack. I now know in very real terms what it means to have the crap scared out of you!

Despite feeling ill all day, I go to visit a few village cooperatives with Clément. He comes to Dagleta to pick me up on his motorcycle and he takes me about 22 kilometers away to a cooperative in the bush. By "bush" I mean remote overgrown areas, which may not be that far from a paved road as the crow flies. Because of the lack of roads, however, these places are very isolated from the rest of the world. To get there we take the paved road, and then we turn onto a dirt road, then onto a smaller and bumpier dirt road, then onto a bush path, and finally onto smaller overgrown trails eroded by rain. We are in the middle of nowhere! At the top of a hill the view of the lush green landscape is beautiful. The vegetation is very green and thick, but it is not high enough to be considered rainforest. There is no sign of civilization. It takes us 45 minutes to get there. As we get closer, Clément stops more frequently to talk to people he knows that we happen to pass on the path. When we stop, a Jehovah's Witness happens to be there and hands me a Watchtower publication in French! Mickey Mouse was right when he said, "It's a small world after all!" This is the last place I would imagine finding a Jehovah's Witness distributing literature.

I feel sick, exhausted, hot, and achy. We visit the head of a local cooperative union under a straw branch roof erected to provide shade. There are five or six members there to greet me. They just started a credit program where they pool their money and make loans to members for income generating activities otherwise known as micro credit. They have a total of $140 from 9 cooperatives or 125 people. They show me their bookkeeping and explain how their group works. I feel overwhelmed because they have so many problems, and I feel inadequately equipped to help them. Already I feel an obligation to not disappoint them. I hope their expectations will not be too great because I am not sure I can deliver. I know it will be hard for me at the beginning because I will be learning so much, but after being at my post for several months, I hope I will be able to make a difference. We are told in training not to expect to accomplish much the first three months at post. During that time we need to get acclimated to living alone at our posts, we need to get to know how things work, and we need to build relationships with the people that we work with. We are told not to jump in head first with all sorts of big ideas. If we do not understand the culture and the people's needs, our ideas will ultimately be rejected because they will not be culturally sensitive or appropriate. Knowing that I should give my self three months before trying to intervene gives me some comfort, because I know I have time to figure out how I will make my contribution.

After we visit the credit union cooperative, we visit a pig-raising cooperative a few miles away, and as I have come to expect, they are very hospitable. I run out of my drinking water. Not knowing where it comes from, I sure as heck do not want to drink anything they give me. Their custom is to offer visitors a bowl of water and everyone drinks out of the same bowl. Clément tells me that to be polite I should pour a few drops of the water on the ground as an offering to the ancestors if I do not want to drink. When they learn that I am sick to my stomach, they are very nice and give me a bunch of coconuts to drink the milk from, and that helps me feel better. Before I leave they give me a big bag of oranges as a gift. I really do not want them because that means I have to carry them in my backpack on a 45-minute motorcycle ride back to Dagleta. Clément explains that if I do not accept the gift, they will think that I see them as too poor to be able to afford giving me the gift. I decide that I will not bring a backpack with me anymore to visit cooperatives. That way I will not be able to carry any large fruit gifts, and I will have a perfect excuse to decline it.

During the meetings I feel lost because everyone speaks Fon, and Clément has to translate into French for me. On the way back Clément stops on the road to buy a live chicken from a woman walking with a basket full of them on her head. He casually drapes the chicken (whose legs are tied together) over the rearview mirror on the handlebar, and we continue on our way.

**November 8th 1995 (Wednesday)** Today I visit Kate, an experienced PCV, at her house in Sékou. I find it very helpful speaking with experienced volunteers because they are very knowledgeable about the realities of living and working in Benin. They know strategies for dealing with the trials and tribulations of day-to-day life, and I learn a lot from them. I realize that the volunteers rely a lot on each other for support. Together they create a strong support network and a surrogate family for us during the time that we are here. This doesn't mean that everyone gets along, and of course there is a lot of gossip. In fact gossiping about other volunteers is the fourth most popular topic of conversation after the three S's = Shit, Sex, and Sustenance. As you can see our hierarchy of needs in Benin is at a much lower level than our needs in the U.S. I think it is understandable considering our living conditions and circumstances.

The food is really starting to get to me because there is so little variety. I have not had any fresh vegetables, and very little meat or dairy products. In addition, Felix rarely has bread for me. Most people eat only pâte, rice, and akassa (fermented cornstarch gelatin).

Tonight there is no moon because it's cloudy, and it is very dark. The previous three nights the moon was almost full. When there is a full moon it is so bright that I do not even need a flashlight to walk around outside.

I miss home, and I am very happy to get several personal letters today delivered to Dagleta by the Peace Corps. Letters make me and the other volunteers so happy. They are our umbilical cord to home. I am sure that letters are enough to get many volunteers through the most difficult times of depression, frustration, loneliness, and feelings of isolation while in Benin. I know they sure cheer me up! The internet and e-mail is just beginning to expand in the U.S., and I have heard that some volunteers have been able to e-mail home from a few locations in Cotonou. However, I have not had the opportunity to do so, and most people I know in the U.S. do not even have e-mail accounts yet.

**November 9th 1995 (Thursday)** I am still blowing mud, and I feel like hell. Felix's dad offers me some of his homemade sodabi. It is a strong, locally made whiskey distilled from fermented palm wine, which is made from palm tree sap. I swear it tastes like gasoline! They claim that I should drink it to help kill the microbes in my stomach that are causing my diarrhea. I do not think it helps any because the rumbling in my bowels goes on full force. I am very uncomfortable and the novelty of village life is definitely wearing off.

Today I visit another cooperative with Clément, and they of course give me another ton of oranges and bananas. To earn money they make sodabi, palm oil, *gari* (cassava flour), soap and they also stock grain to sell during the dry season. I am flattered because when I arrive, there is a big group waiting, and they chant a welcome song for me in Fon. They have a plush chair for me, and I sit in front of them. I feel uncomfortable because the meeting is held on the patio of a nice new building that they built with money they received from a German organization. As I suspect, they ask me over and over if I can get money for them for projects. I explain that my role is for teaching small business skills and not administering projects, but it goes in one collective ear and out the other, and they continue to ask about getting money to fund projects. I doubt if I will be able to work with this type of group, because they already have expectations that Yovos like me will bring them money to build things. It is sad how they have this big fancy building in which to store grain, but it is completely empty. They do not have the capital to buy the grain to fill it! I wonder where the Germans are now, and whether or not they did a feasibility study before they threw money at them. I wonder if they spent much time with them teaching them and encouraging them to use it correctly. Seeing the state that the building is in, I doubt it. On the other hand, I wonder if I teach them the business management skills they need to operate a business effectively, will they succeed, especially if I do not have any start up capital to give them to get started? I can see already that I have got a tough job ahead of me.

**November 10th, 1995 (Friday)** I go to a meeting at the CARDER office to discuss development strategies for several hours in the morning. When I get back to Dagleta, I start doing my laundry, but the children come and finish it for me. The Beninese are extremely hospitable and generous. They are expected to take good care of their guests, and I appreciate it. The children's job is to help the adults and especially the adults' guests. The children are my servants, although I haven't asked them to do anything. They sweep my room, fetch my water, bring my dinner, do my laundry, etc. It is what is expected of them and they do it willingly. I tell Felix how he is being very nice to me, and he says that if he neglects me, the village will mock him and say that he is not a good host. He tells me that some people are already criticizing him because they think that he is responsible for me being sick. It appears there is a lot of social pressure here in this very tight knit community.

Everyone is watching me, and I feel I cannot even go to the bathroom without everyone noticing and talking about it. I bet that's how everyone knows that I am sick. This is what the Peace Corps calls "the Fishbowl Effect." I am the fish and everyone has their eyes on me because I am the only outsider, and I am different and interesting to them.

Tonight I go to take a shower and I find a pig in the shower area, which startles me again! I am really beginning to get sick of the animals running everywhere. I wish that they would pen them up. Not only do they intrude on me at inopportune moments, wake me up at 6 AM, and act as vectors for diseases, but they crap all over the place including the area in front of my door!

Today I feel horrible again, but I am able to eat some dinner so I think I am starting to feel a little better.

In the village I feel really safe. It seems that crime in villages is almost non-existent, except for occasional petty theft.

**November 11th 1995 (Saturday)** Today I am feeling better, and the proof is that I make only three trips to the teak forest all day! Hurray!! I have lost a few pounds already as my appetite has been weak, and I have not exactly been in love with the food. Yesterday I killed at least five cockroaches with my shoe. When I woke up this morning they were gone. I left them on the ground, and the ants came to eat them. I watched as an ant carried the last morsel away. Damn, it's only 8:30 AM and I am sweating already! Sleeping at night is not comfortable because it's so hot, but I sleep well regardless; I am so tired from the heat and many activities during the day.

I have some garbage to throw out today, and I ask Felix what I should do with it. He takes it, and throws it in a garbage pile across the dirt path from my hut. Twenty children come running at full speed from all directions and descend upon it. I can't believe what I am seeing! They are grabbing envelopes, cookie wrappers, sheets of paper, used batteries, and they find my used razor blade. I grab that from them so no one will get hurt. By that time Felix is gone and his father is there observing the chaos, so I give him the razor blade hoping that he will know how to dispose of it properly. Instead he takes it and begins shaving with it on his dry face! I realize at that moment that I have to bury (at night) any garbage that I do not want the whole village playing with.

I am really tired of village life now. I am tired of always having people in my room when I am in my hut. The dirt, lack of privacy, noise, ants, spiders, cockroaches, flies, and mosquitoes in my hut are driving me nuts. There are always babies crying, and it is frustrating for me to not be able to speak Fon. I am so sick of the cockroaches. I have been killing them with my flip-flop every night now. Death to cockroaches!—I'm sure the ants don't mind. I am tired of the heat. I am tired of constantly sweating, and always feeling dirty. I have not seen a thermometer yet, but my guess is that it's about 90 degrees outside and 95 degrees in my hut in the afternoon. I find out that the most Beninese sleep on straw mats on the ground so I know I am lucky to have a mattress.

**November 12ᵗʰ 1995 (Sunday)** I go to Cotonou with Kate by bush taxi to do some shopping. It is a lot fun to get away from the village and have some American companionship.

**November 13ᵗʰ 1995 (Monday)** I hear the Yovo song all the time, and now it's starting to get really annoying. It was cute at first, but not anymore. It's funny how even though I've been in this village for eight days, and I see the same people every day, the novelty of me being a Yovo never seems to wear off. The children still sing the Yovo song, especially when I pass the schoolyard. Even the adults call me Yovo and then giggle.

**November 14ᵗʰ 1995 (Tuesday)** I visit a pineapple producing cooperative, and of course I come back to Dagleta with a pineapple the size of a large watermelon! I don't mind lugging this gift home because they are so delicious and sweet. Unfortunately, I have to bring a backpack in order to carry my water and camera so I cannot refuse. I feel bad because I am visiting all these cooperatives, but I will not have time or transportation means to work with all of them. A bicycle will be my only means of transportation; so many of them are too far for me to get to easily. Peace Corps used to issue motorcycles to volunteers, but because there were so many accidents, they have stopped that practice completely in many countries. Since passable roads and taxis are so hard to find in Benin, they allow volunteers to ride on the back of motorcycles as long as they are wearing their Peace Corps issued helmets. They are so strict about the helmet rule that if you are caught on a motorcycle not wearing one, you are immediately sent back to the United States and your Peace Corps service is over. This is understandable since emergency care is non-existent anywhere outside of Cotonou. The result is that PCV's are immediately identifiable by the motorcycle helmet that is practically attached to our arms when we're walking around cities. We are also forbidden from driving so our transportation options are walking, bicycle, motorcycle taxi, or bush taxi. Unfortunately I don't get a travel allowance so my only every day work related transportation is my mountain bike. The result is I'll only have the time and energy to peddle five miles one way to villages around my house.

**November 15ᵗʰ 1995 (Wednesday)** Today my ten days are up! It is time for me to go back to Lokossa to finish my training before coming back to Allada in two months. I'm anxious to be with the other American trainees and compare experiences. I say good-bye to everyone, and a whole entourage of children helps me carry my bags around a kilometer to the paved road where I need to wave down a bush taxi to take me to Lokossa. It is roughly a 2-hour trip. I am glad to leave because of my uncomfortable living conditions in Dagleta. Despite the discomfort, the ten days went very quickly, and I learned and experienced a lot.

-------------------------------------------------------------------------------

**February 13ᵗʰ 1996** Training has been over now for two months and I'm settling into my house at my post. I am now living in a small three-room cement house with a tin roof on the outskirts of Allada in a neighborhood called Sékoudenou or Adjacomé. Luckily my living conditions are much more comfortable than they were in Dagleta. While I was in Dagleta I thought that Peace Corps was trying to test me by putting me in living conditions that were worse than my future post to make sure I could handle it. I found out that this was not the case because I had the worst living conditions by far among my fellow trainees. It was just the luck of the draw and perhaps some negligence on the part of Peace Corps because they didn't confirm that I would have a latrine to use.

I have gone back to Dagleta to visit a few times already, and now I see how rough I had it. Luckily it was only ten days. Here in Allada my house is much more comfortable because there are several windows that keep it relatively cool. I have screens on the windows and a screen door to keep the bugs, animals, and children out. Luckily there are no cockroaches, but there are plenty of mice and lizards everywhere. I have a latrine in front of the house so I don't have to go to the bathroom in the woods. I have a cement floor in my shower so when I drop the soap, it doesn't get caked with sand. I have electricity, a fan and a few lights. I also do some cooking on my own in my kitchen, so I am able to make a greater variety of foods according to my own hygienic standards. Nonetheless, I have had several bouts of diarrhea since then. Many volunteers say that every few months they have a bout of diarrhea that lasts at least a week. It is something that volunteers have to get used to and accept as a part of living in Benin. To avoid it completely we would have to cook every meal at home and boil all of our drinking water.

I eat street food several meals a week, as cooking here takes a lot of effort. Eating "street food" entails sitting on bench on the side of the road eating a local dish cooked by a woman from town at her house. It is known for being very unsanitary, but I do not have any other options. Not eating street food would mean I would have to cook every meal and never leave Allada!

This was my house for two years after training was over.

This was my favorite rice and beans lady in Allada. She got me through the first few months until I got my kitchen set up and I became comfortable cooking at home. I bought rice and beans from her after that when I wanted to "eat out."

I have made myself relatively comfortable in my new house already. I look back on my stay in Dagleta fondly as a unique experience. Having survived that, I know I can deal with almost anything here and it feels good knowing that. Since this is where I will live for the next two years, I probably will not have the opportunity to live so intimately with the Beninese people in a village setting again. The house where I live now is across a dirt path from a group of at least 40 neighbors, but the distance isolates me from them a little. It is a perfect arrangement because I am far enough from them that I have peace and quiet most of the time. They are close enough to me that they only have to walk across the path to get to my house, and I only have to cross the path to see them. I spend a lot of time with them on my front porch, and they spend a lot of time with me when I visit them at their housing compound. The benefit is that when I go into my house and close the door, they go home, and I have peace and privacy. Privacy is something I would not have if I were living in their housing compound as I did in Dagleta. I am grateful I only had to live in those conditions for only ten days.

# "Working" in Benin

## Why Peace Corps?:

I joined the Peace Corps for many reasons. Prior to joining I had whetted my appetite for travelling and living abroad. While in high school, I lived with a French family in France for a month on an exchange program. In college I went back to France for a month during winter break. During my junior year of college I studied abroad in Spain for a semester, and I lived with a Spanish family. I learned how exciting it is to live in a different country and experience it intimately as a temporary resident, and not as a tourist who only sees its most superficial aspects. I really got to know the people and experienced life as they did. Living abroad opened my eyes to how life can be different in so many ways from life in the United States. These experiences made me realize that the way of life I was accustomed to in America is not necessarily the best way of life, as Americans are often lead to believe. I found living in another country exciting and stimulating because I was learning so much and constantly being exposed to new things. I had to question my values and behaviors as I constantly compared them to those that prevailed in the country I was living in. When I lived abroad, I did so with an open mind and a strong desire to learn as much as I could about the country and the language. The more cultural discoveries I made, and the more relationships I made with the local people, the closer I felt to understanding the culture I was immersed in. I found it very satisfying to possess an intimate knowledge of a foreign land, to speak the language well, and to use both of these skills to forge relationships with the people that I met.

After college I was eager to continue exploring my interest in traveling abroad and learning about other countries. As Western Europe is very similar culturally to the United States, I was ready to live in a country that differed drastically from the U.S. to test myself and expand my horizons. Benin was just what I was looking for. I had a keen interest in language, and I wanted to use the French language skills I had worked hard to acquire since high school. I was also looking forward to learning a local African language. Being fresh out of college I craved adventure, and wanted to live in an exotic African country that most Americans have never heard of. I wanted to test myself to see how much I could adapt to, and I wanted to seek out as many character-building experiences as possible. I wanted to postpone having the major life commitments of adulthood (such as a nine to five job, a house, a family, and two lousy weeks of vacation per year), so I joined Peace Corps right out of college as many volunteers do. I had a strong desire to help people who are not as well off as I am. I was grateful for the education I received and the high standard of living I enjoyed in the United States. I was ready to give back. Helping people in developing countries improve their lives and serving as an American goodwill ambassador is the *raison d'être* of the Peace Corps, so it seemed a good fit for me. I had a strong desire to make a difference in Benin, and although I knew before going that the results of my efforts would be very modest at best, I had no idea how hard it would be to get the Beninese to change and subsequently to see the results of my efforts.

In 1995 Peace Corps Benin had several programs that volunteers were assigned to for their two-year stint. There were English and Science teachers. There were Rural Community Development volunteers who primarily taught hygiene, nutrition and other health related issues like AIDS prevention. In addition, there were Guinea Worm Eradication volunteers, Forestry volunteers, and Small Business Development volunteers. Before they arrive, volunteers are assigned to a program according to their experience, area of study and expertise. Programs phase in and out over the years depending on the needs of the country at a given time. The program I was assigned to was Small Business Development (SBD). As a SBD volunteer, my job was to teach basic small business skills to whoever was interested, but primarily to rural farming cooperatives as per the agreement Peace Corps arranged with the Beninese government. Since Peace Corps required the community to provide the volunteer's housing as a measure to ensure that the community would be interested in utilizing the volunteer's services, they arranged for the union of cooperatives in Allada to pay my $12 a month rent, so there was an expectation that I would work with cooperatives.

## Benin's Young Democratic Capitalistic Economy:

One obstacle I faced teaching small business management techniques was Benin's recent history as a Marxist-Leninist dictatorship, and its history of being colonized by the French for over 61 years that ended only in 1960. The result was that people had little entrepreneurial tradition, felt dependent on handouts, and did not feel self empowered. Mathieu Kérékou was the Marxist-Leninist dictator in power from 1972 to 1990. In 1991 there was a bloodless revolution due to economic pressures, which forced him to accept free elections. He lost the popular vote, and Nicéphore Sogolo was voted in as Benin's first democratically elected president under a capitalist system in 1991. It was remarkable, as Benin was the first country in Africa to have a peaceful transition from a dictatorship to a democracy through elections. In fact, Benin is well know to be an exceptionally peaceful country because there has been no war or major ethnic clashes since the early 70's when Kérékou took power.

When I arrived in 1995, democracy and capitalism had been in place for only four years, and Peace Corps' Small Business Program was only one year old. Since our program was new, there was only one cohort of four new Small Business volunteers who had arrived a few months before us. We were considered pioneers for the program, and because the program was new, Peace Corps had only a rough idea as to what we should do at our posts. The rest we had to figure out on our own and subsequently share with new incoming SBD volunteers.

During the Marxist-Leninist period, most Beninese continued making their living as usual: through subsistence farming and running micro enterprises. However, the government nationalized the few medium and large enterprises that existed (Bianco, David), and this subsequently suppressed Benin's economic growth and entrepreneurial spirit. In 1995 I read a government publication, which said in that Benin, a country of 5 million people at the time, there were only 44 private businesses that had over 20 employees! I found that the Beninese often felt dependent upon the government or numerous non-governmental aid organizations that operated in Benin for assistance. They did not have the "pull yourself up by your boot straps" mentality that countries with a strong tradition of capitalism have. Some of their attitude was based on a history of dependence, but unfortunately a lot was based on the current reality. Most people did not have the basic education needed to run a successful business, and getting anything aside from very small loans was very difficult.

## My Adjustment Period:

Arriving at post was both an exciting and traumatic experience. I was excited to have training end, as we had a very regimented schedule, and for that reason it felt like high school again. I was ready to be on my own and start doing what I came to Benin to do: explore, learn, grow, and help people. We were coddled for our first three months in training. Peace Corps took care of us and provided us with everything we needed. We eight Americans were together all the time, we spoke English amongst ourselves, and were comfortable being around other Americans. The Peace Corps training staff was all Beninese, except for one American trainer sent from Washington. They were very accustomed to Americans, so we could be ourselves with them as well. The only times we were on our own was when we had to live at our posts for ten days (as I described last chapter) and we slept over our Beninese host families' houses. We would go to our host families in the evening and return to our training center the next morning, but this was only for a few weeks. When the Peace Corps vehicle dropped me off at post for good, I had to face Benin head on and alone (or at least it felt that way, since I knew very few people in Allada when I first arrived).

I spent the first three months getting settled in and learning about my new environment. I lived in a small cement house on the edge of town down a very narrow dirt path about a mile from the town's center. I had no electricity for the first few months, and I did not have running water, which was certainly challenging to get used to. I worked on getting settled in my house, and figuring out how to feed myself. I ate street food a lot, but I also learned how to bargain and shop in the market so I could cook at home. I had to get used to the homesickness, loneliness, and cultural isolation of living in a completely foreign environment. I got to know my neighbors well, and I hung out with them when I had free time, or when I wanted to be with other people. I had to quickly learn to speak Fon, as many people spoke very little French or none at all. (In training I learned only the basics of Fon).

I got to know my counterparts at CARDER (the government rural extension agency) who brought me to villages to meet cooperatives that I worked with later on.

I had to deal with a lot of self-doubt as I felt very under qualified. My only business experience was running an exterior house painting business franchise called College Pro Painting during the summers when I was a student at the University of Connecticut. My major, in fact, was Political Science, not business. I guess Peace Corps figured that this didn't matter, as Benin's needs are at such a grass roots level that my limited experience was good enough. I was not so sure, and I hoped the people I worked with would not have high expectations of me.

In terms of "work," Peace Corps suggested we not try to jump in headfirst before three months had passed. We needed to get comfortable and learn about the culture and needs of the people before trying to assess what they needed and how to help them. I also had to establish relationships with people in order to gain their trust before they would be receptive to me. If I had started making assumptions and suggestions before fully understanding their cultural needs, it would not have been well received.

## Challenges to Making "Progress:"

I was assigned to work with a government run rural extension agency called CARDER that was supposed to help me with these adjustments. I worked directly with Clément, a CARDER agent based in Allada. His job was similar to mine in that he was responsible for helping villagers establish cooperatives, motivating them to continue working together, helping them to solve problems, and helping them to increase their profitability. He was called my "counterpart," and he was a really nice guy, but he proved to be of limited help to me once he introduced me to the cooperatives. He was a typical Beninese functionary. He was very, very laid back about his work. I thought it was funny that whenever he took me to cooperatives on his motorcycle, we would stop what seemed like every ten feet to greet people we crossed on the path as we approached the village we were visiting. Invariably it took a long time to get there. Once we arrived, he did little more than socialize. It was very frustrating working with

CARDER because they were never reliable. In the beginning of my service, I was very dependent on them to take me to the villages to introduce me to cooperatives. I was low on their priority list, however, so countless times I made plans with Clément and other CARDER agents to go out to the villages, and they often had to cancel on me for various reasons. When that happened, I would have nothing work related to do the entire day, and I would have to find things to do on my own. Thankfully, this only lasted for the first few months of my service. When they had introduced me to enough cooperatives, and I had learned enough about them, I began working with them on my own. I was happy once I became independent of CARDER, however, I still used them as a resource thereafter from time to time.

Most cooperatives were located in remote villages, and had anywhere from ten to 100 members. They pooled their resources to grow corn, peanuts, cassava, beans, pineapple, and other crops. Some produced soap, red palm oil, *gari*, *klui-klui* (fried peanut butter sticks), and tapioca, while others raised animals. Some provided services such as buying grain after the harvest at a low price and storing it. They stored it in granaries and then resold it at a profit when the price went up in the dry season to turn a profit. On average, the net worth of these groups was only the equivalent of a few hundred dollars, so they were what one calls in the developing world "micro-enterprises." They usually had a president, vice president, secretary, treasurer, a governing charter, and a bank account with the local bank in Allada. The members paid dues to help raise capital for the group's activities. Almost all the men were subsistence farmers by trade. Most of the women bought and resold goods, or produced goods as described above on their own to make money to support their families. Cooperatives served as a secondary source of income for its members, as they usually met as a group only once or twice a week.

This is a cooperative I worked with in a remote village.

I had to ride my mountain bike to the villages, so I worked primarily with the cooperatives that were one to five miles away from my house. Temperatures over 90 degrees, rain, extreme humidity, and terrible roads prevented me from being able to ride any farther. I did not have a phone, and neither did the villagers, so we had to set up appointments one to two weeks in advance in person. The problem was that during the one to two weeks before we met, there were often events that transpired which caused the cooperatives to cancel the meetings. The other problem was that I was never informed beforehand when meetings were cancelled, and I would show up for what one would call in French, a *"faux rendezvous"* (literally, "false meeting"). In other words, I would get stood up. The most common reason my appointments were cancelled was because *"il y avait un mort"* ("there was a death"). When someone dies in a village, the whole village mourns for a week, and for the most part, nothing gets done during that time.

Rain was another reason meetings were cancelled. I did not want to ride my bike in the rain, which is usually very heavy, and the villagers did not want to venture out either. After a heavy rain, the dirt paths leading to the cooperatives became mud bogs making the paths almost impassable. Often our meeting places were under a straw gazebo or a large tree. During the rainy season, the thunderstorms were very strong, and even if people had shown up, it would have been dangerous and impossible to teach anything.

This is a perfect example of the dirt "road" during the rainy season that I had to navigate to get to villages.

If there wasn't a hardship that caused our meeting to be cancelled, members of the cooperatives often forgot there was a meeting because the villagers rarely used calendars, and almost never wrote anything down if they were literate. They rarely owned watches or clocks, so they told time by the position of the sun on the horizon. Using this method has a margin of error of at least one hour. Subsequently, when I arranged to meet with a cooperative, they often showed up a half-hour to an hour and a half late. Waiting was not always an unpleasant experience, however, as there was always someone around with whom I could practice speaking Fon. I could also explore the village while I waited. Unfortunately I could not require them to come to me for meetings in Allada because almost no villagers had cars, very few had motorcycles, and only a handful had bicycles. For these reasons, I was rarely informed of a change in schedule.

When I arrived in a village for a meeting with a cooperative, I was very surprised if the people I was scheduled to meet with showed up at all. I tried to show up 15 minutes late to give them time to assemble before I got there, but almost always no one would be around when I arrived. In that case, I had to find the head of the cooperative, and he in turn rallied everyone to show up. When they did show up, I did my best to informally teach them small business management skills.

While teaching the classes, I had to deal with many distractions, such as crying babies, as all the mothers had to bring them along to the class. They usually didn't have a chalkboard for me to write on, and people riding by on motorcycles often disrupted class as we were working outside. On a couple of occasions, chickens, goats, and pigs wandered by, making noise and distracting everyone. Sometimes the sun baked us, it started to rain, or it was too windy to get much accomplished.

The American definition of "work" is very different from the Beninese definition. Work is work no matter where you go, but what differs is the expectation of how much, how well, and how quickly it gets done. In the U.S. we are very preoccupied with accomplishing tasks efficiently. We value completing tasks on time, and ensuring the work is done well, and done quickly. In Benin personal relationships are much more important than productivity, so when one works in Benin, very often more socializing takes place than work. When individuals showed up for my class, we could never "just get down to business," because it is important to the Beninese to always greet others and shake everyone's hand. It was annoying because if I was in the middle of teaching the group a lesson, and someone came late, the person arriving late usually interrupted me to briefly greet me. I loved the fact that Beninese were very laid back and friendly, but the trade-off was utter inefficiency.

Despite the fact that I was very frustrated with them at times, I could not get angry because the Beninese were so nice. The cooperatives often gave me lunch, gifts of fruit, and they sometimes sang praises about me together as a group. They gave me a lot of respect and viewed me as an expert because I was white and from the United States. I felt uneasy about that because I did not feel I deserved that level of respect because I knew I was no expert. They always offered me water, as is the custom in Benin. I felt obliged to drink it, despite the fact that ten people may have drunk out of the same bowl, as a bowl of water is often passed around among members in a group. If the water was brown, or for some reason I was especially distrustful of it, I would offer some to the ancestors by pouring a little on the ground instead of drinking it. Near the end of the dry season (around March), when it had not rained for more than four months, many villagers' cisterns (tanks that collect rain water) dried up, so they had to fetch their water from *marigots* (low lying ponds). I was sure to tactfully refuse water that time of year, due to the threat of contracting Guinea worm.

Guinea worm is a worm you get by drinking water that contains microscopic Guinea worm eggs. The worms then travel to your legs, grow into a worm, and several months later pop out of a sore. The only way to safely get it out is to wrap it around a matchstick and pull it out slowly over a period of weeks or months! Often painful infections ensue. There have even been accounts of the Guinea worm popping out of people's tongues!!

It was initially very difficult teaching small business skills, because I did not speak Fon well enough to do more than greet them and make smalltalk. Once we got down to business, I had to rely on a member of the group who spoke French to interpret for me. Because the interpreters did not always speak French very well, and were unskilled at interpreting, the interpretations were not always accurate. Sometimes everyone showed up except for my interpreter, making my class next to impossible. I taught them basic concepts such as marketing, product differentiation, bookkeeping, budgeting, cash flow analysis, and profit and loss analysis.

Most of the villagers were uneducated, illiterate, and innumerate, making teaching something as abstract as small business management very difficult to say the least. Usually I had to teach the one or two people in the cooperative who could read or write. I was always afraid that those people would take advantage of the group because those who could not read or write would have a hard time proving someone was being dishonest with the group's money and resources. For a cooperative to be official, they had to register documents with CARDER. Many members had to sign the documents using their inked fingerprints, because they could not even write their own names!

The people's attitudes were also a hindrance to teaching them new skills. They had low expectations of themselves, of their organization, and of me as well. They tended to be fatalistic and were not goal oriented. Sometimes I tried to help them set goals for their cooperative. When nothing got done, they would say, *"il faut attendre un peu,"* meaning "one must wait a little," or "one must be patient." I often got the feeling that the cooperative was a sort of social club where they could earn a little money at the same time. Some cooperatives I worked with told me that they spent all the money they earned during the year on a party in December! I was quick to point out to them that they would never grow their cooperative if they did that, and to me this was another example of how they were not concerned with growth at all. Indeed, most cooperatives had other motives.

Most cooperative members tended to be shortsighted and were concerned primarily with surviving day to day. Business management is all about investing and future benefits from present sacrifices. Because they were not thinking of the long term, and because they had almost nothing to save, I found it very hard to get them to think about the future of their businesses. In fact I often found myself teaching them that what they were doing was in fact a business, and that a business was something that could be measured, analyzed, and controlled, not just some activity they do to survive.

## Skills Versus Capital Dilemma:

I found out that many cooperatives existed mainly for the purpose of meeting the requirements of international and government aid agencies. Unfortunately, these agencies prefer to give grants to cooperatives, and not to individuals. They do this because they want their money to benefit as many people as possible. The result is that they discriminate against individuals who have an idea for small business, and tell them to form a cooperative in order to receive funding. Cooperatives almost always asked me to help get them money for projects, but they were usually very disorganized, and they were often apathetic. For these reasons, I could not help but think that they formed the cooperative solely to act as a front to get money from international aid agencies. I primarily worked with cooperatives that were headed by educated individuals (high school or less), but whose members were poor and illiterate villagers. The lack of trust and transparency between literate and illiterate members often caused tensions and sometimes led cooperatives to disband.

When aid agencies gave out money for projects such as building wells, schools, or workshops, there was always a lot of corruption involved. Often cooperative members tried to find ways to skim money or materials off the top because they knew they could get away with it. As a Peace Corps Volunteer, I was not equipped to help cooperatives obtain funding. My job primarily was to train them in small business skills. I told them from day one that I was there to teach them skills, and not to obtain funding for them, but most of them never believed me. I have a feeling most people attended my training sessions just to humor me, and hoped that they could eventually convince me to get them funding. I could tell because they never stopped asking. I couldn't blame them, as Peace Corps was one of the very few international aid agencies that did not give out money in Benin. Since there were so many that did, the Beninese have learned to equate white people with funded projects.

At times I was resentful of Peace Corps for not providing financial resources for me to award to worthy cooperatives. I know I could have helped them built a lot of things that the villagers could have used. It probably would have made me feel better about what I was doing, as I would have seen more concrete results (no pun intended) from my work had I helped them build a well, a school, or a building used for a cooperative's activities. On the other hand, I knew that there were a lot of problems involved with handing out money. For example, several miles down the narrow dirt path from my house, the scenery was very pristine and untouched by the modern world except for a cement mosque built by a Kuwaiti project, a new village birthing center built by the government, and several wells located at various places. They were paid for by different aid organizations such as UNDP (United Nations Development Program), the French, and the Japanese governments. There were also several broken down and dilapidated German built grain silos that were probably built in the 1970's. I was told that they were never of any use, because they were not built with the local humidity in mind and the corn stored inside rotted. Next to each group of silos was a small building intended for a cooperative to use as a meeting place, but those too were in shambles with no roof. A few of the wells I saw used mechanical pumps to bring the water to the surface, but they were all broken and useless because the people could not get the skilled labor and parts to fix them. Therein lies the problem with funded aid projects in the developing world. The Beninese are delighted to get a gift from the West, but inevitably they are not able to maintain whatever machinery or infrastructure that is provided to them if donors do not build them using "appropriate technology."

"Appropriate technology" means the people understand it, know how to use it, can maintain it, can get replacement parts, can repair it, and it meets their needs. It is also crucial that the recipients are required to participate in the design, funding, and construction of the project, so they have a vested interest in its long-term success.

Generally speaking, funded projects are nothing but a short-term solution to a long-term problem, unless the community plays an integral role in the design, makes a substantial contribution in labor, materials, or money to the project. The people have to want to help themselves in order for handouts to be of any use in the long term. Their vested interest helps insure that they will build upon what was given to them, instead of expecting more handouts as soon as the equipment breaks. Poorly conceived projects only make the recipients more dependent on Western aid, which is the exact opposite result the donors expect. The donors must design projects that use appropriate technology and are in tune with the needs of the local people, taking into consideration cultural and geographical realities. This can only be done with the input of the community. It is arrogant of aid agencies to think that just because a concept works well in the West, it will work well in Benin too, because circumstances are so different there. A classic example is giving farmers tractors. Most farmers in Benin only use hoes and machetes to do their farming. If someone gave them tractors, they would be of little help if they did not know how to use them properly, if they broke down, or if the local farmers who did not receive tractors, sabotaged them because they felt they threatened their livelihood.

The broken down wells and grain silos are perfect examples of hard-learned lessons in international third world development. They were mistakes made when the field of third world development was young and institutions trying to help were learning by trial and error. A majority of the world's colonies (including Benin) was liberated in the 1960's, so the concept of "international development" did not come into existence until shortly after then. Since the 1960's, many lessons have been learned, and luckily most aid agencies today require the local people to contribute at least 20% of the value of the project before the aid agency will agree to contribute the remaining 80%. The aid agencies usually require the local community to initiate, design, and solicit support from them through a competitive application process as opposed to the aid agencies deciding arbitrarily where and how to help. Although donors listen more to the needs of the people today, involve them more in the design and implementation of projects, and promote the use of appropriate technology, the success of funded projects in the long term from what I've seen is still mediocre.

One of the more difficult aspects of being a Peace Corps Volunteer was that most other international aid agencies in Benin funded projects such as digging wells, building schools, meeting halls, storage sheds, workshops, animal pens, latrines, etc. This created an expectation that I would do the same for them, no matter how many times I told them I that I was there to teach small business management skills, not to fund projects. Peace Corps stresses training and teaching, and does little in the way of funding projects. My job was to give people the skills to help them help themselves. When I saw the broken down corn silos, buildings and broken well pumps rusting away, I wished I could make the people see how ineffective funded projects had been, and made them realize the importance of the education I offered. In an ideal situation, I would have offered them both training and money, but unfortunately I did not have the latter. On the other hand, business training does little good if they do not have the capital to start or grow their businesses, and this was very frustrating to me and them. With respect to raising capital, the only thing I could stress to the people I was teaching was the importance of saving and reinvesting their profits. I felt good knowing that the training I was giving them helped them save for the required 20% contribution needed to get a grant. They were more likely to win a grant via the competitive grant soliciting process, as they had improved their organization and made themselves more attractive to the committees selecting grant recipients.

## Training Government Employees:

From my American, results-oriented perspective I found my partner organization, CARDER, to be a very inefficient organization, and its employees were extremely unmotivated. For example, I organized a workshop to teach the CARDER employees the same small business skills that I was teaching to the cooperatives, so they could teach the same skills to the villagers that they worked with. When I went to the head of CARDER, he told me that in order to get the CARDER employees to attend, I would have to pay them. I would have to give them a per diem allowance, I would have to buy them lunch, and pay for the cost of transportation, even if I held the workshop during their normal work hours at the CARDER office!! In essence, he told me that they would require to be paid twice. They would be paid once from their normal salary from CARDER, and once from me, since I was asking them to attend a "training workshop." I could not believe what I was hearing! I told the CARDER head that it would be difficult for me to get funding, and asked him if he could make it mandatory that they attend. He said that if he did, the employees would just find excuses not to come. He also said that if I held the workshop in the CARDER office, they would not be attentive, they would show up late, they would come and go to do errands in town, and they would go to get food. This was the prevailing attitude, as the words "training workshop" entailed lots of perks to the CARDER employees. Most workshops were sponsored by well funded international aid agencies, which brought people together from different parts of the country, and lasted several days. They were used to going off site where they were lodged in a hotel or dorm, were paid per diem, transportation costs, and three meals a day. That was the type of "training workshop" I had to compete with!

Because it would have taken a monumental effort for me to get the funding, I held the workshop as I intended at the CARDER office without any per diem, or meals, or hotels, or reimbursed transportation costs. Everyone showed up, but the head of CARDER was right. They showed up late, they complained about not getting per diem, and they came and went to do errands in town. Nonetheless, I found that they were interested, they seemed to learn a lot, and they were appreciative of my efforts. I was happy about that, but because of my unrealistic expectations, I was disappointed at their attitude.

Working with village cooperatives and CARDER in this unstructured manner was very frustrating and sometimes depressing to say the least. It was very difficult to find enough cooperatives that were receptive to what I had to offer to fill up my schedule, especially in the beginning of my Peace Corps service. As a result I had a lot of free time, and I passed the time by studying Vodun, practicing Fon, reading, writing letters home, writing in my journal, hanging out with other Peace Corps Volunteers in the area, cooking, hanging out with Beninese friends, exploring the area by bike, and taking two to three hour afternoon naps since it was so hot in the afternoon. As time went on, I got to know more cooperatives and I became busier. After a year I saw some results from my work, such as noticing certain cooperatives starting to keep books and creating profit and loss statements. Some made small improvements in the way they ran their cooperatives. Despite these small accomplishments (or perhaps because of them), I decided to change my strategy and work with individual small business owners in Allada. I did this because they were more educated and more dynamic, being that they worked alone and had a greater interest in improving their businesses. They were not constrained by needing the consensus of the group that cooperatives required in order to do anything.

## The Second Year: Shifting Away from Farming Cooperatives:

During my second year, I worked with a traditional savings and loan organization, a welder, a sculptor, a weaver, a carpenter, a small shop owner, a poultry raiser, a vegetable gardener, and a seamstress. I found working with them much more satisfying, as I was able to teach them much more because they had attended high school, and they could read, write, speak French, and do basic math on paper. They were also more willing to adopt the new skills I taught them quickly. I consulted with them one on one and held training workshops for them as a group. I kept my relationship with CARDER as limited as possible due to my frustration with their lax attitude. During my second year I still worked with village cooperatives, but only the ones that were most interested in working with me. Unfortunately, by the time I had become the most effective, my service was ending, and I was heading back to the United States.

My contribution to the individual business owners was limited too, but I saw much better results than I did from working with most cooperatives. I was satisfied that I helped a handful of Beninese people improve their businesses. Because there are so many factors limiting progress in Benin, modest results were all that I could expect. Making a difference in Benin did not come easily, and it required a great deal of time, patience, and resourcefulness.

A few cooperatives and most individual business owners I worked with showed a lot of appreciation for what I taught them, although I felt that my contribution was insignificant. At times I felt guilty because I gained more from my time in Benin than I contributed. I felt they taught me much more about life in Benin than I taught them about small business management. I arrived with the notion that the Beninese needed to learn to be more productive and make more money to improve their lives. I left feeling that relationships are just as important or perhaps more important than monetary progress.

Peace Corps' first mission is the transfer of skills as described above. Its second mission is for its volunteers to be American goodwill ambassadors by making meaningful relationships with the people and teaching them about Americans. I can confidently and proudly say I accomplished the latter.

## Service After my Peace Corps Service:

Peace Corps' third goal is to teach others in the United States what we learned while serving overseas. I did so while I was in Benin through communication with friends and family. When I got back, I gave talks and slide shows of my experiences to schools, retirement homes, and homeless shelters. I spoke about my experiences, (and still do) to family, friends and my students quite frequently. I created a website called "Fon is Fun" (www.fon-is-fun.org) that teaches Fon, as well as cultural information about Benin. When I went back to Benin with my wife seven years after I left (in 2004, see chapter 12), I created a DVD documentary about Benin called "Discovering Benin" that is available on www.Fon-is-Fun. org. I'm finishing this book 14 years after my service ended, and I am still performing Peace Corps' third goal. I do so not out of a sense of obligation to Peace Corps, but out of a personal desire to share such a wonderful, enlightening, and life changing experience.

One of the things that I did not fully comprehend while I was in Benin, was that I would teach others for the rest of my life what I learned there. The results of that are definitely not immediate and not measurable. If I had solely used American criteria for "progress" based on dollars spent to dollars earned to judge my accomplishments while serving in Benin, I certainly would have been a failure.

## The Dilemma of International Development:

Ironically, after gaining a greater appreciation of Beninese culture, I began to question my motives in coming to Benin to "help people" by teaching small business development skills. I was teaching them skills in hopes that they would be able to earn more money, and be able to provide for themselves better. By doing so I was inexorably altering their culture by introducing Western values. Benin is definitely becoming more westernized as new technology and people such as myself expose them to more and more Western ideas. I realized that the potential exists for many modern Western values to displace the positive traditional Beninese culture values like a bulldozer.

As Western values are introduced, things change in Benin. There are some aspects of Benin I do not want to change. I appreciate that the Beninese have so much time to spend with each other. Families are very close, literally and figuratively, because they usually do not move far away in search of work. People are very friendly to each other and are not usually stressed. Some negative Western values I do not want to see take hold in Benin are profit and efficiency becoming more important than personal relationships. Western values teach that finding a better job is more important than living near family members. Work will become less social as the importance of efficiency grows. As the standard of living increases, people will buy more Western goods and will become more materialistic. Materialism will lead people to spend less time with others. As people become accustomed to having more money, they will have to work harder to continue improving their standard of living and will become more stressed. The result will be the Westernization of Benin and a permanent loss of Benin's traditional value system.

At times I felt bad about having a hand in the erosion of traditional Beninese values I had grown to appreciate, and contemplating the negative Western values they would be replaced with. On the other hand, Benin is the 30th poorest country in the world according to the CIA's Factbook (www.cia.gov), so many people suffer abject poverty. Many are barely able to get enough clean water, and nutritious food. Few have access to quality healthcare, many are uneducated, and are not able to save money for their future. I knew that the people I was helping would be able to provide better for themselves and their families due to my efforts. Having better nutrition, having money to pay for healthcare, and improving their living conditions, seems like a fair tradeoff for losing some traditional aspects of their culture. Of course no one knows how Benin will change once it becomes more developed. The jury is out on whether they will be happier in the future than they are now, and therein lies the most fundamental conundrum of a developed country "helping" a less developed country: are we doing more harm than good?

# Market Day in Allada

I am sitting on a small wooden stool in a woman's market stall under a makeshift palm branch shelter. I am writing everything I see, hear, smell, feel and think. Words are pouring from my hand so quickly it seems that I don't have control of it. Every five days the market takes place here, rain or shine, and every time it is once again a momentous occasion like no other. Today is market day. The West African market is a phenomenon that bombards the senses and is an experience few Westerners can ever forget. There is a din of chatter from the thousands of people haggling over prices, greeting each other, honking horns, and cars and motor cycles passing. "Psss . . . *Yovo!!,*" someone calls out to me, but I ignore him. Although I have been living in Benin as a Peace Corps Volunteer for just over two years, the market has never ceased to amaze me. There is nothing like it in the Western world, and my distant memory of the American shopping mall and supermarket seems so foreign and bland compared to this. Now they seem like places I visited on another planet long ago.

People come from dozens of outlying villages within a ten-mile radius to this one spot in the center of my village, Allada, every market day. In the *sous préfecture* (county) of Allada, there are four markets that take place in a continuous cycle, and each market has its designated order. For example, in this region the four local markets are in the villages of Allada, Avakpa, Ouégbo, and Sékou. Avakpa always comes first. The following day is the Allada market, followed by Ouégbo, and finally the Sékou market. The fifth day is *Bossigbe*, or the day of rest, which is mandated by the ancestors and by the traditional religion. "*Psss, Yovo, Donne—moi de l'argent*" (Yovo, give me money!), someone shouts to me from a distance, and again I ignore it. The market is so important in this society that the market cycle is used to measure the passage of time. For example, whenever I try to set up an appointment to meet someone the following week, they always calculate how many Allada market days or Avakpa market days (etc.) away it is. Although the French introduced the Western calendar system here, many people don't pay much attention to it and still measure time by the passage of markets.

## Role of the Market:

Regional markets such as this one play a very important role in the local economy, and are also important social events that bring people together from the entire region. Imagine that the only place in the region where you can go to buy and sell goods for reasonable prices (and still see a decent selection of goods) is here, and it only happens once every five days! For that reason it is as busy as Grand Central Station. There are thousands of people here, and they are all packed into an area about two football fields long. It is relatively small in comparison to urban markets in Benin, which are much larger. The Allada market is lined with several rows of palm branch stalls stretching from one end of the market to the other. The stalls protect the sellers from the searing equatorial sun, but these roofs do little to protect the occupants when it rains hard. Only a few of the more successful sellers can afford to buy corrugated iron sheets to make their stalls rainproof. If it rains, people scramble for cover because in Benin, when it rains, it pours. If it does rain, many vendors do not make much money because all of their customers go home, and if it starts early in the day, people don't come at all, as they do not want to venture out on the muddy dirt roads and paths.

Some people may have come by bush taxi from as far away as the capital city, Cotonou, which is an hour and a half away travelling on one of Benin's few paved roads. People go to Cotonou to buy imported products because Cotonou has the only port and international airport in the country, and imported goods are cheapest at the point of entry into Benin. After buying a relatively small amount of goods in Cotonou, they often transport them by bush taxi to the inland markets to resell them for a small profit. "*Oh . . . Yovo!! . . . Yovo!!*" a kid shouts to me as he walks by. That is how most goods are distributed in Benin, and it is why the market plays such a key role in the economy. There are few wholesalers or distribution companies in Benin, so the small-scale entrepreneur selling in the local market is the only way to get goods to the people around the country. This method of distribution is informal, very haphazard, and is done on a small scale. That is why it is often difficult to find certain imported goods up country and why non-locally produced goods are available sporadically at best. I often buy imported goods, such as wheat flour, from small shops in Allada, and I have become reliant on them for my cooking. It drives me crazy at times because they often tell me *"c'est fini"* (*It ran out*).

## The Link Between Food and Nature:

Here in the market almost all of the food is locally produced. If the average urban or suburban American were asked where his food came from, he would probably not be able to explain in much detail before it arrived at the supermarket. If asked where his water came from, he would say the faucet and perhaps a reservoir if there is one near by. Generally speaking, Americans are very detached from their food because less than 3% of the American population is involved directly in farming, while the figure is about 85% in Benin, due in part to a lack of industrialized farming techniques. In the U.S., most people don't see how food is grown. Since many foods are processed in factories before they are sold, people often don't even know what the primary ingredients look like. Farms are located far away from the urban / suburban centers where most Americans live, and the factories that transform the food are inaccessible to the average person.

In Benin it is quite the opposite. There is a very direct connection between food and nature, and it is evident in the market. Almost all food is grown and processed locally, so everyone knows the origins and processes involved in food production. Most people grow their own food; if not, someone in their family does. After watching their animals grow up, mate, and give birth, they then kill the animals themselves to eat. After killing my first chicken, I realized that killing your own meat really reinforces its origin psychologically. Rationally, Americans know that meat was once a living animal, but it is easy to forget this strolling down the meat aisle in the supermarket. The meat in American supermarkets is clean, neatly cut up, packaged, sealed, and there are few visible signs that it was ever living. We are easily fooled, as anything that could be anatomically identifiable (such heads, feet, fur, feathers, tails, internal organs etc.) are removed. There are very few factories in Benin, so they must transform their own food. For example, after they harvest and dry their corn, they must bring it to the local mill to grind it into flour, while the Westerner would simply buy a bag of pre-ground corn flour. The Beninese can physically see where their water comes from. It falls from the sky onto their roofs and ground and is collected in wells or cisterns (cement collection tanks sunk in the ground). They must pull the water out of the ground by hand and haul it to their house on their heads before they can use it. Sometimes they put large clay pots under the edges of their tin roofs to catch the rainwater if they don't have a cistern, or if theirs is in disrepair.

There are very few pre-prepared foods available to the average person in Benin, because they are imported and too expensive. The foods that are processed are usually made locally, so everyone knows how they were made. Examples are palm oil and *gari* (cassava flour). In every village women buy palm nuts and make oil out of them, which they sell in the market and which people buy for cooking. The same is true of gari. Everyone knows basically how these products are made (even if they haven't done it themselves), as they've had the opportunity to observe others do it. In Benin the only canned foods commonly available are sardines and tomato paste that are imported from Italy or France. Foods are almost never packaged, so people see it in its natural state, and are therefore able to touch it and smell it before purchasing it. Almost all food is grown locally. In the West there is an elaborate distribution system in place, which allows consumers to eat foods that are produced thousands of miles away, including foods that are out of season. Since everything is grown locally here, I have seen the plants or trees that produce almost every type of fruit, vegetable and grain that I eat. In the U.S. the only food we can touch before we bring it home to our kitchens is produce. Being in Benin and learning how my food is grown and processed has strengthened my connection with nature. In the West that connection is very weak (or even nonexistent) because of technology, which strives to control nature and ultimately separates us from it.

## Bargaining:

As I survey the market, I see people in vibrantly colored clothing everywhere. Some are talking, some are arguing, and some are throwing their hands in the air while they haggle over prices. Bargaining is a form of socializing, and definitely adds to the fun of buying things, unless you are a white guy who sellers perceive as having a ton of money. Bargaining can still be lots of fun for me if I am in the mood and I am getting the prices I want. Often Peace Corps Volunteers get ripped off because the Beninese perceive us as being rich (which we obviously are not, as we are paid only $6 a day to live on). Although by local standards, $6 a day is pretty good for one person, it is far less than they perceive us as earning. They assume we are paid like the other white people here who work for various international aid agencies, and are paid much better than Peace Corps Volunteers. When sellers who don't know me see me coming, they usually double their prices, and I have to bargain twice as hard to get close to the "real" market price. Very few people in the market speak French well, so I have to speak Fon which I have gotten pretty good at. Despite the fact that I speak Fon pretty well, it would be much easier if I could bargain in French. The number system in Fon is especially hard. For example 580 francs is *kpon ko nukun aton dola atoon,* which translates to "25 times 23 plus 5!" And there is no easier way of expressing it! Not only do I have to think in Fon, but also I have to do convoluted math in my head at the same time.

It is near impossible for a Yovo to get the "real" price unless you have created a personal relationship with a seller who you have frequented and thus shown some loyalty to. I am grateful because I have been here long enough to have made such relationships. They know me and I know them. I know the price and they know I know the price, so I do not have to worry about bargaining. Volunteers who have been in their villages long enough to enjoy this luxury usually like to brag about how "their" rice and beans mama gives them extra food every time, or how "their" bread seller always gives them a good price. Not getting ripped off makes me feel accepted by the community and proud to have overcome the system that discriminates against outsiders. In fact, I have even spoken to Beninese people from other parts of the country who complain about being overcharged because they are considered outsiders. The people here can easily tell if a person is from another part of the country due to differences in physical appearance, ethnic facial scarification, and accent. I am proud because I have been here long enough to have my own bread seller, two rice and beans mamas (one for lunch and one for dinner), and my egg/ tomato/ onion seller who I call *Noche*—("My Mother"). We chat a little every time I come to buy from them. I am happy to see them, and they are happy to see me. It is a relationship I maintain by buying from them exclusively.

I greet them according to Beninese custom so they don't get offended. If you get down to business with them immediately (as Westerners usually do) they perceive you as being aloof, rude and pushy. The Beninese rarely get down to business without first exchanging a long litany of friendly and warm greetings. For example, when I see my rice and beans Mamma, she is always excited to see me and cries out enthusiastically:

-*Oh Gandaho!* (Gandaho is my name in Fon, which means "Big Chief." I learned that word when I was in training. When they asked my name when I arrived in Allada I thought I'd play a joke and say my name was Gandaho. From then on I was Gandaho.)
-*Noche, a do kede á?* (My Mother! Are you well?)
-*enn, un do gangi.* (Yes, I'm well),
-*Enn* (Yes, pronounced like the "an" in "ant," but it is drawn out and pronounced at least a whole second)
-*A blo kpede á?* (Did you do a little?)
-*Enn, un blo kpede.* (Yes, I did a little)
-*Mi kud'azo.* (Good work)
-*ooooOOOOO* (said like the "O" in "toe" but it increases in pitch and means "I acknowledge your greeting."
-*A wa axime we a?* (Did you come to the market?)
-*Enn, un wa axime.* (Yes, I came to the market)
-*A do fin e á?* (Are you here?) (The Beninese love to state the obvious in their greetings.)
-*Enn, Un do fi.* (Yes, I'm here)
-*Asu towe do gangi á?* (Is your husband well?)
-*Enn, E do gangi. (Yes he's well)*
-*A sa kpede á?* (Did you sell a little?)
-*Enn un sa kpede* (yes, I sold a little)

When you're in a hurry, the extreme friendliness can be a hassle because it takes so long . . . but then again, it's a rare occasion that anyone is in a hurry in Benin. If I am in a hurry, it's usually self-imposed by my American values, and is not dictated by the local culture, as it's always acceptable to be late. The social interaction really makes shopping and eating street food fun. It's a great way to have a few laughs when they tease me or I tease them, all while practicing my Fon, which I enjoy very much. I think back to how cold a feeling it is to shop in the U.S., where the cashiers rarely talk to you, even if they see you every week. Heck, sometimes they don't even look at you if they're busy and tired! People in

Benin are very social, outgoing, and friendly by nature, and I don't have to make much of an effort to strike up a conversation with anyone. Being white also makes me a celebrity, and people are always trying to talk to me whether I want to or not. I could easily spend all day here just chatting with the people I buy from, strangers who want to talk to the Yovo, and acquaintances I've made in town. The Beninese are not so constantly busy (like Westerners), so they have time to be so social and get to know you. Almost no one is in a hurry. They have little money, but they've got all the time in the world, which I feel is the primary reason the personalities of Africans and Westerners are so different.

Because I am a Yovo, I get ripped off all the time outside of Allada since I cannot befriend a seller for everything I buy. When I buy anything outside of Allada, I am usually resigned to pay more because I don't know anyone and I don't always have the energy to bargain hard. Getting ripped off continuously is a sore point for me and all *Yovos* in Benin, especially those of us in the Peace Corps who have to live on a very tight budget. I have come to Benin to help these people, yet it seems all they can think of is how to get more money out of me, and it makes me feel like a walking dollar sign. If I were a tourist it wouldn't be such a big deal, but I want to feel like I am part of the community and want to be treated as such. Unfortunately, most people will never see it that way no matter how long I live here. If I have no idea how much something should cost, I am helpless, because there is no such thing as a price tag. A third party won't tell me how much a local person would pay, in fear of sparking the anger of the seller, who according to custom, has the right to charge whatever she wants without interference from well intentioned bystanders. It drives volunteers absolutely crazy that they try to rip us off, even if it's a question of very little money. I have found myself fighting tooth and nail over 10 CFA (2 cents) because of the principle, not the money. (The CFA is the West African currency which is backed by the French and is universal in most all former French West African colonies.) Paying the going price an issue of pride, wanting to be treated with equality, and not wanting to be discriminated against, even if it is relatively benign form of discrimination. Fortunately for me, racial discrimination is no worse than having to pay a little extra and being called *Yovo*, which is not a malicious term in itself. Luckily the Beninese are not angry towards Americans, or Europeans, as is the case in many countries in the world today.

Bargaining is a real art that you've got to perfect if you want to feel like an "old pro." If you don't know what the real "market" price should be, your starting price may be too high, and if it is, there's no going lower because you've already established the minimum that you're willing to pay. Bargaining is an exercise in compromise. The buyer gives the lowest price that she feels won't offend the seller, or the seller will start at the maximum price she thinks the buyer will entertain without getting angry and walking away. Then the two parties go back and forth until a price in the middle is reached. What works for me is to start by offering one half to one quarter of the price I am willing to pay, and then work my way up.

It was especially frustrating when I was a new volunteer, because some products (such as bread and eggs) are not negotiable, and the vendors would get angry when I tried to get them to lower their price. I have mastered the practice of walking away when I think the price is too high, because usually if the seller is trying to rip me off, she will wave me back willing to sell at the real market price or close to it. *"Bon Soir Yovo!!"* ("Good evening, Whitey!,") a young girl says to me walking by. What really annoys me is that sometimes even though I walk away, and I have offered what I believe to be a fair price, they don't wave me back. Sometimes they are convinced that white people should pay more because they are "rich", so if I am not willing to pay more than everyone else, they won't sell to me at all.

Seasonal price fluctuation on food items is a huge problem for me, because I have no way of telling if the item is really out of season (and thus more expensive), or if the vendor is just trying to pull the wool over my eyes. I have offended several sellers because I did not believe the price was higher because the item was out of season. Even after being here two years, I often get ripped off when I buy something for which I do not know the "real" price, or if I am not in the mood for bargaining. If I don't have the energy to fight, I rationalize paying extra as a tax on being "rich".

## Sounds:

There is an infinite cacophony of sounds coming from all directions: people talking, shouting, calling out to passers by, babies crying, people yelling "Yovo" at me constantly, people asking me if I am going to buy something, if I will give them my Timex wristwatch, if I will give them

50, 100, or 500 Francs, or if I will give them my bike. A woman asks me if I will marry her two-year-old daughter, after which I politely decline. I get offers like this often. It is their attempt at humor, and their way of expressing their desire to see their children with a white man, no matter how young she is, because of the money and status it would bring the family. The tooth stick seller has a big basin of tooth sticks on his head (the Beninese chew on tooth sticks as a way to clean their teeth). They always identify themselves by making a loud obnoxious kissing sound to attract customers, so when you hear that sound you know the tooth stick seller is near. A shoe repair guy walks around making the universal shoe repairman sound: *Thunk . . . . thunk . . . th thunk thunk thunk. Thunk . . . . thunk . . . th thunk thunk thunk.* He does this by tapping a stick on a wooden box that he carries on his shoulder, which contains his shoe polish and tools. *Cling-cling . . . . cling-cling . . . cling-cling* goes the nail clipper with his manicure scissors as he wanders back and forth throughout the market looking for customers. He charges 100 CFA (20 cents) for a manicure and the same for a pedicure. *Honk, Honk* goes the Fan Milk (a local type of ice cream) man honking his bike horn. *Ting, ting, ting, ting, ting, ting ting, ting* goes the medicinal drink seller, tapping a shot glass resting on his finger against the bottle of his potion, as he wanders the market trying to attract customers with his brand of music.

## Smells:

All of the foods for sale are placed out in the open hot air and sun so the smells permeate the air unlike the supermarkets back home, where everything is hermetically sealed and the only smell is that of floor polish. The smells are very strong and diverse throughout the different sections of the market. What you smell depends on what part of the market you're in. A blind person would have no problem making his way around the market navigating by smell alone. The sellers are geographically clustered, so each product has its area of the market where all the vendors of that product sit. They must do that to gang up on market goers, either tempting or assaulting their olfactory senses as they pass by. When I go through the section where they sell smoked fish, I feel nauseous. When I enter the section where they sell hot pepper dried and ground into powder and piled in heaps, it burns my nose and my eyes water as some gets kicked up into the air. When I go past one of the many gris-gris (magic charm) ingredient sellers who have their wares laid out on the ground, the air is permeated with the stench of decaying animals and animal parts that they sell for making magic charms, for Vodun ceremonies, and for Vodun altars. They sell to traditional healers and others who have the skill to use these ingredients in ceremonies used to cure people of illnesses and insure good fortune. They are also used to create magic charms. In another area, there is a strong smell of peanut butter from piles of *klui-klui* (fried peanut butter sticks) stacked three feet high.

As I wander through the market, people are constantly calling out to me: *"Gandaho Wa!"* (Gandaho, come here) or the more annoying and less personal way *"Yovo!! Wa xonu!"* (Whitey, come buy from me!). I rarely recognize people who are calling me, so I just wave and keep going. If I spoke to everyone who wanted to speak to me, I could easily spend all day here! Strangers and people I know are continuously greeting me, and most greetings require a response of "Yes" (Enn) or "I acknowledge your greeting" (oooOOO). My response to most of these greetings is a nearly continuous string of "Enn, oooOOO, Enn, oooOOO, Enn, Enn, oooOOO, Enn, oooOOO, oooOOO." After awhile, it becomes comical.

## Movement:

People are circulating everywhere. If you woke up from a deep sleep here, you would think you were in the middle of some sort of civil unrest, because there is so much commotion. After coming here regularly for a few months, however, you would get used to it, and realize you are witnessing "controlled chaos." It is lively and animated. People are coming and going in every direction. They are shouting, talking, and haggling over prices. Some sections of the market are so crowded that I cannot help bumping into people. In fact sometimes people purposefully reach out and touch me as I pass, because they've never touched white skin before. I guess they are checking to see if it feels the same as theirs, or perhaps they do it just to say they've touched a Yovo. As I maneuver my way through the crowded aisles, pushing my mountain bike along, the hot equatorial sun is pounding me relentlessly, and I feel as if I will melt if I don't find shade quickly.

As I pass one of my sellers she calls to me:
- *Yovo, A do fin e á!* (Whitey, Are you there?)
- *Enn, Un do fi* (Yes, I'm here.)
- *Kwabo Gandaho.* (Welcome Gandaho!)
- *A xo nu kpede á?* (Did you buy a little?)
- *Enn, un xo nu kpede.* (Yes, I bought a little, I reply to the old woman.).
- *Asi towe do gangi á?* (Is your wife well?)
- *Un do asi a.* (I don't have a wife.)
- *Ete Wutu?* (Why not?)
- *Un tuun a.* (I don't know.)

Because I am white and different, people are always staring at me and calling out to me, often asking if I am married. They can never understand why I'm not married at age 23 because most Beninese men my age have at least one wife and a few "second offices," as they say. "Well, why don't you marry a Beninese girl!?" is their usual response.

Vendors are sprawled out along the aisles under their stalls, sitting with their wares spread out in front of them. Some place their goods on simple tables while others lay their goods on the ground on top of plastic rice sacs. Some sellers endure the scorching sun because they cannot afford to pay the 10-cent tax to the town, which allows them to sit under a stall all day. To shade themselves, these women wear huge brimmed straw hats. Other women and children who want to sell, but don't want to pay for a stall or sit still in the hot sun, wander around the market all day looking for customers. By the time I leave the market, the sun and heat will have drained my energy, and I will be ready for my daily afternoon nap because it is 95 degrees and humid in the shade, and 130 degrees in the sun!

As I approach a seller to buy some toilet paper, I hear African Zairois music being played at an ear shattering volume from behind me. I have to shout so the woman can hear me. Playing loud music is form of marketing because it gets everyone's attention. I point to my ear then point to the guy behind me playing the music, and the woman suddenly runs over to him and in a tirade yells at him to "turn that damn music down!!!" She's screaming in Fon at an elevated pace, so I don't understand what she's saying, but I can get the gist from her body language. She is huge and weighs at least 300 pounds, as do many women who sell in the market. She's what we Peace Corps Volunteers call a "Marché Mama." Being overweight is a sign of wealth and status in Benin so successful women in the market tend to be heavy. She has the biggest breasts I have ever seen. I cannot help but notice them because they have slipped out of the cloth, which she loosely wrapped around her chest. Obviously she didn't pay close attention to keeping them tightly in place because in West Africa breasts are not a big deal. In fact, women breast-feed their babies anywhere and everywhere in public without covering up.

In villages, women usually go topless, but in towns, markets, and cities, women make at least a modest effort to cover themselves. After being here for two years, I have become desensitized to seeing women's breasts. It is very common for women to tie their babies to their backs with a piece of cloth. That way they can do what they need to do and have their hands free. Believe it or not I have seen babies breast-feed from their mother's backs by pulling their mothers' very saggy breasts under her arm! This is made possible by giving birth to and breast feeding many children, not wearing a bra and suffering the affects of gravity. Mothers who are not able to do this often just twist the cloth slightly so her baby is more on her side allowing her baby to reach her breast. This way she can continue with her chores and breastfeed her baby without stopping what she's doing. Even though I've been desensitized for the most part to seeing women's breasts in public on a daily basis, it still reminds me how stark the cultural differences are between West Africa and the United States.

The woman is yelling at the guy about his loud music and she is also looking for support from the other people selling around her, which people often do when they have an argument. The person who has a gripe with someone else won't just address their opponent, but will plead his or her case to anyone within earshot and will try to win supporters. The opposing person will do the same. They will try to get onlookers involved in the argument to argue on their behalf. Whoever can win the most support from the crowd usually wins the argument. It is quite an interesting scene, which seems much more civil and community oriented than in the West, where no one wants to get involved in other people's arguments, and often continue on their way ignoring any disturbance or gawking from a safe distance. It is also funny seeing an obviously angry person boisterously pleading her case to strangers and onlookers who have nothing to do with the argument. Seldom do such arguments lead to violence. It is like a spontaneous jury in the street. I patiently wait five minutes for her while she unleashes a storm of fury, and finally intimidates the loud music player to turn it down with support from the neighboring vendors and market goers. At last I am able to hear her. I buy my toilet paper and continue on my way.

## Children and Yovo's:

Because of Benin's astronomical birth rate, there are children everywhere, and there are more children under 15 than there are adults. There are so many that they often seem like ants swarming around me. In the U.S., I do not see small children out in public that often, so here the number of children I see every day is overwhelming. Mothers carry their infants on their backs wherever they go, and as soon as a child can walk, they are out and about playing with their older brothers, sisters, cousins, and friends. The Beninese almost never use birth control, so the women have babies one after another. Having many children is necessary in order to have a large family due to a very high rate of infant mortality. Most women expect at least one or two of their babies to die, so they do not perform the naming ceremony, which initiates the newborn as an official member of the family, until the baby is three months old. The baby is most susceptible to falling ill and dying during those three months, so they try not to get attached to the child until that initial period has passed. Some more traditional women will not leave the area around her house for three months after giving birth, for fear that by leaving she will be attacked by a witch, and the witch will then kill her baby. A few times when I bought something from a woman, I tried to give her the money and she pointed to the table, telling me to put the money on the table instead of directly in her hand. I later found out that this is to protect her and her newborn baby. She believed that if I touched her hand, I could pass an evil spirit to her that would then kill her baby. This woman could not afford to stay home for three months until the naming ceremony, so to her, this was next best way to protect her baby. To a westerner, it sounds funny that a mother believes evil spirits or curses could attack her baby, but by staying home and avoiding contact with strangers, she is doing exactly what many do in the West: protecting her baby from germs. The Beninese just have a different explanation for it.

As I am sitting here in the market, there is a group of children staring at me and singing the *Yovo* song: *"Yovo, Yovo bon soir, ça va bien? Merci."* When I ride my bike through the villages deep in the bush, I usually have 15 or 20 children chasing me because it's such a rare occurrence to have a white guy in their village. They're bored and it offers an interesting form of amusement. They often yell out annoying things to me like, *Yovo, Donne-moi de l'argent!* ("Whitey, give me money!"), or just plain "*Yovo!*" Adults torment us by over charging us and staring at us. Children torment us and have a great time at our expense by singing that hideous *Yovo* song. I must hear it at least 50 times a day, and if I had a franc for every time I've been called "*Yovo*," I would be a millionaire! Sometimes they gang up on me and there is whole chorus of ten children singing as loud as they can "*Yovo, Yovo Bon soir, ça va bien? merci!.*" They often repeat for at least five minutes until they get tired or I leave. Sometimes I have fun with them by pretending I am angry and I start chasing them. The song may sound harmless, but after only a few days of being in Benin, the cuteness wears off and begins to feel disrespectful. I am convinced they sing it out of ignorance, not maliciousness. Seeing a white person is so rare that the children get excited, and they express it by singing the *Yovo* song. They have no idea why it bothers white folks so much.

Many educated adults don't understand why it bothers us either, even after I explain it to them several times. They try to defend the children saying that they are only having fun. Rarely do adults sing the song, but they very often call me "Yovo", which aggravates me even more than when the children do it because I feel that the adults should know better. I have come to accept that they do not know better, and no matter how much I try to explain why it is offensive, they still don't comprehend. Sometimes adults will come up to me and say, "Yovo, how are you?" I explain to them that I don't appreciate being singled out because of the color of my skin, no matter how neutral the meaning of the word is. They always try to defend themselves saying, "I am black and you are white. You can call me *Mewi* (Black person) and I will call you *Yovo*." The problem is that they are ignorant as to what it is to be a minority based on skin color, and what it is like to be singled out continuously because of it. Probably the only way for them to realize their ignorance would be to bring them to the U.S. where they would be a minority. I have learned what it's like to be a minority; however I cannot say I am able to empathize with minorities who have been subjected to a more malicious form of racism. Fortunately the form of racism I have felt here has been no worse than annoying.

Constantly being called "Yovo" is one more example of the extreme difference between American and Beninese culture that I have learned to tolerate. I have been here almost two years, but I am still not used to it. I have merely found ways to cope with it. After being here so long and having heard the "Y" song so many times, it makes my blood boil each time I hear it. I usually try to catch the kids who sing it, and I exact revenge upon them by making mean faces while jokingly yelling after them. If I catch one I say *"Eno a! Un no nyi Yovo a. Un no nyi Gandaho."* (It's not good to call me Yovo. My name is not Yovo! It's Gandaho!) Usually I scare them enough to make them call me Gandaho from them on. I have made it a goal to initiate all the children who live on the road from the center of town to my house (one mile away). As I make this trip several times a day, it is worth it to me to make this effort to prevent being tormented. The problem is that there are so many children that it would take me years to convert all of them. By that time there would be new children getting old enough to join in, so it's really a never-ending battle. These are my playful ways of coping, releasing my frustration and having fun at the same time. I realize that most of the children are harmless and just having fun so I try to return the favor.

A baby's first cognizant encounter with a Yovo could almost be deemed a rite of passage. Until a baby reaches a certain age, somewhere between one and two years old, they don't realize that white people are different. When they do see a white person and realize I am different for the first time, they go crazy screaming and crying in complete terror. Everyone laughs at the baby's naïveté as she clings to her mother seeking shelter from the big ugly white monster coming toward her. The mother usually takes advantage of the situation to have some fun. She will pick up the baby, bring her over to me, and make the baby scream ten times louder by touching the baby's hand to mine. I have fun with it too, so I make some of my infamous baby scaring faces, which every kid in Allada dreads (or so I would like to think). Everyone laughs while the baby continues screaming. That is when the mother teaches the baby the Yovo song, and at this point I interject saying *"Eño a, un no nyi Yovo a !!"* ("That's not good. My name is not Yovo!"), but it never works. The mother never understands why I protest, and surely as soon as I leave, she will continue teaching her baby how to torment white people from a young age.

## Apprentices:

As I sit here observing the market, a girl walks by with six shirts on hangers hooked to the side of a basket that is balanced on her head. "*Kudayijinjon*" (good sitting) she wishes me as she passes by. "*oooOOO*," I reply. Another young girl who couldn't be more than six years old passes me with a metal basin full of mirrors that she's selling. There are many children in the market because they don't go to school. Instead they come to the market to help their mothers buy and sell. If a decision has to be made in a family as to who will go to school and who will not, the boys will go and the girls will work with their mothers, so it is common to see more young girls working in the market than boys. It's really a shame because it only costs a child about $25 a year to send a child to school, which includes the cost for their uniform, school fees, and school supplies! However, $25 a year is a lot of money for a poor Beninese family. Although ignorance and illiteracy are rampant, so many parents resist sending their children to school because of the relatively large expense, and because the children can help earn money for the family working in the market or in the fields. Many students who finish high school and even graduate from the one university in Benin, have difficulty finding work because the economy is so weak. Parents often realize this and unfortunately perceive sending their kids to school as a waste of time and money. Children who do not go to school almost always end up selling in the market or starting an apprenticeship. Many Westerners would label this as child labor and subsequently "wrong." However, the reality is that these children are working with their mothers, and sometimes even for themselves, so it is a far cry from the "sweatshop" often associated by Westerners with the idea of child labor. Their society can rarely afford children the luxury and expense of a carefree childhood that we can in the West.

I see a group of hairdressing apprentices walking in the market. All are girls between roughly 12 and 20 years old. All five are wearing the same brightly patterned clothing, which is the uniform their master chose for them. They are all young girls whose parents pay their master a fee so they may work for free for several years in order to learn the trade. The master has gone through an apprenticeship, finished it successfully, and then opened her own hairdressing business. It may seem unfair that the master benefits from years of free labor and receives fees, but in return the apprentices gain valuable skills. At the end of the apprenticeship, the students will graduate and will be able to set up his or her own shop. They get a practical education, which will help them earn a living for the rest of their lives, so it would be inaccurate to label their situation as wrongful child labor. Apprenticeship is a much lower cost alternative to a technical school, which are almost non-existent in Benin. The apprentice system is used for all trades people such as chauffeurs, welders, carpenters, electricians, masons, radio repairmen, barbers, tailors, shoe repairmen, seamstresses, etc.

It is now noon and school just let out, so school children are easy to spot in the market by their khaki uniforms. Some of the kids are visiting their mothers who are sellers. Others are socializing and buying something to eat for lunch. I am bathed in sweat and I am very uncomfortable, but after being in Benin for so long I have learned to tolerate the heat, as I have so many other inconveniences encompassed by living in a West African village on a meager salary.

## Garbage:

I spot some kids defecating on a garbage pile at the edge of the market, which bothers me because they are doing it right next to a latrine. The problem with the latrine is that it's locked, and they'd have to find the one person wandering around the market who has the key in order to get him to open it. Moreover, the Beninese do not have the habit of using latrines even at home in their villages, as they do not like the smell and they fear the floor will fall in. It is a particularly bad practice here in the market because the uncovered excrement allows flies to land on the uncovered food that is being sold only steps away.

The market is rather dirty with plastic bags and other trash, mostly biodegradable, on the ground because there are no garbage cans. Garbage cans would be useless as there is no municipal trash collection. Children pick up much of the litter and play with it, or goats and pigs come and eat it. The litter that isn't picked up gets swept into garbage piles in random places at the edge of the market. Because products sold in the market are rarely packaged, little trash is generated and litter is not a major problem. This goes to show how little waste one creates in Benin and how little they impact the environment compared to Westerners. In the West we create many times more garbage than they do in Benin, and much of the garbage we create is from food packaging. The downside is however, that food spoils and is contaminated by parasites carried by flies when left uncovered. In general garbage is not a big problem in villages, and small towns such as Allada, but there is a lot of garbage on the streets of Beninese cities and they have some form of garbage collection.

Being a good American, I was initially against littering, but after a few days of carrying garbage around in my pockets and never finding a garbage can, I decided I had to litter like everyone else because there's nowhere else to put it. The definition of litter is to throw garbage where it doesn't belong, but here the only designated place for trash are piles on the sides of the road, so technically I wasn't really littering. Throwing garbage on the ground was a hard at first, and I felt guilty about it, but I got over it. When I am at home, all I can do to get rid of my trash is to give it to the children, burn it, bury it in my yard, or throw it in my latrine.

## Clothes:

You cannot buy new ready to wear clothes here. However, you can buy almost any type of used clothing from the "Dead Yovo" clothing sellers. They call it that because they know that it comes from Westerners, and they cannot imagine why white people would give away their perfectly good clothes unless they were dead; hence the term "dead Yovo clothing." They don't understand the perfectionist, wasteful mentality of Westerners which leads them to throw away clothing because they have a slight imperfection, because they are no longer the latest fashion, or because they simply have too much clothing. The charities we donate clothes to try to sell the best items in the U.S. What they can't sell in the U.S., they sell in bulk to exporters who in turn sell them to African importers in huge bundles. The African importers in turn sell them to the smaller entrepreneurs who sell them in the regional markets in Benin. In fact, almost every market in Benin has some "Dead Yovo" clothes for sale. There is even a huge outdoor market that sells only used Western clothing in Cotonou called Missébo.

Most of the "Dead Yovo" clothes come from the United States, so I have seen people wearing the whole gamut of American clothes from dress suits, to Yankee hats, winter jackets, bowling league shirts, Levis, Nike sneakers, boy scout uniforms, fraternity spring break T-shirts, American

Cancer Society fundraiser T-shirts, Fedex shirts etc. It was funny seeing the Beninese wear T-shirts with sayings they had no idea what they meant, sometimes making sexual references like, "Two is a company, three is kinky," and "Damn I'm good." I even saw a boy walking down a remote dirt road wearing a shirt from UCONN, my alma mater! I had been looking for someone wearing a UCONN T-shirt for some time. I stopped him and tried to explain why I was so excited, but I don't know if he really understood. I knew I would see one eventually, since our basketball team has been so successful, and so has their merchandising. It is such a paradox to see the Beninese wearing clothing that is so uniquely American because America seems light years away in both time and distance.

Even though the Beninese are very poor, dressing well and looking nice takes a high priority. The market is a place to see others as well as be seen, so everyone comes dressed in their Sunday best. A woman passing by comes up to me and says, "*Yovo, Ete a hen wa nu mi?*" (Yovo, what did you bring me?)—"*Nuti!*" ("Nothing!"), I quickly reply. She laughs and continues on her way. The African printed cloth is always very brightly colored and elaborately patterned. I see a few people wearing the outfit made of the fabric chosen for my neighbor's funeral ceremony. All close friends and family usually buy the same patterned cloth and have clothing made for a funeral to show solidarity for the bereaving family. Long after the ceremony, people wear those clothes out in public so it is easy to identify people closely tied to the family of the deceased. I see several stalls where they are selling hundreds of different types of cloth, which are brightly colored and have very flashy designs. The cloth seller always hisses at me yelling "*Yovo, wa!*" ("Whitey, come here!") The concepts of gaudiness or outlandishness are unknown, as you often see people wearing outrageous patterns of orange, green, blue, yellow splashed all over the cloth in geometric patterns. The outfits are usually made uniform, i.e. the top and the bottom are made with the same patterned material. More people wear traditional West African clothing but many wear Dead Yovo clothing too. Dead Yovo clothing is very popular, but it is not considered dressy unless it is a Western dress suit.

This is a photo of my neighbor's funeral ceremony for the matron of the family who died. I was flattered that my neighbors wanted to include me and asked me to wear the ceremonial cloth they chose. Guess which one I am?

If you want new clothes, you have to have them made. After buying the cloth, you have to bring it to a tailor to have him or her make whatever you desire. They often use Chinese sewing machines that are powered by a foot pedal or hand crank. To an American, the concept of custom-made clothing sounds expensive, but it's not here. In Benin, time is not money so labor is very cheap. I can buy four meters of cloth for four or five U.S. dollars, and pay the tailor only about the same amount to make it into clothing. For people with money, or for very special occasions, people buy more expensive cloth to make into outfits that use much more fabric and drapes over the shoulders. Add a matching hat with elaborate embroidery and you could spend $50-$80 (a small fortune in Benin). Women usually wear simple outfits that are composed of a basic blouse, and they wrap the cloth around their waists and tie it to make a dress. To be fancy they wear headdresses that can be tied and wrapped around their heads in an infinite number of ways, which allows them to express their individuality and gives them a uniquely West African look.

## Women and the Market:

There are few men in the market because the market is primarily a woman's domain. A common profession and source of income for a woman is to be a "*Nusato,*" or literally, a "thing seller," meaning she'll sell whatever she can make, find, afford to buy and transport to the market and resell. The problem with this is that more women sell goods than produce them.

Most people who come are not just shoppers, but are here to sell things as well. With the money they earn, they buy things they need before they go home. Some people are sellers by profession (Marché Mammas) and travel to each regional market every day. They have a good size inventory, which they have to pick up and transport home at the end of the day. Many woman also make their own products at home on off market days to sell. They may make palm oil, soap, klui-klui, (fried peanut butter sticks) baskets, pottery, or prepare various other foods.

To get to the market, most women walk several miles with a baby on their backs and carry a heavy basket on their heads. They come from their villages in the bush passing over several miles of narrow and sandy paths that seem to wind endlessly through the thickly vegetated countryside. They do this either barefoot or at best with a cheap pair of flip-flops! My neighbors regularly travel to remote villages on bicycle or on foot to buy goods, and then re-sell them in the market. Women with large metal basins filled with their goods that they have either bought or are going to sell, pass me with their babies on their backs tied snugly with colorful pieces of cloth. I cannot help but admire the ease and grace in which women carry heavy and awkward loads on their heads. They use a coiled cloth to spread out the weight to pad their heads. They are so good at it that they can even urinate standing up with the baby on their backs, and a full basin on their heads! I know this because I have seem them boldly do it in public many times, even in the middle of the capital city, Cotonou! They do it so nonchalantly that to an untrained eye, you wouldn't even know what they were doing!

I knew it was market day when I woke up this morning, as I saw more than the normal number of people walking down the path in front of my house walking toward Allada with goods on their heads. I can never remember on which day the market takes place, as it falls on a different day of the week each time, but all I have to do is look out my door in the morning to tell. On market day, I often see lines of five to ten women walking down the narrow path, single file, in order to allow bicycles and motorcycles to pass them safely. It sometimes reminds me of a parade because there is a constant stream of people. Women come with their children, co-wives (since it's a polygamist society), sisters-in-law, aunts, nieces, friends etc. They must work extra hard on market day because when they get home in the evening, they then have to cook and do other domestic chores such as hauling water, feeding the babies, and doing dishes. The women here are very strong, both mentally and physically. They have more work than the men, and most do not have the luxury of any domestic appliances, or even basic amenities such as running water and electricity.

## Business Philosophy:

Often vendors are slow to "serve" you, or are not even at their stands, which is very frustrating to a Westerner who is used to efficiency and quick service. Fortunately, there is a strong sense of community, and others look out for them if they step away. The Beninese are also very good about watching out for each other's children. Never have I heard of any children being lost or missing in Benin, which is surprising considering how many children are wandering around alone or with other children. There is a wonderful children's book called "It Takes a Village", published by Jane Cowen-Fletcher, a former Benin Peace Corps Volunteer, that clearly demonstrates this.

Each seller in the *marché* (Market) has her own way of attracting customers, but most do nothing but wait. If they are feeling aggressive, they will hiss at you, or wave you over to their stand to get you to take a look. As I stated before, if you are white, then dollar signs go "chachink" in the sellers' eyes and they often become more aggressive, especially if you look timid or even slightly interested in what they are selling. I have learned that if I do not want to be hassled, I don't even look at what she is selling or make eye contact. They sometimes tug on my arm to try to get me to buy from them, and that is why the market can be very frightening for new Peace Corps Volunteers.

At least half a dozen women with metal basins full of *gari* line one of the aisles. A woman bought some *gari* from a vendor sitting next to me. She's putting it in her scarf, and is tying the ends together to carry it home. The seller gave her a *cadeau* (present) of a free handful of *gari*, to encourage her to come back next time. I suppose it's similar to our "baker's dozen." There is perfect competition here because everyone is selling the exact same things. They do not use any sales techniques such as product differentiation or marketing. Instead they compete with other sellers by cultivating personal relationships with their customers to get them to come back out of a sense of loyalty.

There are many Western goods that I long for but cannot get here in Allada, such as vegetables, butter, chocolate, American junk food, and dead meat. Yes . . . dead meat. If you want meat here, you've got to buy it live since there is little refrigeration available, and if it were dead, it would spoil very quickly in the heat. Here in Allada, I cannot buy beef dead or alive and have to go to the capital, Cotonou, once a month to stock up on this and other luxuries. I am very grateful for my Peace Corps issued kerosene refrigerator, which allows me to keep some of these luxuries on hand. It is a real hassle getting goods home from Cotonou, since I have to take a bush taxi to the center of my town, then take a motorcycle taxi to my house, all while carrying 30 pounds of groceries in my backpack! I have perfected the practice of buying butter in Cotonou, putting it in the freezer at the Peace Corps office for a few hours, and then making a mad dash for Allada one hour away before it melts. Usually I make it in time, but not always.

The women lay their goods out in small piles on the ground or on small tables. One woman is selling piles of bright red palm nuts, which are used to make sauces and soap. Piles of green gumbo lie next to the red palm nuts and really hot red peppers, which reminds me of Christmas and makes me sad that I have missed being with my family for two consecutive years. A small boy walks by me carrying a box of Chinese D cell batteries on his head that he is selling. They carry everything on their heads, even a single roll of toilet paper! They do it with such grace and ease that it looks deceptively easy. I am sweating profusely in the shade until . . . ahh . . . a slight breeze passes . . . It feels great. I have learned how to enjoy the simple pleasures of life here.

I feel sorry for the Beninese women, and I also have much admiration for them because they work all day in the hot sun, walk five miles here and back to their villages with heavy loads on their heads and a child on their backs . . . all for maybe 500 to 1000 CFA profit ($1 to $2 a day)!! They earn very little, but the cost of living is very low, and the cost of running their "business" is also very low. Nonetheless, they are very poor. They sell in the market because they have no choice, and it is the only way they can scrape by. Luckily most families do scrape by because men usually have some land that they farm on a subsistence level to produce food. Most farmers produce little more than what their families need, because they do not use machinery. All they use is a hoe to till the land by hand, and a stick to poke holes in the ground where they plant the seeds. The money the women earn in the market is used in the home to buy the things they cannot produce themselves. Over a year, the average family may be able to save $50 to $100, but that will quickly disappear for funeral ceremonies if a relative dies, or if a family member gets sick, so saving anything is next to impossible. Extended families are very large, and the life expectancy is so low that someone in the family is bound to die at least once a year. These ceremonies are a large financial burden on the family, because funerals are usually very lavish, and there is much social and religious pressure to have a "proper" burial for the deceased in order to keep that person's spirit from tormenting the living. Ancestors' spirits are powerful for the Beninese, and they cannot be neglected with impunity.

## Change:

Change is an incessant problem whenever you buy anything, because sellers almost never have enough extra money to be able to keep it on hand. Although we take it for granted, change is actually a form of working capital. The woman selling the *gari* next to me receives a customer. Like most women, she ties her money in the loose cloth she in turn ties around her waist. Upon untying the cloth, she realizes that she does not have change for a 500 franc ($1) note that the customer is offering her, so she asks me if I have change. I do not have change either, so she goes off to ask someone else. Wow, it's 1 PM, and this must be her first customer because if it were not, she would surely have change by now. The change problem is so bad that the 5,000 and 10,000 franc bills ($10 and $20 equivalents) are almost worthless if you want to buy something inexpensive, since no one can give you enough change. It's ironic, but sometimes I feel a 500F note is worth more than a 5000F note because the 5000F note is so unwieldy! When I go to the bank, I need to be extra nice to the cashier, so he will give me more small bills. I need to strategically plan how I will spend the bills I am given. If I spend all of my small bills on more expensive items, I can rarely spend my larger bills for smaller items. When I first arrived in Benin, I got caught in a change trap, and I spent an hour once looking for someone who could break my 5000F note ($10); so I learned quickly!

## Tired Money:

Another oddity about the Beninese Market is "tired money." Yes, "tired" money. Sometimes when I go to buy something, and I hand over the money, the seller will say, "*Ah!! Akwe towe nu ci ko nyi.*" (literally: "your money is tired"). This means the money is rather worn, and she will not accept it. It's clearly a West African CFA coin, but it is a little too worn in her opinion, and she is afraid that the next person will not accept it from her. Sometimes if I am having a bad day, and I am not in a good mood, I will try to make a point by throwing it on the ground and saying, "Well if it's no good then I guess I will throw it away." Their reaction is usually to dive after it. Then I ask, "If my money is no good, why did you chase after it?" Usually they don't get my sarcasm and think it's just another weird thing the Yovo does. Most of the time when I get duped into accepting "tired" money, the only way I can get rid of it is by spending it at night with the street vendors. The street vendors cannot see well at night because they sit outside in the dark with only small kerosene lamps to light their stands. I love it when a seller offers me a "tired coin or bill," and I say to her in Fon "*Ah, Akwe towe nu ci ko nyi,*" and boastfully refuse it just to catch them at their own game. Interestingly enough, this problem exists only in Benin and Togo. When I traveled to Niger and Burkina Faso, there was no problem with "tired" money. Perhaps there they are poorer and willing to accept any money no matter how "tired" it is. When I was in a taxi on my way back into Benin, it was funny to hear the Nigeriens and Burkinabe in the car make fun of the Beninese for this strange behavior. They joked that before crossing the border into Benin, they'd better get rid of all their tired money because it would be useless in there.

## Nicknames:

The Beninese love nicknames, and rarely use each other's real names which they were given at their naming ceremonies. In fact, when I ask my neighbor what one of his family member's name is, someone who lives with him in his family compound, he sometimes doesn't even know! Earlier, one of my neighbors recognized me here in the market and enthusiastically called out to me: "*Oh Gandaho!, Javi!, Tohossi!, Zanvi!, Favi! A wa axime we á?*" I replied, "*Enn, un wa axime*". She called out many of my Fon nicknames and then asked me if I came to the market. I replied, "Yes, I came to the market." I still think it's funny how they ask what is blatantly obvious when greeting people. Sometimes I joke and sarcastically say, "*Eho, un wa axime we á.* (Meaning, "No, I didn't come to the market"), even though I'm standing in the middle of it. They usually think it's funny, and are never offended by my sarcasm. Because I've taken an interest in Vodun and have been researching it avidly, my neighbors have given me many nicknames, which mean that I'm an initiate of each of the cults I have been studying, such as *Ja, Tohossu, Zangbeto and Fah.* The suffixes "vi," "si" at the end means an initiate of those cults. They think it's quite funny that I am so interested in learning about their religion, which most Westerners, a least the many Christian missionaries, shun and erroneously label hedonistic, superstitious and primitive.

My neighbor's name is, Marie, but everyone calls her "Fabricino." Most women are called by the name of her first-born child, and in fact it is impolite to call a woman with children by her first name. Her first-born is named "Fabrice," and the suffix "no" means mother. When it's added to a word as a suffix, it becomes possessive so "Fabricino" means "the mother of Fabrice." Having children is very important in this society, and is also a status symbol. So having the suffix "no" at the end of Fabricino's name is both a title and a status symbol as much as M.D., Esquire, or CEO would be in the West. Men are also given nicknames such as these. For example, Lucien, the father of Tine, is called "Tineto" (the suffix "to" means the father of). Nicknames are also given stating one's profession. For example, one of my neighbors is a mason, and many people call him *xotleto*, which literally means "house builder" or "mason." Nicknames are also given to people stating their ethnicity or origin if they are not from the area, which may explain why everyone loves calling me Yovo. In brief, nicknames state people's role in society, and often point out how the person is different from everyone else. Cultural sensitivity and not pointing out one's minority status is not valued.

## Being a Yovo in Benin:

The Beninese people are so easy going, open, friendly, and generous to everyone, including white people. Someone shouts at me, "American!," to get my attention because he wants to talk to me, but I don't budge. They love white people. It is very surprising that they are so kind to us, considering the French subjected them to more than 60 years of colonization, although many people do see the former colonization as having helped develop Benin. There is no doubt this is true, and the Beninese usually aren't angry about the underlying role of inferiority the colonizer imposed upon them. One reason most Beninese don't feel negatively about white people is because they do not understand the complexities of the global economy, and how we are exploiting them economically. White people have a pretty good reputation, as nearly all white people in Benin work for international aid agencies, are missionaries or work with other charitable organizations that are in Benin to help the Beninese.

I am sitting next to a vendor under her straw roof writing and chatting with her. She's not questioning why I am here or what I am doing. I randomly decided to sit next to her and she gladly offered me her extra stool. I could sit here all day and she wouldn't care because the Beninese aren't particular about their space or privacy as Westerners are. They are very easy going, happy, and jovial, and they love to chat, laugh, and joke all the time. Perhaps she thinks I am going to bring her good luck, or that I will attract the curiosity of other market goers, which will help her sales. Ahh! . . . A cloud just blew over the sun. I can enjoy a 5-degree relief for maybe a minute until the cloud moves on and exposes the sun again.

## Being a Celebrity:

In Allada there are only a few other white people beside myself, but they almost never come to the market because they are well-paid missionaries. They have a car that they use to do most of their shopping in Cotonou. They miss out on many aspects of African life by living in an air conditioned house with running water, electricity, a maid, a cook, a high stone wall around their spacious house, a lawn, and other American amenities such as a VCR, and a TV with a satellite dish. I can't blame them because they intend to live here for 5 to 10 years or more with their children while I'm only here for two years. Living at the level of the local people (by being paid only $6 a day, living in a simple house with no running water, and not having a car) has allowed me to understand the people and culture better. I know, however, that I could not live this way long-term. Living at a higher economic level than the local people alienates you from them, and that is why Peace Corps pays us only $6 a day. It has been an incredible learning experience living as they do, but it has taken its toll on me. I know I could not do it for five years . . . . perhaps three, maybe four, but not five.

I am the only white guy in the entire market of at least several thousand Beninese, yet I feel safer than I would in my own home in the U.S. I never hear of anyone coming into a market in Benin to rob and shoot people as happens in the U.S. There is little crime here, and being white gives me status; unfortunately, it does not guarantee me good prices. I have to pay a price for fame (as famous people do anywhere), because I am constantly being pestered and stared at which at times is quite unnerving. It is also very hard to tell who is a "true friend," and who is being extra nice to me because they want money, gifts, a chance at a visa, a plane ticket to the U.S., or funding for a project sponsored by an international aid agency. If I say "no" to people's blunt requests, they usually insist I provide them with an American pen pal to whom they can ask for favors instead. When I am out in public, people always recognize me, and I seldom recognize them. Once, a man came up to me and said, *"Bonjour Gandaho."* He could tell I did not recognize him, and he then said, "What, don't you recognize me?" I no longer feel compelled to lie and say "Yes, I recognize you", because this happens so often. So I said, "No, sorry, I don't know who you are." He said with an indignant tone, "How could you not remember me? I was the guy sitting on the side of the road eating my *bouillie (porridge),* and when I spilled it, you said, *Doucement* ("be careful" in French) as you were passing by on your bicycle." I didn't know this person at all. I had seen him only once and said only a few words to him, yet he remembered me and expected me to remember him. I said, "There are 10,000 black people who live in this town and there are five white people. Don't you think that it's easier for the black people to know all the white people than it is for the white people to know all the black people?" He agreed, and I continued on my way.

Another reason I receive so much attention here is my Peace Corps issued Trek Mountain Bike. By American standards, it isn't very special or expensive, but here it is ostentatious and is the equivalent of having a Porsche or Ferrari. No one in Benin has one except Yovos, so it is very exotic. The Beninese have one speed Chinese bikes that are as strong as locomotives, but weigh almost as much. I usually get at least ten requests a day to either give someone a ride on my bike, give it to someone, or promise to sell it to someone when I leave Benin. They are also very curious as to what I have in my water bottle, since no one here uses them. I usually tease them by saying it's *Sodabi* (their locally made palm whiskey). I often put on a little show by taking a sip and acting as if it were whiskey by making a face and feigning the need for a chaser. They are usually incredulous, and snatch the bottle from my hand to smell it. We all burst out in laughter when they realize I duped them. I have learned that having a good sense of humor is the only way to deal with living here, and to have some fun at the same time.

### Getting the Goods to Market:

There are several ways in which people and goods get to the market. Taxis bring some people to the market (along with their goods), while others come by *baché* (a small Peugeot pick up truck). These trucks are always crammed to the hilt, to the point where the rear end is sagging close to the ground and it's a wonder the springs don't snap. The roofs of these small pick up trucks are packed with goods 5 feet high, and about 15 to 20 people, not including children, goats, and chickens, will cram into the back under the canopy roof. Those who live in Allada and the near-by villages will come to the market on foot, and if they have a lot of goods to sell, they will bring their goods on a *pousse-pousse* (a two wheeled pushcart).

This is a *baché* (a Peugeot pick up truck) crammed with people and goods on its way to the market.

A man with a cooler on his head is selling popsicles, cold water, and ice. A woman sitting on a tiny stool across from me calls out to me to buy her goods (onions and tomatoes) saying *Waxonu!* (come buy from me). At the edge of the market at least half a dozen *Zemidjan* drivers hang out waiting for customers. *"Zemidjan"* literally means, "Take me quick," or, "motorcycle taxi" in Fon. For less than 20 cents they will "take you quickly" anywhere in town, and for less than a dollar, they will take to outlying villages in the bush within a five-mile radius. They will also take on large amounts of goods for their customers by draping them over the gas tank and handlebars. Sometimes, the passenger will carry a basin on her head and a baby on her back while riding on the back of the motorcycle. She will hold the basin steady with one hand, and hold onto the motorcycle with the other. Sometimes the driver will even put two passengers on the bike! Almost no one (except Peace Corps Volunteers) wears helmets, the roads are bad, and the *Zemidjan* drivers drive like mad, so it is not a very safe way to travel. Patches of deep sand, animals, and pedestrians are the most common cause of accidents. Zemidjans are the major form of transportation in Benin because it is cheap, fast, and many times, it is the only way to get in and out of remote villages, which have paths too narrow or too muddy for anything but a four-wheel drive vehicle.

## Measurement System:

Like everything else in Benin, the measurement system is very imprecise. They use the *Tongolo* for dry measurement. A *Tongolo* is a small bowl identifiable by a red rim, which is piled high with the commodity being sold, usually corn or beans or cassava flour. Because of its inherent imprecision, it becomes a game between the buyer and seller as to the amount of a particular good that is given and accepted. The seller has to be careful; if she is too generous, she won't make any profit, as her profit margin is so low to begin with. On the other hand, if she is too stingy, her clients won't come back. The seller scoops up the corn with the bowl and throws it into the buyer's metal basin quickly, so some of the corn that is falling off the top of the pile is included in the buyer's basin. If the buyer feels that the amount is insufficient, she will ask the seller to start over. Sometimes the seller lets the buyer measure the grain herself to assure she will be happy. If the seller feels she is taking too much, she will make the buyer start over. For liquid measure, they use one liter empty whiskey bottles to measure anything from black market gasoline to peanut oil. Despite the fact that their system of measurement is less than perfect, it works here because people are seldom concerned with being precise.

This woman is using the Tongolo to fill her client's basin with dried corn.

## Resourcefulness:

Nothing is wasted here because resources are so scarce. Odd sized jars, bottles, and containers that Americans throw away by the bin load every week, are sold and used for carrying and storing various liquids and objects. Old bottles are also used to buy, sell, and store cooking things such as oil and kerosene, or the *sodabi* that the old men love to get wasted on. I have seen people who were unfortunate enough not to have a bottle, so they had to buy cooking oil in a plastic bag, which was then tied and carried home very carefully to prevent it from leaking. Vendors sell flip-flops made out of old car tires. Farmers wear them in the fields because sharp sticks and thorns cannot penetrate the soles as they can mass-produced soft-soled flip-flops. Aluminum cook pots are stacked high on a table. They are made out of melted down aluminum cans and aluminum engine parts in a local foundry here in town or they are from factories in Nigeria. A blacksmith sells animal traps that he made out of old car springs. A woman hawks her product: "*Wa xo gali*""Come buy my gari!" A small boy with a wicker basket on his head full of small kerosene lamps and funnels that were made out of tin cans brazed together peddles his wares. Other goods that line the aisles include straw mats that people use to sleep on, yams, and live chickens in baskets sitting on the ground with their feet tied.

As I survey the market, I see very few manufactured goods that were made here in Benin. Most are from Europe, Ghana, and Nigeria, because the industrial revolution has yet to arrive in Benin. Benin, like other West African nations, has been independent only since the early 1960's. After independence, it was ruled by the socialist dictator Mathieu Kérékou. Democracy and free enterprise are fairly new ideas that were made possible by the peaceful revolution in 1991. Since that was only four years ago, private industry and formal businesses are still scarce.

## Dantokpa:

The Allada market is as big as two football fields, but it is puny in comparison to Dantokpa, which is one of the larger markets in West Africa. Dantokpa is located in the economic capital, Cotonou, and it is extremely chaotic. It is gigantic in part due to the healthy cross border trade with neighboring Nigeria, which furnishes the industrially poor Benin with most of its manufactured products. Moneychangers sit on line-up benches holding six-inch thick stacks of Nigerian Naira bills and CFA. Moneychangers' services make the cross border trade possible, since there are few banks and they charge high fees. They operate on the black market, as do approximately 80% of the businesses in Benin. In fact, the Beninese economy is built on black market small business. They are labeled "black market" because they pay no taxes, and do not register with the government. If the government tried to regulate and tax every micro-enterprise, they would not be able to make a profit and the economy would probably collapse. By allowing the black market to flourish, the government is creating an indirect subsidy to the economy. The downside is that the Beninese government can offer few services because it takes in such little revenue.

Dantokpa is so expansive that I feel confident saying, "If you can't buy it in Dantokpa, you can't buy it in Benin," period. Going to Dantokpa is an exhausting experience that one must prepare for both mentally and physically. Because it is so enormous, you need to use reference points outside the market to help navigate your way around. It is an endless maze of stalls where the products are geographically clustered. The rows of people selling the exact same things are so long that you can't even see their ends. There are no maps, signs, or logical ways in which the vendors are organized. The only way to find something specific is to pay someone who really knows the market to take you there. Sometimes you don't even have the choice of accepting a guide, because when they see a white person, they prey on you and won't leave you alone until you either insult them or accept their "friendly" gesture for which they will certainly expect a "tip" later. If you refuse their help and they insist on helping you anyway, they will ask you for a tip later if you do not offer one. If you still refuse to give a tip, they will usually beg, plead, and give you the saddest sob story you've ever heard, making it almost impossible to refuse no matter how resolute you are. The only way to avoid this is to make it look as if you know where you are going and what you are doing. They can sense wide-eyed vulnerability and a lack of confidence a mile away. I have been amazed at how good they are at persuading / extorting money out of me, even though I swore to myself that I would not give in. It is a talent many Beninese have mastered as a means of survival. Luckily the Allada market is much smaller and low key.

## Market Food:

There are many women selling refreshments to thirsty and hungry market goers like me. I hesitate to use the word "shopper", because going to the Beninese market is much more than the mundane chore of "shopping." "Market-goer" is a more appropriate term, because they are participants in an important cultural, social, and economic event. There are several types of locally produced drinks made from corn, fruit, and other ingredients, but I have not dared to try any of them, due to the questionability of the water used to make them. If I am thirsty, I usually opt for oranges. Because the oranges are fibrous, people don't eat them, but suck on them. Orange peels are very bitter and the zest is pungent, so they cut away the top layer of the peel with a razor blade, and then cut a hole in the top from which you suck the juice as you slowly squeeze it. Not surprisingly, the ground at the market is littered with orange peels.

In the market there is plenty of cheap food to be found, hot and ready to eat, such as *akassa* wrapped in teak leaves. It is an almost tasteless gelatin like ball of slightly fermented cornstarch, which is eaten with hot pepper sauce. Fried dough balls, fried yams, and fried plantains are common too, always accompanied by extremely spicy hot pepper sauce. It is comical for me to buy these foods wrapped in leaves, random pieces of paper, or pieces of cement bags! Once, when I was in a bush taxi heading north, I bought some fried sweet potatoes on the side of the road through my taxi window. The girl who sold them to me wrapped them in a piece of a high school student's homework paper complete with his name, grade level, date, and the grade he received on it! That's the reason I burn or throw down my latrine anything I do not want made public and circulated around the country. The woman who sells me my fried dough balls here in Allada always tears off a piece of brown paper from an empty cement bag, and then slaps it to remove the cement dust before putting my food on it. I don't have a problem with it, as I've resigned myself to the lower level of hygiene since I've been in Benin. Unfortunately, I do not really have a choice. The only alternative to eating street food is for me to cook everything from scratch at home, which would not be practical, as I would not be able to leave home for more than a few hours at a time. Food in Benin suffers from poor hygiene, not only from being wrapped in things such as cement bags, but also because it is often left uncovered allowing flies to land on it. In addition, it is never refrigerated, which allows bacteria to easily grow in the hot climate. The plates and utensils are washed in cold filthy water that is re-used for most of the day, which also spreads microbes and parasites. The septic conditions have sent me running to my latrine countless times during my two years here.

Other types of food ready to eat in the market are rice and beans (my favorite), barbecued turkey parts, *pâte* (corn flour mush, pronounced like "pot" so newcomers to Benin often think we're talking about marijuana), barbecued mystery meat kabobs, and omelets made on demand by a guy using a small kerosene stove sitting at a picnic bench. Like most things in Benin, food is very inexpensive, and I can eat until I am ready to pop for 200-300F (40-60 cents), provided I do not purchase any meat or fish. A woman with a large pot of rice and beans on her head and a stool in her hand circulates through the market. When she finds a customer, she puts the tray on the stool, serves the customer, and waits until he is done eating. When her customer finishes, she packs up the food, puts it back on her head, and continues making her rounds through the market. Traditionally, the Beninese eat with their right hand without any utensil, but rice and beans is a meal that people use spoons and forks for today. Food is usually very spicy to make up for the bland ingredients, and the spice makes me feel ten degrees hotter, which can be quite unpleasant considering how hot it is already.

A woman is selling tins of sardines at her stand, and on them it says, in English and French, "Gift of Germany. Not for resale." The seller probably received these sardines from her local women's center as an incentive to bring her baby in to get weighed and have its health checked. She probably also received healthcare classes. She likely decided to sell them for a profit, instead of giving them to her family. Very few people here even know how to read, let alone speak English, so it causes her no guilt.

For cooking at home, many ingredients, such as sugar, piles of salt, and meat flavored Maggi bouillon cubes, which are used in sauces because most people can't afford meat, are sold packaged in plastic bags. One thing I cannot buy in the market is papaya. Because they are so prevalent, no one wants to buy them except me because I do not have any in my yard. I did plant some, but they have not begun to give fruit yet. In the market they sell whole bunches of bananas cut straight from the tree, coconuts, and pineapples the size of watermelons. Allada is the pineapple capital of Benin, and it is the region's cash crop. Palm nuts are southern Benin's other cash crop, but producing them is a large, government controlled industry. The local people cannot compete with the government in palm oil production, because they are unable to produce a sufficient quantity for exportation. Palm oil produced locally by small cottage industry is therefore sold and consumed locally. Many types of Western imported alcohol are sold in the market, such as Schnapps, Gin, Scotch, Pastis, Vodka, and Rum. There are at least five types of dry beans and rice sold.

In Benin, meat is usually purchased for special occasions only, unless you're wealthy, although whole smoked fish is quite common. The most common meats eaten are chicken, bush rat (something like a more furry version of an opossum), goat, lamb, pork, beef, turkey and guinea fowl (in that order). Because meat is so expensive, people here eat just about any meat they can find crawling in the bush, such as snake, squirrel, rabbit, guinea pigs, snails and of course bush rat, which is a specialty of Allada. Bush rat doesn't taste bad, but the way it is presented is nauseating because they hack the animal into anatomically identifiable parts, such as the posterior with the tail attached, legs with feet attached, and the head with its shoulder and forelegs attached. They waste no part of the animal and eat everything including the head and the skin. What really turns me off is the furry rat butt. They burn off the fur to be able to eat it with the skin, but sometimes not all the fur burns off. Peace Corps Volunteers have affectionately named my town the "Rat Butt Capital of Benin," as the major North-South road in Benin runs through the middle of Allada, and all the Peace Corps Volunteers who travel north must pass through my town. The taxi invariably stops here, and when it does, several women brandishing large platters of cooked rat butt as well as assorted other rat parts swarm the taxi trying to sell it to them. Invariably, the windows are open, so they try to stick it right under their noses to try to entice them to buy some. A common, less expensive alternative to meat is fish. Fish here are usually bony minnows that are fried or smoked several days prior, and then re-cooked in a sauce. The result is a far cry from a fresh boneless filet we're accustomed to in the U.S. People who live near the ocean or lakes have a much better supply of fish than those in Allada, and the fish there are generally fresh.

These women are waiting on the side of the road in the center of Allada, waiting to sell their bush rat to passengers in taxis who pull up. Notice the tails sticking up on the left and the whole bush rat on the right.

## Vodun in the Market:

I look up from my writing to see a man suddenly grabbing a hand full of *gari* and a couple of palm nuts from the woman's stall I'm occupying. I was afraid that he was a *voleur* (thief), and I was perplexed that the woman didn't become irate that this person was stealing her food and didn't start screaming *ajoto!* (Thief!). He walked away casually without paying for the food, and I was absolutely dumbfounded because I had never seen anything like it before. The legal system, which the Beninese inherited from the French, is ineffective due to corruption and incompetence, so the Beninese have little faith in it. The result is that thieves are often victims of vigilante justice. The accused face being beaten (sometimes to death), stoned, or burned alive by angry mobs who are intolerant of thieves, and feel the only way to attain justice and control in their community is to administer it themselves. One night when I was in Cotonou leaving a restaurant, a man snatched a fellow Peace Corps Volunteer's purse. Another volunteer and I started chasing him. Other Beninese people saw what happened and suddenly came out of the woodwork to aid us in the chase. With their help, we quickly apprehended him and got the purse back. A crowd quickly formed around him and people started picking up rocks to throw at him. We protested, and requested that they not harm him, after which an argument broke out as to what to do with him. We did not want to be embroiled in a potentially dangerous situation, and felt powerless, so we left. We heard the next day that the thief was beaten and almost killed, but a French expatriate who had a car offered him a ride out of the area to safety. Usually thieves are only killed for serious crimes, such as stealing a car, or ones who have a reputation of committing many smaller thefts. Ironically, it is the thief who needs to be protected by the police; that is if the police show up in time. That is why I am so astonished that this man who I perceive as being a thief walked away unharmed.

In my broken Fon, I ask the woman what was going on, but she doesn't understand me or at least I do not understand her response. I then ask several people in French to get a clear answer, and it turns out that the man is taking collections from the sellers to make an offering to the altar of the god Legba that was also in Dagleta. Legba is a god who is in charge of protecting villages and the market. In the market he ensures that all vendors have good fortune. In a sense, the woman was praying to the god and asking for his goodwill in making an offering to him. The food she gave will be put on the Legba altar in the center of the market. It is a mound of hardened mud covered with cement topped by an overturned clay pot and, as do all Legba altars, it has a large metal penis protruding from it in the anatomically correct location. It was consecrated in a ceremony by a Vodun priest on which he made an animal sacrifice to invoke the gods and ancestors to reside in it. If the altar is neglected, according to the Beninese, the gods will become angry, there will be thieves, it will rain, people won't buy, and the vendors will make no profit. When food and drink are placed on the altar and prayers are said, Legba will be placated and he will bring good fortune to all.

One can tell Vodun is very prevalent here by the many Vodun initiates who pass by. They are easily identified by the scars they have all over their bodies, and by the special necklaces they wear which prove they were initiated. It reminds me of the interesting Vodun ceremony I saw last week in town, and I am very curious about this secretive, elaborate, and enigmatic religion that is difficult to gain access to.

**Products & Packaging:**

There are many products sold in the market, and some are unidentifiable to a newcomer to Benin. I am curious, and have asked many questions so I have learned what just about everything is. The Beninese are very cleanly, so traditional soap is sold in all shapes, sizes and colors throughout the market. At first I couldn't tell what it was and had to ask. I make my way to my favorite egg seller and in Fon, I say to her enthusiastically,

-Azinsatoche! (My egg seller!)
-*Oh Gandaho!*, She replies happily.
-*Azinsatoche! A do gangi a?* (My egg seller! Are you well!?)
-*Un do gangi* (I'm well),
-*A sa nu kpede a?* (Did you sell some things?)
-*Enn, un sa kpede.* (Yes, I sold a little.)
-*Asu towe lo? E do gangi á* (And your husband? Is he well?)
-*Enn, e do gangi.* (Yes, he's doing well.)
-*Vi towele lo?* (And your kids?)
-*Ye do gangi.* (They are fine.)
-*Lame towe do gangi á?* (Is your health well?)
-*Enn, lanmeche do gangi.* (Yes, my health is well.)

As usual, she gives me the eggs in a plastic bag. Now I face the challenge of getting them home without breaking them packed among the other groceries in my bike bag, while passing over the bumpy dirt roads leading to my house. It is a difficult task, which has resulted in many broken eggs in the past.

Some women sell very strong medicines in the market that would only be sold by prescription in the West, and these women have never been to school in their lives! The buyer needs no prescription and can buy birth control pills, injectable penicillin, aspirin, Fansidar (a strong anti malarial drug), Paracetamol, quinine, Nivaquine, and many other powerful drugs. They've been sitting out in the sun for who knows how long, and are usually sold in small plastic bags without the packaging and instructions. Even if they did have instructions, few people could read them. What people know about the effect of different drugs, what drug to use for what illness, and what quantity to take is from hearsay or from people at the municipal women's center who have had very little training. There are a miniscule number of doctors in Benin, and there are very few people who can afford to see them even though they only charge a few dollars per visit. Most people only go when they are severely ill. What really made me cringe was when I was in a *buvette* (an outdoor bar that also serves food) once, and they were selling these drugs alongside beer and hard alcohol! There is one formal pharmacy in Allada, but their prices are much higher than here in the market.

It is interesting to me that Benin is less developed than most of the neighboring countries, yet it still attracts immigrants looking to make a better living. It's also interesting how people from certain countries here tend to sell or produce the same products. For example, the Nigerians in Benin sell cheesy posters as well as stickers that adorn most bush taxi bumpers and motorcycles. They say things like "Who knows the future?", "Be quiet Jealous", "Thank God", and "Only God knows the future." A man shouts to me, "Anisara!" (meaning "whitey" in Arabic). I think every African culture has a word for us white folk. He sells plain cloth for dress clothes. He is a Nigerien, a person from Niger, not to be mistaken with a "Nigerian," (someone from Nigeria). Both countries border Benin, so try to keep that one straight in French! The Nigeriens sell cloth for dress clothes and cheap watches. In addition, they often cook and sell "mystery meat" kabobs on the side of the road. The Ghanaians have a reputation for doing shoe repair and selling tooth sticks.

Other sundry goods for sale in the market are plastic buckets, cooking utensils, backpacks, motorcycle parts, and bike parts. Cigarettes such as Marlboro, Bond, and Rothman's are for sale all over, but luckily they aren't very popular since people cannot afford them. They are usually sold by the individual cigarette and not by the pack, since so few people can afford to buy a whole pack at once. Few people smoke, but the cigarette companies are trying hard to get them to start with their advertising. There are billboards around, as well as promotional items with their logo on them such as drinking glasses, signs, trays, matches, and clocks. The worst part is that there is so little healthcare available for those who do get sick from smoking. The medical community often turns away patients who have cancer, because they don't have the skill or resources to treat it, or even diagnose it properly! If they did have the skill and resources, few patients would be able to afford it.

A child with a metal basin full of firewood passes me. You can be sure it will be used for cooking and not heating, because it never gets colder than 70 degrees here. A woman passes me selling bags of cold water in a cooler on her head. The buyer must pinch a small hole on a corner of the plastic bag and suck the water out. Another woman is carrying a box of European *Lait Sucré* (sweetened condensed milk) on her head. It is used copiously in coffee: a quarter cup of sweetened condensed milk to three-quarters cup of coffee. Down one aisle is a very nice old Ghanaian man who I have become friendly with. Amazingly, he sells slingshots for little kids to play with, and rat poison! His way of attracting customers is to blow a bike horn at passers by. With his dark sunglasses and funny hat, he is quite comical sitting on his stool. When it's not market day, he sits under a tree in the middle of town where I pass every day. I usually greet him and chat for a while because he is one of few people I can speak English with in Allada. Ghanaians speak English because it was a British colony; however, it is challenging to understand his version of English. Nigerian English is equally difficult.

## *Fou's:*

Every town has at least one high profile mentally ill person who roams the streets begging. The Beninese affectionately call them in French *"fou"* (French for "crazy person"), since political correctness is unknown here, nor is there much knowledge of mental disorders or mental health in general. Fortunately, Allada's *Fou* is not a "naked *fou*" like there are in some towns. He is a very dirty and ragged looking person who stumbles along attracting scorn from everyone. He stops to beg from a vendor, and she subsequently shoos him away. Beninese extended families usually offer a very strong social net, but it's not infallible. Often in cases of emotional disorders, families are ashamed and ostracize the person. Adrien, one of my neighbors has a mental illness, perhaps schizophrenia, and luckily his family is supportive of him. There are few institutions in Benin to help mentally disturbed people, so they are forced to wander aimlessly through villages begging and possibly doing odd jobs to earn some money. Many physically handicapped people suffer the same fate. In Cotonou they congregate at intersections where there are traffic lights because they can easily beg from the occupants of the stopped cars.

## Primary Resources:

Oranges are in season, so there are huge piles of them. They are so prevalent that many go to waste because sellers can barely give them away. Waste would be eliminated if there were factories that could transform primary resources such as oranges into finished products such as orange juice, but there are few such factories in Benin. It is a travesty that they are forced to import large amounts of tomato paste from Italy, because during the rainy season tomatoes are very abundant, and many go to waste. This is a common problem of the developing world: they can produce the primary resources, but they do not have the capital or expertise to build the industries to transform them into finished products. They sell the raw materials at low prices, and then buy them back as finished value-added products at much higher prices. Fortunately, the staple corn does not go to waste because it is dried and can be easily stored in granaries for long periods. Corn is an absolute necessity to get them through the five month long dry season from November to March. The price however, goes up two or three times at the end of the dry season when supplies are dangerously low and demand is high.

An abundance of oranges for sale in the market when they were in season.

The cost of transporting goods in Benin is great due to the poor infrastructure and underdeveloped distribution systems. For example, pineapples are very prevalent and cheap in the south and are rare and expensive in the north, which is only a few hundred miles away. The opposite it true of beef. It is very cheap in the north and expensive in the south. This is because there is ample grazing land for cattle in the north, unlike the south where the land is densely vegetated and densely populated. The result is that there is little variety of foods available compared to in the U.S.

At this point, I am exhausted from the heat, shopping, and socializing. I have bought everything I need, so I return home for my afternoon *sieste*. By dusk the whole market will clear out, and the entire area will be deserted and lifeless for five days until the next market takes place. I can't help but compare this amazing experience to the humdrum, mundane task of going to the Supermarket in the U.S.

\* Note: In chapter eleven I will discuss my reaction to the American supermarket in detail after returning from Benin.

# THE BUSH TAXI RIDE FROM HELL

**July 28<sup>th</sup> 1996**—I just spent the last four days at Shelly's house in Djougou with other Peace Corps Volunteers from our training group. We cooked, ate, drank, relaxed, had lots of laughs, and explored the town. We have all been at our posts in different parts of Benin for the past seven months, and this was a well-needed escape from our daily routines and jobs at our posts. It was nice to spend time with the volunteers from my training group who I spent every day with for the first three months I was in Benin. Since then we have only seen each other once or twice in Cotonou. None of us feel lonely at post, because there are always Beninese people around, and we all have Beninese friends; however, we often feel isolated due to the significant cultural and linguistic barriers. Spending time with other Americans every few weeks is something we have to do to maintain our sanity. It's especially cathartic to share our frustrations, experiences, feelings, and coping strategies, because living in Benin is extremely difficult on so many levels.

Djougou is in Northern Benin, and now I have to return to my home in Allada. It sounds funny calling Allada "home" because when I arrived I never would have thought a small town in Benin, West Africa would ever feel like home. Now that I have been living there seven months, and I have learned so much about the country, I have settled in, and I am proud to say it is my home. I have made many friends, I have made my house fairly comfortable, and I have established my routines. Allada is 240 miles south of Djougou, but it might as well be 1,000 miles, considering how arduous and slow travel is in Benin. In the United States, people don't think twice about traveling 240 miles. In most places in the U.S., highways abound and the trip can be done with ease and comfort in about four hours. Americans would not appreciate the ease of travel on such a trip, especially if they hit minimal traffic along the way. However, after travelling a fair amount in Benin, I appreciate how easy it is to get around in the U.S., and how I took it for granted. When I get back to the U.S., I will certainly have a newfound appreciation for our efficient transportation system. I don't have a car here, and there are no trains or buses making the trip to Allada from Djougou, so my only way of getting home is to take a bush taxi. I have a lot of experience taking bush taxis because as a Peace Corps Volunteer, we are not allowed to drive, and we don't have enough money to rent an entire taxi. We are allowed to take *zemidjans* (motorcycle taxis), but they are for short distances only.

I am really tired, because the north is Muslim country, and from 4 to 4:30 AM, and again from 5 to 5:30 AM, the local mosque blares its call to prayer "*Allaha Akbar!*" ("Allah is great!") over and over through a loudspeaker on top of the nearby minaret, practically shaking me out of bed. Shelly says that she sleeps through it now, as she has become accustomed to it.

She is well acquainted with the process of getting a bush taxi in her town to travel south, as she has done many times. She said that if I go to the taxi station early, around 8 AM, the taxi will probably fill up and leave by 10 or 11, and the trip will take at most 8 hours so I am hoping to be home by about 7 PM. I go to the taxi station at 8 AM and I quickly find a taxi driver who is going south. I take Shelly's advice and I tell the driver to pick me up at her house as soon as he's ready to leave. I tell him to pick me up at the white volunteer's house who rides a bicycle and lives over "that way." He knows exactly who I am talking about as there are only a few white people here and she is the only one with a bike.

For shorter trips, 30-50 mile trips maximum, you can usually wait on the side of the road and wave a taxi down, but not for a trip of this length. For long trips you have to go to *la gare routière* (taxi station). Normally when you walk into a large taxi station, the drivers swarm you like hungry piranhas. They are all competing with each other to fill up their taxis so they can leave sooner and save time. They wave and hiss at you to get your attention. Sometimes they grab your arm or your bag and ask, "Where are you going? . . . Come take my taxi." I have learned that once you give them your bag, you are done for. You may think that the driver is being nice by helping with your bag, but from his perspective, when you let him take your bag, you are tacitly agreeing to go with him even though you don't pay in full until you get to your destination. To prevent this problem, you have to hold onto your bag tightly until you are sure that you want to go with a certain driver. Once he puts your bag in the trunk of his taxi, you will have to fight like hell to get it back if you change your mind about going with him.

One of the biggest annoyances involved with taking bush taxis in Benin is never knowing when you will be leaving, since there are no schedules. When you leave is when the taxi is full. That could be in five minutes, or it could be in five hours! The most common game the drivers play is responding, *"toute de suite"* (right away), when they see you are getting impatient about leaving and you ask them, "When are we leaving?" The reality is they will not leave until the taxi is full. They can only guess when that will be, and the passengers who are waiting can only hope it will be soon.

The first thing a bush taxi passenger needs to do is inspect the car and make sure it is in good condition before agreeing to go with a particular driver. You also need to know how many places are in the car, and how many people are already waiting to go in that taxi. By "places" I do not mean seats, because they cram passengers into cars like sardines, and they put at least two people per "seat" (as we would define a seat in the U.S). If there are twelve places to be filled and you are the first passenger, then you will probably have a long wait. Choosing the taxi with the most passengers in it already insures the shortest wait. This can be difficult, however, as the passengers are often not in the car, but sitting elsewhere or walking around to kill time. The goal is to be the last passenger to get in, so you do not have to wait at all. Taxi drivers are aware of this and often play games. They have other taxi drivers or their apprentices sit in the car to fool travelers into thinking there are more passengers in the taxi than there really are.

When I get to the taxi station, there is only one taxi going south, so I don't have any of these hassles . . . but I also don't have any choice. Unfortunately, I am only the second passenger in the driver's 12 seater Peugeot station wagon, and I am afraid that I will have a very *loooong* wait.

From all my traveling in Benin, I have spent many hours in taxi stations sitting and waiting. What I have discovered is that waiting takes a very long time when you have no idea when the taxi is leaving. If it's 8 AM and you know you're going to leave at 10 AM, you can find ways to make two hours pass pretty quickly. If it is 8 AM and you have no idea when you are going to leave, by 10 AM your frustration compounds your boredom, and the time really drags. Think of it this way: every time you have to take a long distance taxi ride in Benin, it's like being stuck in an airport when your flight is delayed due to weather, a mechanical problem, or a computer glitch, and no one can give you a clear answer as to how and when the problem will be fixed. The Beninese deal with waiting under these circumstances all the time and have come to expect it. Usually it's only the impatient Yovos who get flustered.

Luckily Shelly's house is close to the taxi station, and the driver knows where it is. If he didn't, I would be stuck sitting on a wooden bench in the taxi station waiting for hours in a dirt parking lot full of cars, exhaust, people, and animals. I was stuck waiting for five hours in a taxi station in Parakou on my way up here, and I almost went out of my mind! What drove me crazy the most was that whenever I asked the driver when he was leaving, he would invariably give me the "*toute de suite*" line. While I was sitting there, the town "*fou*" (crazy person) pestered me, as did young children and beggars. While I was waiting, a goat happened to wander near me. It then stopped in its tracks and gave birth! I must admit that was interesting, especially when I noticed no one else thought anything of it.

I reserve my seat in the taxi by giving the driver my word that I will go with him. Then I go back to Shelly's and wait. Two hours go by and I am getting worried that he left without me, so I go back to check with him. The taxi now has four people plus me, but it still needs seven more before it will leave! I go back to Shelly's and I wait, and wait, and wait and wait . . . and then I wait some more. Eleven, twelve, and one o'clock roll by. I am getting so impatient at this blasted bush taxi system, because I am thinking that I may never get home! The taxi finally comes to get me at 2PM . . . at last!!!

## On the Road—Finally!

I say goodbye to Shelly, and I hope to be home in about 8 hours (or 10 PM). Finally I'm on my way home! The first thing I notice once we get going is that the driver starts going the wrong way! "*What is he doing?*," I think to myself as he pulls into a gas station to fill up. "This guy has been waiting for six hours to fill his blasted taxi up with people, yet he waited until now to get gas!" This happens all the time, and at first I had no idea why. Eventually I figured out that the drivers ask for a small portion of the fare in advance to pay for the gas, and they cannot get enough money until the car is full with passengers.

Almost all of the bush taxis in Benin are old beat up 1970's Peugeots that were taken off the road in France because they were unsafe and dilapidated. Instead of crushing them or sending them to junkyards for parts, the French sell them to the poor folks in West Africa for an outrageous price (primarily due to shipping costs). The taxi I am in is a nine seater, so named because of the number of people it was designed to hold in France. In Benin, however, they squeeze in at least 12 people! Therefore, I find it quite funny that the Beninese still call them "nine seaters." The taxi drivers use these "nine seater" station wagons for longer trips. For shorter trips they use smaller Peugeot 504 cars that have five seats and they cram seven, sometimes eight people into those. On occasion, when drivers want to make extra money, they put a fourth person in the front seat! When they do, the driver has to share the leg space around the gas pedal with the leg of the fourth person, as the fourth person needs to straddle the gearshift and transmission hump.

Bush taxis often break down, leaving the driver and the passengers stranded on the side of the road, usually in the middle of nowhere. Often there are holes in the floor, so you can see the road beneath you. Sometimes the seats are bare rotting foam rubber. The windshields are sometimes cracked. The driver may have to hot-wire the car to start it, or even resort to push starting it. A few times I saw drivers use bungee cords to hold doors closed. I have been in only one taxi that had working seat belts. Healthcare is practically non-existent in Benin, so I doubt that many bush taxi drivers have been to an eye doctor and I'm sure many do not have 20/20 vision. For these reasons, as well as the terrible condition of the roads, and the reckless driving, that we Peace Corps Volunteers affectionately call the front seat the "death seat." I always make sure that I sit in the back.

Taxi drivers are notorious for overcharging *Yovos* for taxi rides. It's hard to know what the going rate is, because there are so many possibilities for start and end points. I have enough knowledge of the prices, and I always ask an unbiased person the price if I am unsure before getting in a taxi in order to keep from being ripped off. Today I pay the going rate of about 5,000 CFA, or around $10, for this trip.

Luckily Shelly lives here, and she knows what the real price is so I don't have to worry that I'm getting ripped off. 5,000 CFA is not a lot, so the taxi driver cannot afford to waste any space in his vehicle if he is going to make a profit.

As I expect, there are twelve of us in this particular "nine seater," and the roof is packed as high as the car is tall with everyone's baggage. We are packed into the car like sardines, and we are jammed into the seats so close to the person next to us that our hips are pressed together tightly. Some passengers have to sit forward, because there is not enough room for everyone's shoulders if we all sit back at once. It feels as if everyone inhaled at once, the doors would pop open. I feel lucky this time that none of the passengers is overweight. There have been times when I had an overweight woman sitting next to me, and she took up one and a half seats, but only paid for one. Of course the taxi driver put four of us back there, and the rest of us had to make due with one and a third butt cheeks on the seat. That was downright uncomfortable. At times my legs and butt fell asleep, and I had no space to move, so I used the frequent stops to walk around and try to regain circulation.

Believe it or not, I have seen worse conditions than these. Often groups of people who are going on a trip together rent out small covered Peugeot pickup trucks, and they squeeze in God knows how many people in the truck bed. When everyone gets out, it literally looks like a clown car from the circus! Most Beninese cannot afford the high price of comfort, but the ones who can, sometimes opt to buy two seats in the bush taxi. Unfortunately, I am a poor Peace Corps Volunteer. I am used to roughing it, so I pay for only one seat and I get to know my traveling companions intimately.

Besides the twelve people in the car, I can't forget to mention the two babies sitting on their mother's laps and the live chickens on the floor that eventually crap on people's feet. One time, when I was in a bush taxi, one of the passengers put his live chicken in the back window of the car, and of course it crapped on another passenger's shoulder. After it did, the owner of the chicken casually plucked a feather from the chicken's tail, scraped off the poop, and threw it out the window. The guy who had crap on his shoulder didn't even flinch, which goes to show how common it is to share a bush taxi with live animals, and how easygoing the Beninese are. A volunteer friend of mine in Mali told me how she was once in a taxi that had goats tied to the roof, and she suddenly felt warm rain on a clear, sunny day. She then realized that it was goat urine streaming off the roof that had blown into her face by the wind! I was once in a car with screaming hog-tied goats in the trunk, which made for quite an unpleasant ride. Luckily we have only a few chickens this time.

I have been eating all sorts of new foods here up north, and I cannot help but wonder if something will irritate my digestive system on my ride home. Luckily I have been feeling well lately, but as I have learned many times, that can change very quickly. I have not had to travel while suffering from diarrhea. I am sure it would not only be very unpleasant, but also very inconvenient if I had to ask the driver to keep stopping. It would be very embarrassing because my only choice would be to go on the side of the road. I will keep my fingers crossed.

Some of the passengers engage in lively and boisterous conversations in several different languages. I recognize a conversation in Fon, but only some words. I cannot understand what they are saying because my Fon is not very good, and they are speaking rather quickly. All of this loud chatter around me, in languages I do not understand, certainly gets annoying.

I have no problem with French, but only a few passengers speak it well. Benin is a country about the size of Pennsylvania, and its inhabitants speak 50 indigenous African languages! These are the languages that people learn at home, and are spoken in particular regions of Benin, such as Fon, the local language of southern Benin. Some of those local languages are similar and can be understood by speakers of other indigenous languages in the same region, but many are very different from one another and cannot be understood by people from other regions. Perhaps some of my fellow passengers are speaking Yom, the language from Djougou, or Bariba, another common language here in Northern Benin, although they could be speaking several of more than a dozen languages spoken in the north. French is the colonial language of Benin, and it is very useful to anyone in Benin because without it, people from one region could not speak to people from another, despite the fact that the two regions may only be several miles away! French also allows people from other former West African French colonies such as Senegal, Mali, Ivory Coast, Mauritania, Burkina Faso, Niger, Togo, and Benin to communicate easily with each other. Unfortunately, the only people who speak French are the people who have gone to school, and many have not, so often I cannot communicate with them. If I need to speak to them, I find someone who speaks French, and I ask him or her to interpret for me.

We certainly do not have air conditioning in the taxi, and the temperature is about 95 and humid. As a matter of fact, it's safe to say that no bush taxi in Benin has air conditioning. What makes it worse is that the taxis almost never have window cranks that work, and the drivers often only leave the windows open a crack in case it rains. If you're driver has one, you can ask him to give you the hand crank to open or close your window. The Beninese are very clean people, and they generally bathe daily, but when you're sweating in those hot conditions for hours on end, the odor in the air gets unpleasant quickly.

Benin suffers from terrible infrastructure, which makes it quite arduous to travel. In the entire country, there are only four major roads that are paved, and they are all undivided. Almost all of the other roads are dirt, full of potholes, ditches, and bone rattling washboard. Because the taxis are usually overloaded and have bad suspensions, they often bottom out going over the big potholes and jolt my entire skeleton. Even in the capital city, Cotonou, most of the roads are dirt or deep sand. When it rains the roads become insufferable mud bogs that increase your travel time considerably. Sometimes smaller dirt roads become completely impassible during the rainy season, even in a four-wheel drive vehicle. The paved roads are unsafe because there are no dividers, guard rails, or break down lanes, and people routinely drive at 70 plus miles per hour. The dirt roads are safer because the drivers are forced to go much slower, but they are a lot less comfortable due to all of the bumps and dust.

This is the biggest and most important road in Benin. It is paved but is narrow and undivided.

There are speed limits posted, but there is no way to enforce them since the police do not have radar detectors. Even if they did have radar detectors, they do not have cars fast enough to chase down the speeders. There are occasional speed limit signs, but due to the lack of enforcement, they are merely suggestions. Often the cars' and trucks' brakes are not in good condition, and the roads are curvy in places. Due to all of these bad conditions, there are, not surprisingly, many accidents. On the way up north, I must have seen fifty wrecked cars on the side of the road. Often, the Beninese just leave the wreckage there because there are no tow trucks, and no one has the money to haul away a vehicle unless it is actually salvageable. The lack of good roads not only makes traveling in Benin dangerous and miserable, but it hinders Benin's economic growth because people and goods cannot easily get to markets.

As we are barreling down the dirt road, the driver is constantly honking his horn. I think this is very rude and annoying, until I realize that he is not doing it out of anger, but as a safety precaution to avoid all the pedestrians, motorcyclists, errant goats, pigs, cyclists, stopped cars, and children along the road. In places the road is a veritable obstacle course, and the driver veers and swerves. These roads often cut right through the centers of towns and villages, and the taxi drivers do not slow down, so it is better that they honk a lot. One time when I was on my way to Cotonou, I was reading a magazine in the back seat when the driver unexpectedly stopped. I thought nothing of it because they stop so frequently to pick up passengers, get gas, stop for police roadblocks, etc. The next thing I knew, he was putting the bloody body of a dead young girl, who was probably nine or ten years old, in the front seat! I was shocked! I looked back and saw a group of people, and another taxi that had hit the girl as she was crossing the road. The driver of that taxi waved our taxi down for help. After they put her in the front seat, they argued about what to do. I pleaded with them to take her to a hospital, but they said that she was already dead and it was not necessary. Besides, they argued, the nearest hospital was about an hour away. The two drivers then discussed the issue further, and they decided to take the girl out of the taxi, and put her back on the ground until the police got there. Soon after, my taxi left and took me to Cotonou. When I was in Cotonou, I saw another volunteer who arrived about an hour after me, and had been traveling on the same road. She said that she saw the same thing, and apparently the girl was still lying on the side of the road with a group of people milling around an hour after I had seen her. It goes to show how poor the emergency care is in Benin. There are no ambulances or a 911 system. There are no Life Star helicopters and only the ultra-wealthy have cell phones to call for help. I realize how lucky I am living in the U.S, because if I am in an accident, EMT's, ambulances, police, Life Star helicopters, and high tech hospitals are all about ten minutes away in most urban areas. Luckily, I have not been in an accident here, and I'm keeping my fingers crossed. Thinking of that accident, I am glad that the driver is honking every time he sees pedestrians, despite the fact it can be annoying.

Because these taxis are so old, overloaded, and poorly maintained, they often break down. I'm praying that we don't have any mechanical problems on this trip. We are traveling on a dirt road now, and if we have a mechanical problem, it will be a lot harder to find a new taxi passing by because there are so few of them on this road. I often see drivers removing the rear ends of their pickup trucks on the side of the road because they overloaded them and something broke. There are no tow trucks or AAA to tow them. It is very dangerous when they break down, because there is no break down lane. They are very resourceful, however, and instead of using flares, they put branches on the road to signal a broken down car to the oncoming drivers. One volunteer told me a story about how a wheel fell off the taxi they were in as it was speeding down the road!

I once saw a broken down bus in Allada that was coming from Niger and going to Togo. The passengers had to camp on the side of the road for three days while the driver rebuilt the transmission! The bus driver could not refund them their money, probably because he didn't have it, so all of the passengers who could not afford to pay for a bush taxi to take them the rest of the way had to wait there for three days! Taxi drivers never replace belts, hoses, tires etc., as preventative maintenance. It is cheaper for them to be stuck on the side of the road somewhere for four hours than change a perfectly good belt that still has one, or maybe 1,000 miles of life in it. This is because time is less valuable than money in Benin. They have a lot of time, but very little money. In the end, the passengers pay the price, but surprisingly almost no one complains . . . aside from me, (but only once in a while), the impatient white guy who is always in a hurry.

Beninese resourcefulness really amazes me. The fact that they can keep these old cars running with so little money, tools and parts is no small feat. Because spare parts are expensive and hard to find, they have to make due with what parts they have lying around. I have seen an old tomato paste can with holes poked in it put over the carburetor to serve as an air filter. I'm guessing they have to rebuild their engines every month or so when they utilize this technique, considering all the dirt that gets kicked up on these roads and invariably gets sucked into the engines. They also have to make due with limited tools. I once saw an old engine block and a long wooden pole used as a lever to lift up one end of a car to change its tires.

We have been on the road for about an hour when suddenly . . . we get a flat tire. We all get out and the driver notifies us that he doesn't have a jack! It blows my mind that the driver is so irresponsible! "*How are we going to fix this!?*" I think. Then the driver motions for everyone to grab the bumper and lift! "*Un, deux, trois, levez!*" He yells. I help too, and believe it or not, we are able to help the driver change the tire by lifting the car. Soon we are back on the road, but no more than

20 or 30 minutes goes by before we stop again. We stop to get the flat tire fixed, so we will have a spare in case of another flat. That takes at least a half-hour. We are stopped in front of a guy sitting on the side of the road with a toolbox in a small village called Basila. He fixes the tire while the rest of us go to the bathroom and get some street food. Soon we are on the road again, but this is only the first of many, many stops.

Along the way we periodically come upon local police stops, *gendarme* (national police) stops and forestry stops. We stop for a gendarme and he has the driver open the back of the car to look for "contraband," whatever that may be. As the driver opens the rear hatch, one of the passenger's chickens flies out and onto the ground. The chicken's legs come untied and it runs into the woods. The angry owner jumps out of the car, and we all end up getting out to help him look for it for 20 minutes, further prolonging our trip. The gendarme discourages the search and tells us with a big grin, "You will never find it!" After we give up looking, the gendarme boldly says that the chicken will inevitably come back at night, and tells us how he will catch it and eat it! Since it was a big chicken, I am sure the owner is upset.

The police, gendarme, and forestry stops seem random, and each time we go through one, we have to wait five or ten minutes, so that alone adds an hour to our trip. They place signs on the road to signal to the drivers to stop. These roadblocks are everywhere around Benin and West Africa. Ostensibly they are there to enforce the laws. In reality they are there to collect bribes to augment officials' meager salaries. They take advantage of their power to harass drivers and extort money from them. If the drivers do not pay the normal expected bribe, then the gendarme will start looking for infractions, and will hold up the driver until he gives in and pays the bribe. Almost every bush taxi in Benin could be charged with dozens of violations, such as having too many passengers and too much baggage, not having a fire extinguisher, not having a first aid kit, and not having the proper insurance or documentation etc. The taxi drivers know that there is no way that they can follow all the regulations and still make a profit. They could never afford to make all the necessary repairs, and if they carried less passengers and baggage to comply with the laws, they would have to charge more and would not be able to find passengers. Paying a small bribe is a much more economical solution for them.

The police and gendarmes don't actually block the roads, but there are usually one or two officers sitting on chairs with their automatic weapons at their sides, so the taxi drivers take them seriously and stop. I have heard that the police often do not have enough money for bullets, but the taxi drivers do not want to chance that. The taxi driver has to get out of the car and show the official his car registration and license, and possibly other documents along with the standard 200 CFA tucked inside. The official will give the papers and the car a perfunctory look over, discretely take the money, and then let him go. It is a form of institutionalized extortion, but it only costs the drivers 200F, or about forty cents, so they usually accept it and just build the price of the bribes into the taxi fare. I guess one can think of it as an informal toll.

Forty cents doesn't sound like much for a police officer, but they probably only make a few dollars a day in salary. Forty cents is not bad at all, especially when you multiply it by dozens or more drivers every day. It is a racket because it is unfair for the taxi drivers and the passengers. On the other hand, the bribery subsidizes the officials' salaries and motivates them to work since the government cannot afford to pay them a fair salary. One can see it as a progressive tax since only those who use the roads have to pay it. On the other hand, bribery undermines the laws that are in place. Either way it is not an ideal situation.

If the driver knows that his taxi is in violation of many laws, such as being grossly overloaded or having a very dilapidated car, he might increase the bribe for good measure. In one instance, the police went so far as to tell our driver that he could not continue on, and that he had to turn back. That forced all of us to be stuck on the side of the road to wave down another taxi. Perhaps our driver was feeling ornery, and refused to pay the gendarme a sweet enough bribe to be granted passage. Luckily there are always taxis going by, at least on the paved roads, and they always stop if they have room. Officially, bribery is illegal in Benin so it has to be done discretely. Nonetheless, it is rampant.

Some drivers have fewer problems than others do at these roadblocks, depending on how often they pass and how well they know the police or gendarmes who are on duty. One time I was in a taxi that was overloaded, so the driver had two passengers get out before the roadblock and walk past the police to avoid being in violation and having to pay a higher bribe. Sometimes if the gendarmes are feeling their oats, they will come and check the passenger's identification, and may ask a passenger for a bribe if something is not in order. I never experienced this in Benin, but I did in the Ivory Coast. There a police officer checked the passports and identification papers of everyone in the taxi, and he found that one person did not have an I.D. He first tried to scare all of us and wielded his power by saying that he could make us all wait there "until the issue was resolved." i.e. until he got the bribe that he wanted. We waited for about ten minutes, and finally he came back and said something to the effect of, "since I'm being nice today, I'm going to let you all go." We thanked him for his "generosity," and we were on our way. I suspect however, that the driver paid him a high enough bribe to resolve the situation.

On a later trip when I was in a taxi in Abidjan, Ivory Coast with a friend, we were pulled over and the police asked for our passports. We gave them to him thinking nothing of it. He came back and said to my friend in the front seat, "You were not wearing your seatbelts. I will have to keep your passports, and you will have to come to the police station to collect them and pay a 10,000 CFA fine. "10,000 CFA ($20 U.S.)," we thought. "That is outrageous! We only earn 3,000 CFA ($6) a day as volunteers, and we are only spending about 5,000 CFA per day on this trip." We were shocked and afraid that we would have problems getting our passports back. He then said, "Well if you each pay me 2,000 CFA, I won't have to take your passports and you can go." We politely protested that it was a lot of money, and also that the taxi driver never told us we were supposed to wear our seatbelts. Besides, we live in Benin, and taxis never have working seatbelts. His response was, "OK, if you pay me 1,000 CFA, we can forget the whole thing." We were very angry, and felt that it was very unfair, but this was a simple and inexpensive solution to a potentially time consuming and complicated situation. We decided to pay him and we were on our way. In a strange way we felt satisfied that at least we bargained him down on the "fine."

On that same trip, from Ghana to the Ivory Coast, was also an absolute nightmare as far as stops and roadblocks were concerned, which made the trip seem interminable. From Takoradi, Ghana to Abidjan, Ivory Coast, I counted 20 stops! I had heard from other volunteers that it would be bad, so I decided to keep a tally. We had to stop four times for gendarmes, six times for police, one time for a forestry check, once for another customs check, twice for no apparent reason, once for a food stop, twice for gas, and once to let people out. That trip was only 150 miles and it took over 8 hours! That averages out to a speed of about 18 miles per hour. If I were in good shape, I could have completed the trip just as fast on my bike!

Crossing borders in a bush taxi is usually a very lengthy process. Later, when I traveled from Niger to Burkina Faso, it took three hours to cross the border!! We arrived at the border at 1:30 PM from Niamey in a crowded bush taxi van. On the Niger side everyone had to get out of the van and give our passports to the gendarmes, who took them inside and brought them back a half hour later stamped with our exit information. We all got back in the van, and drove a half-hour or so before coming to the Burkina Faso border town. First we had to pass through customs, and everyone had to get out while all of the baggage on the van was unloaded. Each passenger had to carry his luggage over to be inspected, and then carry it about a hundred yards back to the minibus again. I was told that this was required to make sure that people could not put their bags back in the car without getting them inspected first. Customs took an hour because some people had duties to pay. After everyone was through the border, and the car was loaded up again, we were off! . . . to the gendarmes down the road. Everyone had to get out again. The gendarme looked at the passports and collected a 100F fee from each of us. Everyone got back in and we were off . . . to the police down the road! We all got out, and they took our passports to stamp them. "God, this process is !@#$%^&* ridiculous!!" I thought. The customs officials, gendarmes, and police were not working together because they would not be able to make as much money that way, and this gave them all something to do. We were finally on our way in Burkina Faso at 4:30. I could not help but think the reason Burkina Faso is so poor is because it takes forever to get in or out! I thank my lucky stars there are no borders to cross on this trip back to Allada.

Often bush taxis run out of gas due to bad planning and broken gas gauges. To check the gas level they often have a piece of metal strapping to use as a dipstick. After a taxi runs out of gas and the driver gets it refilled, they usually remove the gas line from the carburetor and suck on it to remove the air. He siphons gas in his mouth, injects it into the carburetor, and reconnects the gas line. When I once commented to a driver regarding the dangers of ingesting gasoline, he responded that it kills intestinal parasites, and suggested I try some! Amazingly, the cars always seem to start on the first crank of the engine after the driver does this. Gas is usually sold black market style in Benin, often by little kids and their mothers on the side of the road and packaged in whiskey bottles and plastic jugs. The government obviously does not care as they often sell it right in front of the government owned gas stations. I am hoping we will not run out of gas on this trip.

As we are driving along, our driver suddenly speeds up abruptly, swerves, and hits something in the road. The taxi comes to a quick stop, and we start going in reverse. "What is this crazy driver doing?," I think to myself. He jumps out of the car, and proudly picks up a very long black snake from the road that he just ran over. Some people get out of the car to inspect it. The driver is planning to keep the snake to eat, but one of the passengers offers to buy it from him. I ask the man who buys the snake what he is going to do with it. He says that he is going to use the head to create gris-gris (a magic charm), or use it as an ingredient in a traditional healing remedy. He puts it in a bag, stows it on the roof with the other baggage, and we continue on.

I heard from another volunteer once that he took a long taxi ride at night, and there were a lot of bush rats and other animals crossing the road. The taxi driver did the same thing, swerving to intentionally hit and kill the animals. Each time the driver hit an animal, everyone in the taxi cheered because it was Christmas Eve, and the driver was giving the animals to his passengers as a gift. By the time they reached Cotonou, the driver had hit enough rabbits, bush rats, and snakes that every passenger got one! They even offered one to the American volunteer, but he politely declined. The passengers were more than happy to receive such a nice gift, as they cannot afford to buy meat on a regular basis.

I see that down the road in front of our taxi there is a group of men standing on both sides of the road holding a rope across it with a red flag attached to signal us to stop. I am worried that they are going to rob us. The driver slows down and just as we reach the rope, the men drop it to the ground so we can cross. We stop and the men approach the car. I get very nervous, but everyone else in the taxi seems unusually calm, so I take solace in their body language. The men speak with the driver briefly, he gives them a few coins, and we are on our way again. After further investigation, I find out that they are a group of local people who fill the potholes in the road with dirt, and they are trying to coerce the drivers to pay them a small contribution. I find that very resourceful since the government is not going to fix the road any time soon, and the local people know that the drivers benefit from their work. On subsequent taxi rides I have seen fights occur when workers harass the drivers who refuse to pay. Often the drivers, especially on faster roads, just blow through these roadblocks, and it seems like a game of chicken to me, as the men holding the rope do not drop it until the very last second. Men in Allada have done this on remote roads on market day and try to charge everyone coming to the market, including cyclists, pedestrians and motorcyclists. They choose market day because there are many more people traveling than any other day.

After more bouncing up and down over washboarded dirt road, suffering the hot dusty and cramped conditions, we stop again, this time to pray at a mosque. The driver and a few passengers are Muslim, and it is prayer time, so here we are. Luckily this takes only 20 minutes. As a passenger in a bush taxi, you are at the driver's whim and mercy. You often never know why he is stopping. Usually it is for a good reason, but sometimes they stop to see their friends or pick up a few things for dinner at a roadside stand while all of the passengers are waiting. Sometimes the drivers are very nice, and make personal stops for the passengers, such as when a passenger sees something for sale on the side of the road and wants to buy it. The downside of course, is that it holds everyone else up. As a passenger, it is very frustrating to be cooped up in a hot taxi and not know why you are waiting. Believe me, when the taxi stops, it gets hot quickly, especially if the driver stops in the sun and you're stuck in between two or more people. When the taxi stops in the center of a larger town, women and children selling a variety of foods swarm the taxi selling food and other goods so you don't even need to get out to do some shopping. If you need to go to the bathroom or stretch your legs, you usually have to have to ask the driver to let you out because the door handle is usually broken on the inside. In bush taxis my discomfort is often exacerbated by the drivers playing repetitive African music very loudly, and I usually have to make multiple requests that he turn it down.

Children selling bananas and peanuts to us when we stopped.

Taxi drivers have been known to pull stunts on their passengers, such as not taking them all the way to the agreed upon destination. They always refund any remaining money you have prepaid, but you are then left to find a new taxi, which can take many more hours of waiting. They do this because they know that if they tell you that they are not going all the way to your destination, you will not go with them. This driver says he is going to Cotonou, and will let me out in Allada, but I cannot be sure from past experiences.

After about five hours of driving, we finally reach the paved road! The road is fairly smooth . . . hurray!! This is all well and good, but this means the chauffeur can drive like a maniac now. Like all the drivers, he often passes cars near the crests of hills or curves at 70 mph even if he can't see if there is on-coming traffic. In this situation, you either have to close your eyes and pray, or plead with him to go "*doucement*" (take it easy). By this time I am covered from head to toe with red dirt from the dust that the passing cars kicked up. I am sitting next to the window so I bear that brunt of it. I take my sunglasses off, and look in the side view mirror. Not surprisingly I look like a raccoon from all the dirt sticking to my sweaty face. I am ecstatic, because there will be no more dust, no more bouncing up and down on potholes and having my bones jarred by the washboard road surface. It is also starting to get dark. Peace Corps advises volunteers to travel only during the day because there are less accidents in daylight, but that is next to impossible on a long trip like this. Traveling at night is just one more reason for me to be anxious, but I try to be resigned to my fate and be as relaxed as the other passengers.

I am thinking that the rest of this trip will go smoothly and quickly, because we will be on a paved road the rest of the way. But alas . . . we get another flat tire!! Once again, the driver yells "*Un, deux, trois, levez*" ("1,2.3, lift!"), we lift, he changes the tire, and a half hour later we are on our way. I cannot believe how long and miserable this trip is! It is already 10 PM and I thought I would have been home an hour ago. However, we are still at least two hours away!

I am listening to my Walkman to keep me from going insane, and I notice that the passenger next to me is sleeping on my shoulder. "Oh well, no big deal," I think. I might need him to return the favor later. One time when I was on a shorter taxi ride, I was sitting next to a guy who was coughing regularly. I asked him if he had seen a doctor. He said yes, and then proceeded to tell me that he had tuberculosis! I was scared that I would catch it from him so I tried to lean the other way. Luckily nothing came of it, and I'm glad the guy sleeping on my shoulder on this trip seems healthy.

We are nearing southern Benin, and the air becomes more humid and the vegetation becomes greener, as there is more rain in southern Benin than in the arid North. We stop in Bohicon for a late street food dinner, and it takes over half an hour. Finally, the taxi pulls into Allada a little after 1 AM! I then have to find a zemidjan to take me the one-mile trip to my house down the pitch-black narrow dirt path on the outskirts of town. I am absolutely exhausted, and completely filthy. I ache all over from being crushed by the other passengers, and from being bounced up and down for eleven hours. I am grimy from sweating and getting sandblasted by dust.

After counting, I realize that we stopped a total of 16 times along the way! Two times to fix flat tires, once to get the tire patched, twice to get gas, twice for food, once to pray at the mosque, once to let someone out, once to collect a dead snake, once to pay the road repairers, and five times for official roadblocks. If you include the time I spent waiting for the taxi to leave, this trip took me seventeen and a half hours, all to go 240 stinking miles! That's an average speed of only eleven miles per hour! Our average speed from when we left to when I arrived was only eighteen miles per hour, and we didn't cross a border. Although it's scary to think, it actually could have been worse.

It is terrible having to wait six hours and then ride eleven hours in these difficult conditions, but it makes me realize how resourceful the Beninese are, keeping these old beat up cars running with so little money and spare parts. It also makes me realize how lucky we are in the U.S. to have our own cars, and public transportation, which are usually quick and reliable. I am impressed at how rarely the Beninese complain. On this trip for example, I did not hear one complaint, or even one sigh of frustration. I admire them for their patience, and for how friendly they are to me and to everyone else. In the U.S., I have seen people become angry, and ultimately rude, because they had to wait just a few minutes in a line that was not moving as fast as they would like. In Benin, people are accustomed to inefficiency, and are almost always good-natured about it. On the other hand, I was fuming the entire way on this trip, and was trying hard to hold it in. Looking back it was quite an adventure. It was truly a bush taxi ride from hell, and worse than most of the others I have experienced.

When I told this story to other volunteers, I was shocked when one told me that the same trip took her 23 hours one time! Her taxi broke down and she ended up sleeping on the side of the road for a few hours while they fixed it. Benin volunteers almost never have "perfect" taxi rides. I would define the "perfect" bush taxi ride as one with no more than a few necessary stops, and no difficulties of any sort. In my two years in Benin, I only had one such ride in a bush taxi. As with any trip in West Africa, getting there is half the adventure (or more). So if you visit Benin, be sure not to miss the true bush taxi experience!

# A Visit to Melissa

Being a PCV is an intense experience. We experience the highest of highs and the lowest of lows. Having been here over a year, I have come a long way in terms of adapting to my new environment and forging relationships with with the Beninese. I have had some modest work related successes working with cooperatives but it is frustrating at times. From what I hear, the greatest and most fulfilling successes don't happen until the second year. So far I have made myself comfortable in my new environment. I have made many Beninese friends, established professional relationships, learned Fon, and learned a lot about the culture. I learned my way around, adapted to the food, the heat and the microorganisms in the food and water. I'm starting to feel well adapted to life here, but I'm feeling down for some reason.

Some reasons for feeling glum are, just to name a few: being sick, being homesick, wondering what am I accomplishing here, wanting more visible results from the business skills I'm teaching, being isolated from people who understand me, wondering what I'll do after Peace Corps, dealing with language barriers, not fitting in, not understanding the culture enough, being frustrated with Beninese inefficiency, not liking the food, and suffering in high heat and humidity. Despite these hardships and reasons to be depressed, for the most part I am positive. I'm usually more positive about being here than now because I can feel myself growing from testing myself and pushing myself to my limit.

It has been several weeks since I've seen another American aside from my postmate in Allada. I need to spend some time with another American to unwind a little and hopefully a short getaway will cheer me up. I decide to pay a visit to a new Peace Corps Volunteer named Melissa, who just arrived at her post, which is only about a ten mile mountain bike ride from my house.

## The Bush Postal System:

I want to let Melissa know of my arrival ahead of time to make sure she will be home. Since Peace Corps' philosophy is for its volunteers to live on or close to the level of the local people, I have neither a car nor a telephone, and neither does she. She has a post office box, but I don't know what it is yet, so I used a more traditional method to send her a message. Melissa's village is called Bopa, and people from Bopa and Allada both frequent the large regional market in the neighboring village, Avakpa. Monday morning was the market day in Avakpa, so I went to the bush taxi station in town and found a Peugeot *baché* (a small French pick up truck), which was packed with people, as well as numerous goods, stowed on top. I gave the driver a letter for Melissa. I asked him to give it to a market woman who comes from Bopa, and to ask her to give it to Melissa. On the envelope I wrote in French "Melissa, Peace Corps Volunteer—Social Center, Bopa" (where she works). The taxi driver gladly accepted and took the letter. I wasn't sure if this would work or not, but I've heard that other volunteers have used this method to get messages to each other with success, so I thought I would give it a shot considering I had no other way of getting in touch with her. If it didn't work, and she wasn't home when I arrived, I would stay with my neighbors' relatives who live in a village near Bopa.

## The Dry Season and Water:

A few days later, I prepare to leave in the late afternoon after the intense equatorial heat dies down (Benin lies only eight degrees above the equator). I leave my house waving goodbye to my neighbors, and begin my journey through the ten miles of thickly vegetated, remote African bush. The dirt path leading away from my house is only slightly wider than the width of a small car. On this stretch of the bush path, I usually see at least several hundred children playing, and pass numerous people carrying loads on their heads, as well as other cyclists, motorcyclists, cars, and farmers working in their fields. It's surprising that so many people live back here, as this area seems so uninhabitable and remote, and there are so few resources available. There is no electricity, no running water, no mail service, no public transportation, and no official businesses.

Along the way I pedal through several traditional African villages such as Lissegazoun, Dedomé and Dékanmé. I see many things that Westerners imagine as stereotypical of Africa, including small thatched roof mud huts clustered together into housing compounds under banana, palm, and coconut trees. Next to the huts there are many tall cylindrical hut-like structures that are made of palm branches, wood and bamboo. They have thatch roofs and the floor is elevated above the ground. These are corn granaries and are essential to the villagers' food security during the long dry season. They usually store their corn in them and rely on them to keep the rain and vermin out. The villages are cut out of the thick vegetation, and appear and disappear quickly as I pedal my way down the long serpentine path. In the villages near any housing compound the air is always filled with wood smoke from cooking fires. The huts are surrounded by dirt, as their owners always kill any grass. If they were surrounded by grass, they risk altercations with snakes, which are abundant in Benin and are often very deadly.

It is February and it is the dry season. With the dry season comes the Harmattan, which is a wind that blows south from the Sahara desert, bringing with it loads of dust making the air very hazy. During the Harmattan the air is much drier. It makes the mornings and evenings cooler than usual, but hotter than average at mid-day. Some volunteers who live farther north say that it gets so hot in their houses this time of year that their candles warp, and they must sleep outside! Fortunately, it doesn't get quite that hot in southern Benin. During the rest of the year, the weather here rarely changes, so even a slight change in temperature or humidity is easily noticed. It's really funny seeing Beninese people wearing winter clothing this time of year when it drops to a bone chilling 70 degrees in the early morning or evening. They wear sweaters, long pants, winter jackets, gloves, and ski hats, all Dead Yovo clothing sold in the market. One time I saw a motorcycle taxi driver wearing a ski mask! I have to admit that I consider 75 degrees cold now that I have been here over a year, as I am used to an average temperature of 85 to 90 degrees. Nonetheless, no matter how cold it gets, I have sworn to never wear a winter jacket while I am in Africa.

Now is a particularly difficult time of year for the southern Beninese people, as the dry season has been going on for four months. Since the dry season started, it has rained briefly only a few times, and no crops can be grown until the first rain in March or April. Water for drinking, washing, and bathing has become a scarce commodity for villagers, as their cisterns have dried up, and they must rely on the very few wells that exist for their water. There are lines at the wells this time of year, and the village women and children must often wait hours to fetch water because of the great demand. The wells are very deep, going down as far as 150 feet, so it takes a long time to fill a large basin when all they're using is a three gallon rubber bag attached to a rope. Sometimes they have a pulley or a hand cranked roller to pull the water out of the ground but not always. Each person uses at least one basin of water per day, so they spend a great deal of time fetching water this time of year.

These women and children must wait in line at this well, pull the water bucket up by hand because there is no pulley, then they have to carry it home on their heads.

If they don't want to wait, or if there aren't any wells nearby, they may resort to drinking dirty pond water, which can be found several kilometers away down narrow bush paths on steep hills. The pond water transmits the Guinea worm parasite. When an infected person steps into the water, the worm pops out of the skin and lays eggs into the water. When the next person drinks water containing the eggs, the cycle is completed. Thankfully, in 2004 Guinea worm was completely eradicated (Carter

Center.org) in Benin by teaching people how to filter their water. I have seen water from these ponds, and it is usually brown with mud that is kicked up by people stepping in it to scoop it up. Once the rainy season starts, they collect the rainwater in their cisterns and large ceramic pots placed under their gutters. At that time, they will rely less on well and pond water, and they will have to haul the water shorter distances to get it back to their huts. Often villagers cannot afford to maintain their cisterns. The gutter pipes rust and the cement liner cracks so they are not able to collect much water. In that case, even during the rainy season, they may have to walk some distance to fetch water.

I admire the Beninese for the strength that is required to carry large basins of water. It is an every day task for women and children living in villages, because they never have running water, and fetching water is considered a woman's job in Benin. Some people are lucky enough to live near a well, or to have an operational cistern near their house, but often they have to carry the water long distances. My neighbors and I are lucky because my landlord has a functioning cistern in front of my house that holds enough water for me to have water even through the dry season. He sells water to my neighbors, so there is a din of people in my front yard for several hours every afternoon. Last year I worried that he would sell too much water, and I would subsequently run out. If it did run out, I would have had to pay someone to fetch water for me down the road. I could not have asked him to stop selling it because it would have created a hardship for my neighbors. Luckily he did stop selling it once when the level got down to about three feet near the end of the dry season, and it was enough water to last me until the rainy season started in April.

When he stopped selling the water at my house, my neighbors had to walk half a kilometer to buy tap water at my landlord's house. The woman and children had to make at least one trip a day, every day, with a basin of water on their heads until the rains started in earnest. My guess is that each basin of water holds about five gallons of water. A gallon of water weighs about eight pounds, so they have to carry 40 pounds of water on their heads one to two kilometers a day for two months!

I was so impressed that I tried it once. After about 50 yards, my arms, neck and shoulders were screaming, and I had to stop. Not only does carrying water take strength, but it also takes a lot of skill. After you fill your basin with water, you coil a piece of cloth, and put it on your head for padding. Sometimes they put branches with leaves in the water to prevent it from sloshing around. Then they squat down, and with the help of another person, they lift the basin on their heads and then stand up slowly. When I did this, I immediately felt the pressure on my head, neck, shoulders and back . . . . and then I felt the pain. Walking with good posture is crucial to keeping the water from spilling, and takes a lot of skill. I must have spilled about a quarter of my water in the 50 yards I tried to carry it. The children, only five or six years old, start carrying water with smaller basins so they have time to work up to the larger five gallon ones. Most villagers don't live in walking distance to municipal water sources so they have to carry it on their heads up steep hills, as the ponds tend to be located in valleys. I can only imagine how hard that is.

This is Claire carrying water home on the 1KM long path to her hut.

Even though men don't usually carry water, they carry other things on their heads. I've seen men carry big logs on their heads, boxes, cases of beer etc. On the other end of the spectrum, I've seen people walk with just a roll of toilet paper on their heads although they weren't carrying anything else in their hands. I guess it's just a habit that allows them to keep their hands free. They are always very graceful and almost never need to use their hands to balance the item they are carrying because they have had so much practice.

For obvious reasons the Beninese are very conservative with the amount of water they use. Being the rich Yovo, I pay my neighbor, Nestor, to fetch the water from my cistern every day. I keep a five gallon bucket in the kitchen, a five gallon bucket in the shower, and I rarely use more than that in a day. In the United States, older toilets use 5-7 gallons in one flush, not to mention what a ten minute shower uses! I have ceramic filters in the bucket in the kitchen, as I drink, cook, and do the dishes with that water. I am glad for those filters, because my cistern has only woven palm branches to keep debris out. There are many gaps and I have seen dead lizards floating in the water after they fell into the cistern.

## The Bush Path:

During the rainy season, the road or, more accurately, the "bush path" I'm riding on becomes a serpentine obstacle course of huge mud puddles. They often span the entire width of the road, forcing travelers to either take small paths to circumnavigate the puddles, or to go straight through them. On several occasions I have sunk knee deep, as I mistakenly chose the deep side of the puddle. It is a gamble because there is no way of telling which is the shallow side. For cars, the path becomes almost impassible due to the horrible conditions. During rainy seasons I have crossed mud bogs so thick on this road that the mud jammed between my wheels and fenders, preventing them from turning. The mud caked two inches thick on the bottom of my shoes, making the path as slippery as ice! Pushing my mud-laden bike along the path while my feet were slipping all over and the wheels did not turn, was not exactly pleasant.

I am thankful that it is the dry season now because all the mud and puddles have dried up allowing me a much more enjoyable ride. The only disadvantage is the dust that blows in my face when an occasional motorcycle or car passes by me.

As I ride, I see many people. In the villages they are milling around, many are sitting on wood benches in front of their huts, and there are children playing everywhere. I see goats, chickens, and pigs wandering around foraging for food. There are people everywhere because the Beninese do not live in their houses. Villagers live outside and use their huts only for storing their few belongings and for sleeping at night. They spend little time indoors because it is so hot. It is dark inside because they usually have only a few small windows. During the day people spend most of their time under *paillottes* (straw roofs without walls similar to a gazebo). They offer protection from the searing equatorial sun while allowing the breeze to pass through. Paillotes also offer plenty of light. When lounging under a paillote, occupants have the advantage of seeing people pass by, which is a favorite pastime of the Beninese.

I feel a sense of accomplishment, because over the past year and a half, I have successfully learned my way through this maze of remote overgrown bush paths. They are indeed paths and certainly not roads, so they do not have names, and no one living on them has an address. If someone wants to tell you where he lives out here, he has to tell you the name of the village and the name of the agglomeration of huts. When you get close to the person's hut, you have to ask for directions. If people here want to receive mail, they have to get a post office box in Allada, and travel the five to ten miles each way to check it. The paths are very narrow, and frequently split off in different directions, and there are almost never any signs indicating where a particular path leads. I have learned the paths through trial and error, from studying a hard to find map, and from Clément, my Beninese counterpart, who has taken me to some of these villages on his motorcycle to introduce me to cooperatives.

As I enter the village of Lissegazoun, I pass groups of men sitting under trees playing a traditional board game called *Adji* (AKA Woale, Mancala, etc., as it is called in other parts of Africa). As I've said before, people in Benin are very friendly, and in villages they take friendliness to an extreme. They are especially friendly during the dry season, when the men who traditionally do all the farming are idle. Almost everyone I pass says at least *"Kwabo"* (Welcome). The groups of men often jump up, calling me energetically, trying to get me to stop and talk. They are usually bored and are looking for something interesting to do. Seeing a *Yovo* riding a fancy mountain bike through their village is a sure opportunity for some entertainment. Probably the last time they saw a Yovo pass by in anything other than a four-wheel drive international aid vehicle was the last time they saw me ride by a few months ago.

133

By the way people react when I ride by (especially children), one would think that I am a Martian who just landed his UFO in front of their huts. Children playing in a group spot me coming from a distance and quickly say to the others, "Hey look! A Yovo is coming . . . A Yovo is coming . . . A Yovo is coming!" Then all the children start yelling and screaming with delight, and run behind me as fast as they can chanting their insidious song, *"Yovo Yovo bon soir Ça va bien? Merci!"* This song (as well as being called *Yovo*) burns me up, and I know that when my two years here are up, it will be one aspect of Benin I certainly will not miss.

I see a few children who appear to be malnourished or may have parasites because they have very swollen stomachs. Most children are barefoot and are only wearing underwear. They are very poor but the Beninese are very good at surviving at a subsistence level. I've never heard of anyone dying from starvation in Benin as most people have access to land to grow corn and cassava. Their strong family networks help keep people fed in times of crisis. Luckily there have been no major droughts, floods, famine, wars or epidemics recently that are seemingly so common in Africa.

The Adji players hiss at me and yell, *"Yovo Wa!"* (Come here whitey!). When I was green and I had been in Benin for only a short while, I heeded their seemingly innocent pleas not knowing what they wanted. Now I know better. I could probably recite word for word what they would say if I stopped. First they would greet me in a variety of ways, and then ask me where I was going. They would admire my mountain bike and ask where they could get one, and then ask me if I would sell them the bike when I go back to the U.S. Sometimes they would flat out ask if I would give it to them. If they don't ask for my bike, they ask me for money. In the U.S., if someone said to me "give me your money" or "give me your bike," I would do as requested to potentially spare my life. However, here in Benin I have learned that people are very peace loving, and crime beyond petty theft is very rare. For this reason I often ask my self, "who is more uncivilized, these 'primitive' Beninese people, or people in the West, where people get shot and killed for stupid things like looking at someone the wrong way, cutting someone off on the highway or taking someone's parking spot?" I never feel threatened when people ask me for money, or when they ask me for anything else for that matter. They are only begging, although they are not beggars by trade. They only beg when they see a white person, as they see the occasion as an irresistible opportunity to "earn" a quick franc.

The path I am riding on is a veritable obstacle course, not only because I have to avoid ruts, holes, chickens, goats, children, motorcycles, people on bicycles, and pedestrians, but also because I have to watch out for occasional cars passing. The path is only as wide as a small car, and when a car approaches, I am obliged to stop and pull over into the brush to let it pass. The cars are usually bush taxis filled with sacs of corn or pineapples that women from Cotonou have come to buy from the villagers to resell for a profit in the city. I have to skillfully negotiate both the patches of thick sand when the path turns into beach, as well as the deep ruts cut from trucks that passed during the rainy season. Many women walk on the path, either coming from or going to the market, with basins full of goods on their heads and sometimes water if they're coming from a well. In order to avoid hitting the people and animals on the path, I am obliged to constantly ring my bell. In the U.S. a bell is usually a toy that parents put on children's bikes for fun, but here it is as necessary as a front wheel. Riding my bike down a dirt path in Benin is like riding my bike down a city sidewalk back home. Just for kicks I sometimes yell out *"Yovo Jawe"* (The whitey is coming) as I'm approaching people from behind. They usually get out of my way quickly, and we all get a good laugh as I pass by them.

It is precisely these treacherous paths that make the villages in Benin what they are. If there were paved roads and other infrastructure, then goods, information, and people would flow much more freely, and dispel the isolation and ignorance that defines a village. A road in the West may only seem to be a means of transportation, but in isolated areas such as this, roads are an important means of communication to the outside world. They are much more important for communication than in the West because here in the bush, no one has telephones, electricity, TVs, or mail service. In fact, there are only a few people who have battery operated radios. The one Beninese radio station broadcasts most of the day in French, and only a few hours in Fon, so most uneducated villagers don't understand a majority of the broadcasts.

## The Isolation of Village Life:

This village is five miles from Allada, but since the only means of transportation most people have is their feet or a bicycle, the distance is substantial. The village is like an island, and the bush like an ocean. The horizon for the villagers is only as far as they can walk or ride their bike if they are fortunate enough to own one. Only the wealthiest villagers have motorcycles.

When I speak with them, I can see very quickly how limited their understanding of the world is past their local area. The few people who have a little money may have taken a bush taxi or a motorcycle taxi as far as regional cities, but many, especially women and children, have never even had that opportunity. Conversely few strangers venture back here because of the bad roads, and there is nothing back here except people and fields.

When I visit remote villages such as this, I notice right away the difference between the village mentality and the town mentality of the people in Allada, where I live. In these remote villages, it feels like I've stepped back in time, and very little has changed for centuries. Most people are illiterate. Some have attended school, but only a few years of elementary school. Many older people, especially women, have never gone to school at all. Few people speak French, and even fewer write it well. Allada is a town of about 10,000 people, and is located on the major north-south paved road that runs through the center of the country. Because of the paved road, people can come and go with relative ease by bush taxi, and many people pass through on their way to points north. Trucks can deliver goods, and Allada is strategically located to receive some of the scarce government resources, such as telephone access, electricity, and running water. There are government institutions such as a post office, a bank, boutiques, buvettes, a municipal cultural center, a police station, a hospital, churches, and schools. On average people in Allada are more educated than villagers, and most speak at least some French. All of this is made possible by the paved road. Although towns and cities in Benin are more modern than villages, they are much less developed than their Western equivalents.

As soon as you ride five miles down one of these bush paths, you feel how much slower the pace of life is, and how time is so inconsequential because there is so little opportunity. Ignorance and illiteracy are rampant. In the villages traditional values prevail, and parents rarely promote education. If a child wants to go to school past the elementary level, he will have to either walk or bike many miles to the closest high school every day, or he will have to live with relatives who live near a high school.

Sometimes high school students rent rooms with other students if they live too far away and can afford it. Unbelievably, there are only two high schools in the entire *sous-prefecture* (county)! Traditionally when parents don't have enough money to send all of their children to school, they send only the boys. They do this because girls are supposed to get married and have many children. Fortunately this is slowly starting to change. Now many government and non-government organizations are encouraging girls to be educated and stay in school.

I have a new appreciation of being literate. Having worked primarily with illiterate people in the villages my first year, trying to teach them small business skills, I have come to realize that being able to read is a sixth sense that literate people take for granted. Literacy offers an important source of outside stimuli, as do any of our other five senses, and many villagers lack this extra sense.

## Rural Life:

As I turn a corner I see a group of men and children digging up the path. They are hard at work moving dirt to fill in a large ditch. Two men are holding up a rope across the path blocking my passage, and they blow a whistle signaling me to stop as if the rope wasn't a clear signal. This is the same phenomenon that I saw on my bush taxi ride from Djougou. They expect me to give them money, as they do of everyone who passes, while they are there working. I give the men 50 francs (10 cents), which I am sure is more than most people give. They lower the rope and wave me through. They are happy, and I go on my way without being harassed.

Benin is so poor that the government can barely maintain the paved roads and the major dirt roads, so maintenance of these remote bush paths by the government is totally out of the question. I admire the villagers' resourcefulness for repairing their own paths. However, they often make matters worse, because all they have to work with are hoes and metal basins to carry the dirt in. They may fill in a hole, or create a drainage channel for the water, but they don't really solve the problem because as soon as it rains again, the loosely packed soil turns to mud and washes away. Sometimes I get annoyed because they've essentially appointed themselves tax collectors, and if you don't want to pay, they try to pressure you and extort money from you. They obviously understand the concept of supply and demand, because it is market day and many people must pass over this road, whether by foot, bicycle, car, or motorcycle taxi to get to the market.

Fixing things improperly is a constant dilemma in Benin, as resources are so scarce. The cost of labor is much cheaper than equipment and spare parts, so it's more economical to keep fixing things shoddily when they break, and then fix them again, and again, and again, because they were never fixed properly the first time. I have been a victim of this phenomenon several times while trying to get my radio fixed, or the jury-rigged electric wire leading to my house, and of course bush taxis that are always breaking down.

I pass a few buildings and wells that have signs indicating they were paid for by different international aid agencies or foreign governments. I wonder if they feel embarrassed that they must rely on so much help from other countries, but from what I have seen and heard, they are not. On the other hand, they do not have the national pride and confidence that Americans do. In fact many Beninese have expressed their feeling of inferiority to Westerners, which I find sad and try to discourage.

As I ride along under the palm trees and through the thick green bush, I can't help but admire the villagers' slow-paced, stress-free life style. On the other hand, I pity their lack of self-actualization. They feel so helpless to change their current life style and situation. Being extremely poor, uneducated, and illiterate in a country whose government offers next to no services, leaves them few options, and their attitudes about improving their situation is usually commensurate. They are resigned to the whim of fate and nature, thus living more or less as their ancestors did centuries ago. The upside is that their circumstances allow them to live close to nature, close to its forces and to its rhythms. Living in harmony with nature allows the Beninese many benefits that we in the West are deprived of. The people here are more relaxed, and they enjoy an uncomplicated life. They are more content with what they have, and they have a strong sense of community. They must rely on each other, rather than technology, wealth, and government systems, as we do in the West. Westerners on the other hand, try to control their fate and natural environment with technology, which ultimately complicates our lives, and often creates as many problems as it solves.

Often, for the uneducated Beninese person, the only way he feels he can control nature or his fate is through religion. For that reason they are much more accepting of misfortunes such as illness, accidents, death, and other events, as they ascribe these events to the will of the spirits, ancestors, and gods. I am sure much of their fatalistic attitude stems from their religion and culture. Also to blame is 60 years of French colonization and domination. Another explanation may be "environmental determinism." The theory of environmental determinism claims that climate (the distance a group lives from the equator) affects the values and economic development of societies. Today anthropologists discount this theory as being too simplistic, and it has been replaced by the theory of "environmental possibilism." It is a more dynamic theory that states that culture is shaped by how people interact with the opportunities and limits climate puts on them (Briney, Amanda). I believe climate has something to do with their lack of development. Because Benin has a tropical climate, year round survival is relatively easy. Food is easy to grow. Houses are made of mud and straw and building one is very inexpensive. In colder climates people must be more innovative in order to survive, which leads them to produce more and have stronger economies. People in the colder regions are often more industrious and innovative. They often value living beyond the basic subsistence level. Many Beninese seem resigned to living at a subsistence level, and don't try very hard to better themselves, nor do they push their children to better themselves. Tradition and the ways of the ancestors are highly respected. They are strong forces inhibiting change and "progress." Another reason why the Beninese lag so far behind the rest of the world economically is because the rest of the world is already so far ahead of them. Being an underdog makes it difficult for Benin to compete in the global economy, and even harder for them to catch up.

I ride past some farmers who are in their fields getting a head start on clearing them. They are readying them for planting as soon as the first rain comes at the end of next month. It is backbreaking labor, as they use no machines and the intense equatorial sun and humidity makes it that much more unpleasant. The only tools they do use are hoes, machetes, axes to cut stumps and sticks to poke holes in the ground to sow seeds. With only these simple implements, they clear the brush and loosen the soil, sow seeds, weed, and harvest. Sometimes if a field is very thickly grown over, they resort to burning it to clear the land which is not good for the soil. Because of such limited technology and tremendous inefficiency, the average farmer is lucky if he produces only slightly more than he and his family can consume. If there is any surplus, he will have his wife sell it at the market. I wonder what they would think riding along in an Iowa farmer's tractor that can produce hundreds of times more corn than the single Beninese subsistence farmer. Almost everyone here is a subsistence farmer, and even government employees have plots of land that they either work themselves or pay someone to work for them for extra income. Proof of this can be found in the small signs which mark people's fields, such as one that reads: "Jean Akpolgan, School teacher in Allada."

I find the state of farming in Benin sad, as their ancestors have been farming the same way for centuries, yet they have not yet devised better techniques, tools, or machines to increase productivity. It is a perfect example of how people here are content living at a subsistence level, and how tradition holds them back. I admire the simple lifestyle that subsistence level living and respect for tradition provides them. The downside, of course, is their dependence on the weather, and their subsequent lack of food security made worse by a growing population that is slowly becoming more urbanized. If there is either not enough rain or too much, their food supplies are put in grave danger.

Along the path I pass a few exceptionally large pineapple fields of several acres each, which are run by a village cooperative. The pineapples grown in Benin are delicious, and they are a cash crop of the region. I love the fact that I can buy one the size of a watermelon for only 200 CFA (40 cents)! In a village named Dèdomé, I stop to take a picture of a huge Baobab tree. Its trunk is disproportionately fat relative to its height, making it an interesting sight to see. Large trees are considered sacred in Benin, and there are a few Vodun altars at its base that I investigate. Southern Benin is the birthplace of Vodun, and many slaves were taken from this area to Haiti. In Haiti Vodun mixed with Christianity, which was imposed on the slaves by their owners, and the mixture formed "Vaudou," (Voodoo in French). Many Haitians still practice Vaudou today. I've developed a keen interest in Vodun, and I make a point to seek it out and learn more about it wherever I go, so I can compare what I see from one area to another. I've attended many Vodun ceremonies, and interviewed many Vodun priests and initiates in my spare time. It has become a hobby, and I consider myself an amateur anthropologist when it comes to Vodun. I have also read a lot of books on Vodun that I've found in the bookstores in Cotonou. I've discovered that Vodun is indeed a religion, and not just black magic and zombies that Hollywood movies make it out to be.

## *Yovo Se Fongbe*!!

When I pull out my camera, 20 small children instantly come running from every direction trying desperately to squeeze in the picture, hoping to get a copy from me one day. I know they're talking about me, but because they're speaking so fast, I can't pick up more than "Yovo this" and "Yovo that." I briefly greet them in Fon. They all yell and scream with delight because the Yovo can speak their language! They are astonished and say things such as:

*-Mawu, Yovo se fongbe bi!!* (My god, the white guy can speak Fon really well!)
*-A tinkpon din!* (You've really made an effort!)
*-Wa, Yovo se Fongbe!!* (Come here. The Yovo speaks Fon!)
*-Wa se Yovo doxo do Fongbeme!!* (Come here and listen to the Yovo speak Fon!)

More adults and children come over, and they start asking me questions to see what I'm all about and test how well I really speak Fon.

*-Fite a nono de?* (Where do you live?)
*-Un nono do Allada* (I live in Allada)
*-Fite a noyi de?* (Where are you going?)
*-Un na yi mo xontonce do Bopa* (I'm going to see my friend in Bopa)
*-Azote a no wa?* (What do you do for work?)
*-Un no kplon glesile* (I teach farmers)
*-Hwetenu a wa do Benin?* (How long have you been in Benin?)
*-Un wa do Benin azan xwe dokpo adade* (I came to Benin a year and a half ago)
*-Vi nabi a do?* (How many kids do you have?)
*-Un do vi sukpo din!* (I have tons of kids)
*-Asi nabi a do?* (How many wives do you have?)
*-Un do asi Gban! Un do asi dokpo do gbe dokpo do sun dokpo.* (I've got 30 wives! One for every day of the month!)

They all break out in hysterical laughter at my joke, and then I go on:

*Dinyo asicele ye ku bi! Azetole ye du asicele bi, eño nu mi à.* (Now all of my wives are dead because they were killed by witches so I'm not happy.) (Everyone bursts out in cries of delight and laughter again).

Then pointing to young girl I say:
-*We o, a na da mi a?* (You there, do you want to marry me?)
Again everyone laughs and giggles.
-*Enn, na dawe* (Yes, I'll marry you she shyly replies)

I have gone through this same scenario hundreds of times, so it has become routine, and I answer every question perfectly. They just look at me dumbfounded. I call it the *"Mawu! E se Fongbe!"* routine ("My God! . . . He speaks Fon!" routine). I have perfected the responses, making them think I speak better than I really do. It gets annoying to go through the same conversation time and time again, so I depart from the truth a bit in order to have some fun. In fact, lying is a favorite pastime of people here. Because life can be so monotonous, people love to lead others on as long as they can. It's a game I've learned to play well, and lying keeps me from getting irritated at the same damn questions I hear over and over. Each time I make up different answers, and sometimes I reuse the good ones, such as telling my interrogators that I have a wife for every day of the month but they were all killed by witches.

I realize that I am adapting to their culture, because I would never ask someone in the West to marry me casually as a joke, and I would never lie just for fun to strangers. It is something I have learned from them. On many occasions people have asked me if I have a wife, and I said no. Because it is rare for someone my age (although I'm only 23) not to have a wife in Benin, they always ask me why. I've grown tired of trying to make them understand the Western way, which is incomprehensible to them, so I just make a joke about it by giving them exaggerated lies.

On many occasions girls have casually asked me to marry them and embarrassed me, so now I preempt them by asking first. I joke that I have many wives and children. This is a polygamist society, and having many wives and children is an important status symbol. Usually only wealthy and successful men can afford more than one wife. My joke about witches killing my wives plays off their superstitions because they still blame witches when people die prematurely or from mysterious causes. It's all in fun, and everyone knows it because of my gross exaggerations. These are just two examples of how different Beninese personalities and senses of humor are compared to Westerners.

## Adapting to my Surroundings:

Because I have been adapting my personality to Benin for the last year, I feel as if I have an alter ego now. I have a distinct personality and identity adapted to Benin (who is "*Gandaho*," my nickname in Fon). I still have my American personality of course, which I assume when I see other Americans from time to time, and when I'm alone. I know my American personality is changing because of my experiences, and it is odd to think how different Gandaho is from Chris. I suspect that who I am is not fundamentally changing, but I know certain aspects of me are. I have to do and say many things I would not normally do as a coping techniques to help me navigate through the more challenging aspects of life in Benin. The result of those coping techniques is that I have assumed a new Beninese personality as I described above. When I have visited other PCV's at their posts, and I have seen them interacting with the Beninese, I have noticed the same thing about them. Seeing how they have adapted their personalities helped me realize what I am feeling is normal.

Knowing my personality is changing to adapt to the culture here makes me worry about returning to the U.S. in less than a year. What will I be like when I return? How will I have changed and in what ways? I know I am changing, but how much I am changing is hard to tell. I suspect I won't know how much I have changed until I go back to the United States, and then I'll be able to compare my old self with my new self. Will I go back to being my old self after being home for a few months or will it take years? Will the identity I created here cease to exist once I leave Benin? My guess is that some aspects of my new self that I picked up in Benin will stick, and the ones that were merely coping techniques will fall by the wayside. I am worried about going back to the U.S. because I don't know if I will fit in after what I have experienced here. Will I feel like a stranger in my own country? I have heard stories of PCV's having a tough time with reentry shock, and I if I feel this way after having been here only a year, I am betting that returning to the U.S. will be difficult a year from now. I have even had nightmares about returning home and not fitting in. It goes to show that culture is such a powerful a force that it can change people very quickly.

Because I am white, I always make a spectacle wherever I go, and when I start speaking Fon, the effect is multiplied several fold. I haven't met any Westerners here who speak Fon well, so most Beninese probably haven't met one either. I learned Fon because I am pretty good at learning and speaking languages, and I have worked hard at it. Although I learned minimal Fon in training, since arriving at post, I have spoken Fon to my neighbors every day. Most of them do not speak French, so I have no other choice. Peace Corps reimburses me as a matter of policy, 5,000 CFA a month ($10) for private language lessons. I pay my neighbor Angelo to give me lessons a few hours a week.

I was fortunate because when I arrived in Benin, I already spoke French well. I passed the mandatory French test required by the Peace Corps that all Benin PCV's must pass before going to post. A few weeks later I was able to start learning Fon, as soon as Peace Corps determined I would be living in a Fon speaking area of Benin. However, I probably had less than a dozen Fon lessons during training, so most of what I know, I learned on my own by speaking with anyone and everyone I met. Being able to speak Fon has been a great advantage to me since so many people speak French poorly, if at all. Most Peace Corps Volunteers must concentrate their efforts on improving their French during their two years in Benin, so they usually do not have the luxury of dedicating their efforts solely to learning the local language in-depth the way that I have. The exception is the volunteers who are posted in very remote areas up north, where almost no one speaks French. They are forced to use their local language almost exclusively.

Historically the Westerners who have been in Benin were French, and are known for their superior attitude towards the Beninese, which is not surprising considering they imposed colonial rule for 60 years. They pushed their language and culture on the Beninese, teaching them that their own culture and language were inferior to those of the West. Sadly enough, Fon is not even taught in their public schools today! It is amusing and flattering for me to see how happy and amazed people get when they see I can speak their language fairly well. In fact, there are only about a million people in the world who speak Fon. For practical reasons it does not make sense for a foreigner to learn Fon unless he is going to live among the people for an extended period of time as Peace Corps Volunteers and missionaries do.

After the loud cries and laughter die down, I wish the citizens of Dèdomé farewell in Fon as I get back on my bike. By now there are at least 30 people surrounding me. As I ride out of the village, the children run behind me and next to me. They manage to keep up with me for quite a distance, laughing and giggling until they finally get tired. Looking back I see them waving good-bye to me, and they are as happy as can be that a *Yovo* came to their remote village. This is part of my job as a Peace Corps Volunteer: spreading American goodwill and teaching them about Americans. I do this not by giving handouts, but by living on the level of the people to promote mutual understanding, and showing them that I am not above them. If I had a superior attitude, I would not bother learning Fon, and I would be in a four-wheel vehicle. That is why they are so happy that I speak Fon with them. It shows that I respect them, their culture, and their language. They are surprised because respect is something they have rarely received from Westerners. The Beninese are used to being looked down upon, and are often portrayed as incompetent and backwards. Their inferiority complex is compounded by their colonial history, through the realization that most of the world is wealthier and more powerful than they are, and by their dependence on Western aid. By showing them that I respect them, I hope it makes them feel more equal to Westerners, and proud to be Beninese.

## The Zangbeto Vodun Ceremony:

As I round the bend, the road starts to descend and a beautiful view of Lake Ahèmé appears below. By the side of the lake, I can see the tin roofs of the mud huts in the village of Dèkanmé where I intend to take a *pirogue* (large canoe) across the lake to Bopa. The houses are surrounded by palm trees, and as far as the eye can see, there is lush green vegetation in all directions from atop this magnificent hill,

Arriving in the village down below, I see a beautifully painted cement wall that surrounds a Vodun convent dedicated to the god Zangbeto. I briefly admire it and ask the owner if I can take a picture. He says only if I pay 1,000 F (or $2.00.) "Ahh! 1,000 francs!" I shriek in dismay and turn away. 1,000 francs is two day's salary for a farm worker, and he wants that much for only one picture! As I am talking, a Zemidjan driver is looking on and overhears our conversation. He tells me that there is a public Zangbeto ceremony in a village called Kpago about 5 km south of here. Wow! I have been looking for an opportunity to go to a Zangbeto ceremony for a long time, so I immediately jump at the chance.

I ride my bike there and upon arriving, I am led to the center of the village where the ceremony is gearing up. There is a large sand square surrounded by the same type of painted wall I had seen in Dèkanmé. The paintings are of the Zangbeto god's "huts." Their "huts" are costumes, which resemble haystacks, into which the Zangbeto spirits are invoked by a sacred ceremony and drumming music. Once a spirit occupies the haystack, they begin to dance and twirl around. Also painted on the wall are a few village scenes and portraits of elders of the Vodun society. People are starting to arrive and others are setting down benches for the distinguished guests to sit on. I ask one of the heads of the Zangbeto group if I can take pictures, and of course, he states his price. He explains that they had just spent a lot of money on the Zangbeto haystacks and on having the murals painted on the wall. I agree to pay 1,000 CFA, which isn't much, considering I can take as many pictures as I want, and this will be a big ceremony. Vodun is fascinating to me because it is purely African, and has suffered very little Western influence, unlike many other aspects of the culture here. One of the Zangbeto initiates is very friendly and offers to explain to me what is going on as we both watch the ceremony.

At about five PM the ceremony begins. The drumming starts and a group of women begin to dance and sing energetically to the beat. Four or five tiers of people surround the entire square. It seems like the whole village is here as well as many people from neighboring villages, so there are probably 1,000 people present. It's odd to look around and realize that I'm the only white person in sight. Being the only white person in this crowd saliently reminds me where I am. As I look around I notice that almost everyone stares at me intermittently, to see what the Yovo is doing, and they're probably wondering why in the world I'm at their Vodun ceremony out in this remote village. Being constantly stared at by 1,000 people is quite unnerving when I'm not supposed to be the center of attention; however I am used to being the sideshow wherever I go. Despite the uneasiness I feel from being stared at so much, I feel very much at ease, as I know I am perfectly safe, and I know from experience that the Beninese harbor no animosity towards Americans. They may be envious of Yovos and overcharge us when we buy anything, but they are not aggressive or malicious toward us. I know I'm only being stared at because people are curious to see what a Yovo looks like, and they want to see what I do. It makes me realize how much I've adapted to being the stark minority here, because I would never have ventured here alone when I first arrived in Benin. It also helps me empathize with minorities in the U.S., as I have never been a minority before.

I feel very satisfied that I am the only Yovo at this ceremony because I know that what I will see will be completely authentic and not something contrived for tourists. I feel privileged because I know it is something so few other Westerners will ever see. In fact, most people here don't even know what a tourist is, because so few come to Benin, and almost all Yovos in Benin are international aid employees like myself or embassy officials. The tourists who do visit Benin generally stick to a few easily accessible destinations.

This Vodun ceremony is not just an amusing activity, but is part of their religious beliefs. They believe that spirits control all aspects of their lives, known as "animism," and they worship spirits such as Zangbeto. In Fon, "Zangbeto" literally means "person of the night," and is a spirit who comes out at night to scare thieves away, as well as to protect the villages from evil spirits. Only a few times a year do the Zangbeto come out to entertain the public during the day, so it is a very special occasion that few people miss. Some people may question whether there really is a person inside the costume, but to say so would be blasphemous, so no one ever challenges it. An analogous example in the West is that no one jumps up during the Eucharistic portion of a Christian mass, claiming that the bread and wine supposedly converted to the body and blood of Christ are still only bread and wine.

A few minutes after the drumming starts, a procession of men parades into the square with a wooden box on their heads, and places it on a table in front of the elder Vodun chiefs. They remove from the box sacred objects made out of wood, seashells, cloth, and feathers, all of which have been sprinkled with sacrificial chicken blood to consecrate them. My new friend explains that these objects are the sacred objects that contain the spirit of Zangbeto. Soon after, the drumming starts, and the dancing haystacks come out one by one from behind the wall, twirling and rocking back and forth around the square. Accompanying each haystack is its guide who carries a stick to hit the unruly spectators, usually children, who get too close. The guides also make sure the Zangbeto don't bump into anything. It is very bad luck to touch a Zangbeto, so theoretically, the person carrying the stick and hitting the children is actually protecting them. All of the people who come to the ceremony are enthralled by the scene, and they scream and cheer when the Zangbeto perform spectacular moves. The drumming music and women singing are enrapturing. I find it hard to stand still to such an energetic rhythm. Most villagers are too poor to afford entertainment, so this provides them with lots of free fun. It is also a religious experience that renews their belief that the spiritual world is constantly interacting with the living world. It reconfirms their faith that the spirits are watching out for them.

After the Zangbeto come out and dance around to the orchestra of drumming music, they sit down in the center of the square while one of them performs a miracle. The idea is to prove to the audience that there is indeed a spirit in the haystack, and not a person, as skeptics may believe.

First they put a small straw mat on the sand in the middle of the square. Then one of the Zangbetoes moves over it and sits down. Some of the initiates of the cult come over and tap their hands on the outside of the haystack. Then one of the initiates blows a whistle, which marks a sacred moment. They quickly lift the costume off the ground, and beneath it on the straw mat is a live turtle! The Zangbeto spirit transformed itself into the turtle! The crowd roars with delight and amazement. I too am astonished and I cheer loudly. Although my rational mind had me convinced there was a person inside, I saw nothing suspicious such as a person either entering or exiting from under the haystack. The hay is attached to a conical wooden frame, and underneath is empty space. They proceed to parade the haystack on its side around the square to show everyone that indeed nothing is hiding inside. They put the haystack back on the mat with the turtle underneath, tap on it again, they blow the whistle, and suddenly the Zangbeto gets up and starts energetically dancing around the square to the drumming. The turtle is nowhere to be seen! Again the crowd roars with delight to see that there are indeed powerful Vodun gods who are capable of amazing feats. They perform this ceremony again, but the second time a puppy appears from under the Zangbeto instead of a turtle. This feat of divine intervention reassures them that the Vodun gods are capable of protecting them from harm and answering their prayers.

## Crossing Lake Aheme in a Pirogue:

I want to stay longer, but it is starting to get dark. I have to leave so I can get back to Dèkanmé where I intend to take the pirogue across the lake. I hope it is not too late. I thank my new friend for explaining to me what was happening, and I leave the crowd behind. They will surely be enraptured with the Zangbeto dancing and music until after dark. On the way back to Dèkanmé, I bump into the handicapped guy in a three-wheeled wheel chair who has stopped by my house several times in the past to beg. He is very friendly, and I am shocked to see him here, because I always assumed he lived closer to me, not ten miles away in this remote village. I feel sorry for him because he cannot speak, but he does well with his own simple version of sign language. He clearly remembers me, smiles, and waves. Because the roads are so bad, and smooth sidewalks are almost non-existent in Benin, two-wheeled wheel chairs are very uncommon. The three-wheeled wheel chair is adapted to Benin. It uses a bicycle crank with pedals connected to a chain, and the occupant turns the cranks with his hands to propel it. I can't believe how he gets around on that thing, considering all of the bad roads and dirt paths he must travel on. I can only imagine how he gets over the treacherous bush path leading to my house. I get to the edge of the lake and it is almost dark. I am concerned about finding someone to take me across. The lake is several miles long so it is impractical to circumnavigate it. Because there are no bridges or motorized ferryboats, the local people have adapted by offering an informal service to get the job done. It is neither fast nor efficient, but at least you can cross the lake, which is about two miles wide. Luckily I find an *aklokunto* (gondolier—for lack of a better word) at the side of the lake, and I negotiate a price of 400 F (90 cents) with him for a one-way trip for my bike and me. I paid only 300 F last time, but I am not in the mood to haggle, considering it is getting dark. Shortly before we leave, a man with three hog-tied goats on the back of his bike pulls up wanting to cross too. The gondolier puts our bikes in the boat, retrieves a long palm branch pole, which is at least ten feet long, and he pushes us off. Since the lake is shallow all the way across, the gondolier uses nothing more than the pole to propel us. I start speaking Fon to them, and of course I get the usual "*Mawu!. E se Fongbe!*" routine, which lasts at least ten minutes.

It is very beautiful and peaceful crossing the lake at dusk. There is no sunset due to the dust and haze that the Harmattan winds brought.

This handmade wooden boat is bigger than the average canoe, and could probably hold ten people if they didn't have much baggage. I ask the gondolier why no one on this lake has ever thought of buying a motor to propel these boats across at twice the speed we're travelling. He said that someone did try once, and it worked very well for a short time. Quickly he took the business from all the other gondoliers so someone vandalized the engine. Not surprisingly, that was the end of motorized transport on Lake Ahèmé! There are dozens of people on both sides of the lake who make their living by taking people back and forth, so the vandal was only protecting his livelihood. There are many people who go back and forth to the Bopa, Avakpa and Allada markets on either side of the lake, so on market days the gondoliers have plenty of business.

This is the pirogue I took to cross lake Ahèmé on my return trip.

I have crossed this lake several times before and I love it. I feel it is the quintessential African experience. One of the reasons why I love living in a small West African town is because it allows me to almost completely escape signs of Western culture, which are so prevalent almost everywhere in the world. Relative to other countries, Western influence in Benin is minimal, which is exemplified by the fact that you cannot use credit cards anywhere, except in a few of the most exclusive hotels and restaurants in

Cotonou. There is not one American chain store in the whole country! There is no Macdonald's, no Taco Bell, and no Kentucky Fried Chicken, etc. Less innocuous examples of Western culture do abound in Benin such as automobiles, some Western music, some Western clothes, the postal system, Western style government, the school system, the French language, and imported goods. However, when I am on this boat, it gives me goose bumps to think I could easily be 500 years in the past. There is absolutely no trace of Western culture that I can see from here. It is as if I stepped into a time machine. I relish the feeling of knowing there are few places in the world where I can be this detached from the influence of Western culture.

As it gets dark, it seems as if my sense of smell and hearing become sharper. I can feel the boat rock rhythmically as the gondolier stands at the stern, pushing the boat along with the long pole. I can hear the calm water lap softly up against the boat, and the water dripping off the pole as he pulls it out of the water after every lunge. Unfortunately, the peace is disrupted periodically by the shrill screeching of the hog-tied goats that are lying on the floor of the boat by my feet. I am amazed that such small creatures can cry so loud. Obviously they do not approve of their travel conditions, and they are worried about their fate. I have to plug my ear at times, because the screaming is so loud and piercing.

I can see small brush fires burning from afar on the other side of the lake, which create orange spots on the dim horizon. A farmer probably lit them to clear his field as the growing season is approaching. The lake doesn't seem very wide, but because we only move by pole power, it takes about an hour to cross. It once took me almost two hours, as there was a strong head wind, not to mention the thunderstorm we were caught in. I have been told that there is one last hippopotamus in this lake. I have never seen it, and I certainly don't want to, especially not from this boat, because they can be very dangerous. I have seen local fishermen who have created wind chimes out of old metal plates and rocks attached to strings that they carry in their boats to scare off this beast. There is also a Vodun fetish in the lake that protects the fishermen from the Hippo.

I watch the shore in the distance slowly get closer and closer in the dim light until we finally arrive. I bid farewell to the gondolier, and the man with the hog-tied goats, and head off to find Melissa. I have no idea where she lives, but I know it won't be hard to find her since Yovos never go unnoticed. I look for a group of children, because they always have time to help a Yovo in need. I quickly spot a group playing near the market, and I ask them where the Yovo with the bike lives. Although Bopa is a pretty big village, Melissa is one of very few white people living here, and I know she is the only one who rides a bike. All Yovos in Benin, other than Peace Corps Volunteers, have cars or motorcycles. As I know they would, they take me directly to her house. She is surprised and happy to see me because she thought that I would not cross the lake in the dark, and she assumed I wasn't coming. I am happily surprised that she got my letter, and amused by the simple fact that a message could be carried to its destination in such an informal way.

We enjoy each other's company, discussing the many trials and tribulations of being an American volunteer in Benin. We get caught up on Peace Corps gossip relating to the other 80 or so Americans volunteers living in different parts of Benin. She shows me around her village and introduces me to her Beninese friends. My return trip to Allada the next evening is a similar adventure and I return to Allada with renewed enthusiasm for the challenges that face me.

# A Visit to the not so Traditional, "Traditional" Healer

## Meeting Mr. Hinonvi:

I am chatting with a gris-gris (magic charm) ingredient seller in the Allada market who has his wares spread out on the ground on a large canvas tarp. The stench is overwhelming because he primarily sells small, dead, dried animals, or dried parts of larger ones. There are dead dried chameleons and bats, as well as different types of birds, various skulls, monkey paws, snakes, and other things that I cannot identify. There are also a lot of dried plant objects, such as seeds, leaves, stones, beads, and objects used to create Vodun altars. In addition, there are supplies for various Vodun ceremonies. As I ask him to explain what one does with a dried viper's head, the skin of an electric fish, and a dried dog's head, a gentleman named Mr. Hihonvi comes over to us. He introduces himself as a traditional healer from Sékou, a village only a few kilometers down the paved road towards the capital city Cotonou. The gris-gris ingredient seller's stall is the best spot to meet traditional healers. They all come here to buy the hard to find ingredients necessary for healing ceremonies and to make the potions they use to cure their patients. Vodun priests also come here to buy ingredients and implements for Vodun ceremonies. Like most Beninese, Mr. Hihonvi is very friendly and talkative. I explain to him that I am interested in learning about traditional healing, and he is very accommodating, adding to the gris-gris seller's explanations as to what all the different ingredients are for and how they are used. He speaks French well, and he tells me that he studied chemistry for two years at the University of Benin. He explains that "Hihonvi" means "born of light," and is a name he gave to himself and to his medical practice. He takes out a photocopied flyer from his bag, and proudly presents it to me. It is a flyer for his medical practice. It makes some very interesting claims, stating how he is able to cure asthma, respiratory illnesses, sterility (both male and female), hemorrhoids, heart problems, impotence, malaria, madness, diabetes, and a slew of other diseases that we've yet to find cures for in the developed world. It sparks my interest, so I decide to schedule a time to see him to learn more about traditional medicine, and to see if he can diagnose a strange illness that I contracted three weeks after I arrived in Benin.

## My Inexplicable Illness:

After being in Benin only three weeks, I suddenly lost my hearing in my left ear for no apparent reason, accompanied by ringing and vertigo. The Peace Corps doctor communicated with an ear nose and throat doctor in Washington, D.C. via fax, and they treated me with steroids, but nothing changed. It wasn't until two months later, when my training was over, that they medevaced me to Washington, D.C. to see specialists. The doctors suspected that a virus damaged my inner ear, but they needed to do an MRI to rule out a cancerous growth on the auditory nerve. Understandably, I was very worried, and after two weeks of doctor visits in D.C., they diagnosed it as sudden nerve deafness caused by a virus. I was extremely relieved to learn that I did not have a tumor. However, I was told that there is neither a cure nor a chance of recovery. I had permanently lost 80% of my hearing in my left ear. I was told that this happens to people in the United States too so I couldn't blame it on an exotic African disease. I was very glad to find out the chance of it happening in the other ear was extremely slim. Knowing that my hearing loss was not necessarily caused by an "African" disease, and that the chances of it happening to the other ear was very slim, made it much easier for me to return to Benin. When I was given the option to be medically separated from the Peace Corps (the equivalent of an honorable discharge for medical reasons), I didn't need to think twice about it. I needed to finish what I had started. Before returning to Benin, I took advantage of being in the United States, and I visited my parents for a few days.

It really does suck being deaf in one ear, and it is upsetting to say the least. Some PCV's said that they would not have returned to Benin after such a life-altering setback, so ultimately, I proved my conviction to serve in Benin. I was too determined to give up my dream of being a Peace Corps Volunteer for the next two years in one of the poorest countries in the world. I was thirsty for adventure, and filled with the hope that I could help people, and I wanted to grow personally from the experience. I knew that if I didn't do it then, I would probably never have another chance, especially once I did something foolish, like starting a career, getting married, having children, and buying a house. Oddly, I was almost as worried about not being able to come back to Benin due to my hearing loss as I was worried about my health. I know this because I had nightmares about not being able to return to Benin during the two months after I lost my hearing before I was sent back to the U.S.

As I said, losing half my hearing has been very difficult for me, and at this point, I am looking for any remedy I can find since Western medicine has told me there is nothing they can do. I figure if modern medicine cannot cure it, then maybe the traditional African perspective will be more affective. Going to see Mr. Hihonvi will also, if nothing else, give me a chance to learn more about traditional Beninese medicine, or at least his version of traditional medicine.

I have some knowledge of traditional healers in Benin. From what I have learned, they usually do their diagnosis using geomantic divination, which is called "Fah" in Benin. Fah is a way of communicating with spirits and gods to reveal the unknown. It could be compared to Tarot card reading, palm reading, Ouijah boards, crystal ball reading, or other forms of communicating with the supernatural world. To read a person's Fah, the healer or Fah priest throws two strings that have eight seedpods on each string. The seedpods are concave, so there is an up side and a down side to each pod. If it lands with the convex side up, it symbolizes a one. If it lands with the concave side up, it symbolizes a two. The combinations of ones and twos make different Fah symbols and combined there are 256 different combinations. It is up to the Fah priest or healer to interpret the symbols and how they relate to the person's problem or illness.

Once he determines the cause of the patient's problem, the healer may prescribe an infusion, basically a tea made from specific tree leaves, which the patient drinks. If he determines that the cause is evil spirits attacking the person, he will exorcise him. He will have the person wash in a tea infusion, and will leave both the water and the matt the person stood on at the side of the road at an intersection. The spirits that were washed out of the person and into the water will then take the path away from the person's house.

Often the cause of an illness is a neglected god or ancestor that is exacting revenge on the person. People have altars at their houses for certain gods, and also for their deceased ancestors. To pray to them and venerate them, they have to make sacrifices on a regular basis. The most typical sacrifice is animal blood, such as chicken, goat or pig blood. Ancestors and gods like to symbolically eat the same things they did when they were living, so people may put bottles of sodabi, whiskey, water, soda, cigarettes, corn meal, palm oil, cola nuts, powder, or perfume on the altars. If people do this regularly, then it will help appease the gods and their ancestors. If they do not, they risk retribution. If a traditional healer determines that a client's illness is due to not making sacrifices, then making an animal sacrifice and placing some food and drink on the altar can usually cure them. From talking to Mr. Hihonvi, I get the sense that he does things a bit differently than the average traditional healer, and I want to know more.

## The Consultation and Free Demonstration:

A week later I take a bush taxi to Sékou, only a few kilometers from Allada, to see Mr. Hihonvi. I notice a metal sign on the side of the road that says "*Cabinet de Soins*" (Medical Clinic). Upon arriving at a house a few feet from the paved road, he warmly greets me in the usual protracted Beninese fashion. Shaking my hands he asks, "How are you? And your work? And your health? Did you have a good trip here? And your family? Are they well?" He leads me to his "office," which is very business like and professional, unlike the other traditional healers who I've gone to see in neighboring villages. Most traditional healers work out of their houses and don't have an office as Mr. Hihonvi does. It is a small cement block room with a tin roof, and is nestled among a compound of mud huts in which he and his family live. The room is very simple. There is no electricity, running water, or medical equipment, or machines of any type that a Westerner would expect to find in a medical office. There is only a desk, a few chairs, and a shelf full of bottles containing medicines that he produced himself. They each have a photocopied label, and are clean and carefully lined up.

I am fortunate enough to get a first hand demonstration of how he treats his patients before I let him treat me as his 12 year old son is sick and lying on the cement floor, using only a straw mat for padding. "He has stomach pains and vomiting," Mr. Hihonvi explains to me as he sits me down in front of his desk. As he is consulting with me about my hearing problem in his "*Cabinet de Soins,*" and explaining how he treats people, he keeps interrupting our conversation in order to attend to his son. He gets up and takes a bottle off the shelf behind him, and gives his son something from the bottle. "Here, chew on these cloves, they will lower your fever." He sits down and continues explaining how, "Western medicine does nothing for evil spells. My approach is based on traditional African methods as well as Western scientific medicine. I'm an intellectual . . . Excuse me," he interrupts. "Son, how do you feel now? Are you feeling better? Is your fever going down?" His son woefully shakes his head. (Note that he only told his son to eat the cloves two minutes ago!) "Come here," he says to the boy. His son reluctantly pulls himself up off the floor and Mr. Hihonvi takes a small brown bottle from the shelf, tilts his son's head back, and puts a few drops of the liquid into his son's nose, which he explains will help his headache. He pours a green colored liquid out of a jug, and has his son drink it. "It's a leaf infusion," he explains. "Lie down," he instructs his beleaguered son.

Mr. Hihonvi goes back to the shelf of potions and medicines, most of which he made himself from extracting substances from plants, roots, leaves, oils, and other various ingredients. He chooses one, walks over to his son and says, "Tilt your head back and open your mouth." He then pours some of its contents down the boy's throat. "It's honey with special spices," he proudly explains to me. He rubs a foul smelling garlic concentrate cream over his son's chest and face. It is so potent that I almost feel the need to leave the room. "The cream is for chasing evil spirits away. You never know, with my work, I deal with a lot of evil spirits, and one may have attacked my son." He returns to explaining his medical philosophies, but after only five minutes he asks the boy, "How do you feel now?" His son just shakes his head, and is still lying in a heap on the floor, so it's obvious he is not feeling any better yet. Mr. Hihonvi is convinced that his efforts aren't working, so he goes outside and picks some leaves off a tree in the yard and says, "Here, chew on these leaves. They'll chase away evil spirits." Ten seconds later the boy leans over and vomits on the floor, which is certainly not surprising to me. "Oh, I will give him medicine to stop his vomiting," he says after throwing sand on the mess. "Give him some water to stay hydrated," I suggest, since that was what I was taught to do in my Peace Corps health training. "No, it's better not to drink if you're vomiting, because you'll just throw it up again," he replies. I don't argue as he is the healer and I am the patient.

"Come here," he says to his son who is sitting two feet away on the floor, while Mr. Hihonvi sits in a chair. Again his son slowly pulls himself up, and staggers over to where we are sitting. Mr. Hihonvi opens a dried hot pepper pod, dumps the seeds in his son's hand, and tells him to eat them. He faithfully obeys. At this point, I can't help but wonder if he is giving him all these different treatments to help his son or to show off to me. "Now go walk around outside before you vomit in the house again."

"The hot pepper seeds will kill the microbes in his stomach," he explains. "It's a type of antibiotic." A few minutes later the boy comes back inside and lies down. He is shivering from the effects of the fever, despite the fact it's probably 95 degrees inside. Mr. Hihonvi then gets up and pours some imported olive oil into his son's mouth as he is lying down. "For physical strength," he comments.

"What do you think he has?" I ask. "Oh, he's just physically fatigued," he replies. That's funny, I think to myself. From the treatments and explanations he's given so far, it seems that he either has microbes in his stomach, or he's being afflicted by evil spirits. I am also surprised that he doesn't say he has malaria. It is such a common illness in Benin that whenever anyone has a fever, the Beninese almost always assume it to be "*le pallu*" (malaria).

"Son, come here," he commands again. He feels his son's head to see if the fever is going down. "OK, go lie down." I can't help but think he should let the poor boy rest for God's sake! But I bite my tongue. "Get up," "sit down," "come here," "go there," "eat this," "drink that," every two minutes. "Do you feel better yet?" "No?" "What's wrong?" "How about now? Do you feel better yet?" "Yes? Good. Lay down." The whole scenario is quite comical. I know that a Western doctor would find this . . . um . . . well . . . unorthodox to say the least . . . but, what do I know about medicine? Who am I to criticize? Besides, this is quite entertaining. It's obvious Mr. Hihonvi cares deeply about his son, and is trying his best to help him. And his son senses this, despite the fact the cure is far worse than the disease. Suddenly my latest bout of West African stomach parasites acts up. No toilets here, so I quickly run out to the woods behind the "*Cabinet de Soins.*"

After I return, Mr. Hinhonvi explains that the hot pepper will raise his temperature, and he will no longer have the chills. The boy is finally calm and falls asleep, but as soon as he does, Mr. Hihonvi says, "How do you feel son?" The boy can only moan. Mr. Hihonvi gets up, goes outside, and comes back a few minutes later with the branch of a tree, which he then gives to his son. "Chew on this, it's a source of vitamin C," he instructs him. "He's been playing too much over the school vacation, and his fatigue has accumulated," he utters to me. "I will make another leaf infusion to cure him later. What I've been giving him up until now has only been to cure the symptoms, not the cause."

"How do you diagnose the illnesses of your patients?" I ask. "I meditate," he replies.

"I don't use the traditional form of divination called Fah, as other traditional healers do in the area because I am Christian, and Fah communicates with Vodun gods. Fah is for the villagers and illiterates. In meditation I communicate with Jesus and other spirits who tell me what's wrong with my patients. I can't believe what I heard on Radio France International the other day! They said that the white people in your country want to blow up an old 747 in order to try to figure out how the airplane (TWA Flight 800) crashed. Why don't they just consult oracles, or a divination priest as we do here? It would be much more simple and inexpensive. Hey, son, how's your fever? Is it going up or is it going down? Do you feel better yet?" He keeps asking the boy every 30 seconds, as if he is really expecting spontaneous results from his efforts. After a while the boy starts replying with a distressed "*oui*" to avoid any further treatment.

We continue our conversation. "Ninety-nine percent of all illnesses in Africa are caused by witchcraft (curses) and angry Vodun gods, while only one percent is natural," he says. He continues, "Very few diseases are of natural causes because the Beninese are very distrustful, jealous, and malicious towards each other. They often go see a Vodun priest to put curses on their neighbors to harm or even kill them. Curses work by turning evil spirits against someone you want harmed. Vodun gods who are angry about being neglected by their worshipers can be to blame for making people sick, and so can errant evil spirits who attack people at random." "Well then what is an example of a naturally caused disease?," I ask. "Malaria," he answers. It is as prevalent as the common cold is in the West, so how could it be anything but natural?, I think.

"I cure most of my patients using leaves because they have the power to drive away evil spirits which cause illnesses," explains Mr. Hihonvi. "In addition to leaves, I use 'scientific' methods to cure disease as well. Spirits who cause illness reside inside you, and eat part of the food that you do.

If you remove what they eat from your diet, then the spirit will starve and will leave you, thus curing you. For example, cancer eats protein. If you suffer from cancer, all you need to do is remove all protein from your diet and you'll be healed. I can cure cancer in 92 days if the patient stops eating meat, fish, eggs and fruit juice. Some diseases are of natural origin from causes such as bacteria or viruses, but Western medicine only calms symptoms and does nothing to cure illness caused by curses. I use decoctions, infusions, potions, creams, eye drops, nose drops, throat drops etc. that I make myself. If he (referring to his son) shivers again, I will give him a cola nut because it's a stimulant."

I'm sure his son overhears him, because the boy doesn't shiver again. "I'm a Christian, but I still believe that Vodun spirits have the power to harm others. I don't worship them, nor do I have Vodun altars." Nevertheless, he does believe they exist, and does fear them, as do most Christians in southern Benin. He goes on, "To exorcise evil spirits from my patients, I use the power of God and Jesus, as well as the power of leaves." He enters the back room, and gets a piece of charcoal. He lights it, and explains that he is doing so to help chase any evil spirits away that may be harming his son.

"Besides diagnosing and healing illnesses, I make gris-gris to protect people against disease, and all types of misfortunes. I can make a magic ring worn on the finger to keep a girl from getting pregnant. Often a father will pay a substantial fee for his daughter to become an apprentice as a seamstress, or hairdresser, and in order for his investment in her not to be lost, he has to insure that she doesn't become pregnant. A father may also want to prevent her from becoming pregnant to keep her in school." He goes on to explain that the ring acts as a magical chastity belt preventing the male from penetrating her.

"Another method is if the father doesn't like the man his daughter is seeing, I can do a ceremony to drive him away using spirits." He makes it clear that he doesn't actually harm anyone with his magic and medicine, as most traditional healers proclaim vehemently as well. It is very important for anyone claiming to possess magical powers or expertise to prevent rumors that they are using them for malevolent purposes. If not, they may be blamed for inexplicable misfortunes in the community. The consequences of being accused of practicing witchcraft (placing curses on people) could be grave, to say the least. I heard a story and even saw a picture of a person who was accused of being a witch, and was he was beaten to death by a group of people from a neighboring village not long ago.

By this point in the conversation, I lose faith that he can heal my ear because of his, um, shall we say . . . shaky and inconsistent methodology. I am thoroughly entertained, however, and I am curious to see how imaginative his diagnosis and treatment of my ear will be. He says my hearing loss could be caused by a curse, a change in climate, or possibly an evil spirit that haphazardly attacked me. I tell him that doctors in the U.S. said it was a virus, and there is nothing they could do to help me. He replies, "When it's spirits that are the culprit causing a disease, white people can't understand it. When they can't figure out the cause of an illness with their science, they call it a virus, when in reality evil spirits are causing the illness." I think it is funny because when Africans can't scientifically explain an illness, they label the cause as evil spirits, while Western medicine's version of evil spirits are viruses.

"The problem with your ear is likely caused by the brain, because any problem in the area of the head is caused by the brain. It's probably not a curse that's causing your problem," Mr. Hihonvi explains. He then shows me a notebook in which he recorded his past client's names, ages, weight, professions, ailments, and also how he treated them in an effort to convince me of his level of experience. So much for confidentiality, I think. I bet he'll be telling future customers how he healed a *Yovo* from the Peace Corps once. One case from his book was that of a woman needing treatment for asthma. He determined that it was because a man was interested in her, but she wasn't interested in him, so the man used an evil gris-gris (magic charm) against her to make her ill. He claims to have healed her.

"I can predict a person's future illnesses, and can tell a person what his aptitudes are in order to help him make career decisions. Sometimes parents want to know this for their children, so they know whether to send them to school or have them become an apprentice," he says. "I know remedies for nightmares, bed wetting, and obesity. I can also do scarifications behind the ear to protect people from witches." As he is talking he points out that I am wearing glasses, and says he has a bottle of eye drops that he sells for only 375 CFA (60 cents) that will cure me of the need to wear them anymore. "Your eyes will get worse if you don't follow my advice. Your 'nature' doesn't like to wear glasses, so you should only wear them when you have to."

"Uh . . . I think I'll wait for now on the eye drops," I reply politely.

Although he is obviously trying to make a sale, he is also being very nice by telling me so much about his practice. I can tell that he isn't a swindler, and that he truly believes in what he's selling. The average Beninese person, who is just looking for money from the seemingly rich white guy, would have already asked directly and pressured me for money, and probably would have tried to con me several times by now. He hasn't yet, so this is a pleasant surprise.

He doesn't seem like he is in a rush, as I am probably the only customer he has had all day, if not all week, so he continues, "I'm capable of memory enhancement. Often in polygamist families, a co-wife will get jealous of her fellow co-wife's child, and in turn close the child's mind with a curse that prevents him from learning and being able to do well in school. I can feed the child's brain with garlic, and use a gris-gris called 'ylo' (meaning "to call" in Fon) to attract the sympathy of the teacher to the student without the teacher knowing it. The teacher will be less stringent when grading, and will give the student more attention in the classroom. The student must put a powder on his hand and lick it and eat it. The same powder works to help vendors to sell more in the market by attracting clients."

He says he likes to be referred to as "Doto" (a derivative of the English word "Doctor"), which means a Western type doctor in Fon. He does not like to be called "*azondato*," which means "traditional healer" in Fon. To him the term is insulting because most are uneducated and illiterate. He accuses traditional healers of being swindlers who actually make people sick, and then ask for money to cure the same illness they caused. "I want to gain recognition for the profession of traditional medicine in Benin, and I'm working hard towards this," he proclaims. "I understand Westerners and the West." He claims to be different from other Beninese because he's educated, and, unlike most others, he has traveled outside Benin.

"I've done a lot of research in my field, and I have successfully cured AIDS. When I was practicing in the Ivory Coast, I wrote on a sign outside my *Cabinet de Soins* that I could cure AIDS, but unfortunately the people didn't believe me, and it didn't go over well with them. They threatened to burn me alive so I had to come back to Benin." I noted that there was nothing which mentioned being able to cure AIDS on his sign, or on the pamphlet he gave me. "I can cure AIDS in 14-28 weeks with leaf infusion baths, and I have already cured two people," he says.

I ask him how much he charges for consultations, and he says 500 CFA ($1.00) for the diagnosis, 1,000 CFA ($2.00) for determining how to cure the illness, and then additional costs for the treatment, which can vary depending on what the treatment is. His prices are only a little higher than the average village healers I've seen, so I don't mind. He assures me that if he is not able to cure me, he will send me to someone who can. For the diagnosis, he writes down my personal information: my name, age, weight, profession, and a brief history of the problem so he can meditate on it. We set up a time for me to come back in three days, and I return to Allada.

## The Diagnosis and Prescribed Treatment:

Three days later I return to his "office," and he explains to me his findings without having done any type of physical examination or testing. He tells me the meditation séance, which he did early that morning before I came, only took a few hours. This is what he came up with: "It is neither an illness nor a curse. Evil spirits can't attack you because you're immune," he says, and then gives allegories to explain. "A cat can't attack a lion, and an ant can't swallow a lizard," implying that I am the lion and the lizard, hence invincible with respect to evil spirits. After hearing this, I am flattered. "You are a double person because you have the spirit of your twin brother within you. He was never born, because he wanted to stay in your shadow to fight for you and protect you against all evil." "Wow!," I say. "I never had any idea about having an unborn twin brother."

He goes on to describe the diagnosis: "While I meditated I met your guardian spirits, your mother's spirit and Jesus. (Note: My mother is living) Your spirits were complaining, and your mother was suffering. Your mother didn't want you to come to Africa because you're too young to leave her, and she's suffering in your absence. Since love can move mountains, the power of her love is causing your illness." I can't quite follow his rationale and he doesn't elaborate. He continues, "A secondary cause is that people are like boats that have crews of guardian ancestor spirits, and when your boat left America, most of your crew stayed home, because they didn't want to go to Africa. Your boat is undermanned, and your hearing loss is a symptom. You're in a state of spiritual imbalance. One reason why your guardian ancestor spirits mutinied was because you failed to forewarn them of your departure, and many were left behind." This is a bit too much for me, and I snidely think to myself—"OK, fine, next time I go anywhere, I will send my ancestral guardian spirits a press release!"

He continues, "Some of your ancestors' spirits did follow you here, but they aren't happy in Benin. They don't like to travel, and they don't like Africa. Your spirits can travel up to three months but two years, (the length of my Peace Corps duty) is too long for you to be so far away from home." I almost laugh out loud when I think about how I don't like it in Benin sometimes. But if I can make do in these conditions, so can my guardian spirits!

He then specifies what my ancestors' spirits don't like about Africa: "Your guardian spirits don't like the food here," noting that the spirits eat the same food I do as I'm consuming it. "Your guardian spirits don't like the hot climate and they are racist as well."

I think to myself, "What? My spirits don't like Africans!? Imagine that! I've got racist guardian spirits!?" To top it all off, he says that my spirits don't like the smell of latrines, which happens to be a place I frequent quite often.

Finally he gets to the most important part: the remedy for my hearing loss in one ear: "For your remedy you have to drink and wash with specially treated water for 21 days, and during the treatment, you're not to swim or wash in the ocean, a river, or a stream." He tells me that he will bless the water by invoking benevolent spirits into it by praying and by marking the route to the water with candles. "Every three days you'll have to come here to get refills. Because you're my friend, I will give you a discount," he says. Hmm, that sounds familiar, I think. Where have I heard that before? "Normally I'd ask 21,700 CFA ($40) for it, but instead I'll give it to you for only 7,100 CFA ($14)."

"Because you've already ingested too much African poison, you will need to buy 12 bottles of this anti-poison potion called 'Teyayo,' (he pulls one off the shelf behind him to show me), and you must take a spoonful in the morning, noon, and night until the 12 bottles are used up. The anti-poison costs 500 CFA (1$) per bottle. It is made from palm oil, leaves, and garlic, and it rids you of the poisons you've eaten. You must start eating more American food, or at least four out of seven days of the week. The other days you can eat African food, or you can eat every meal half Beninese, half American. Your ancestors don't like the food, and don't like you to eat with your hand either, so make sure you use a fork."

(Note that in Benin people often eat with their right hand and do not use utensils).

Mr. Hihonvi continues, "You need to avoid the heat. Use a fan more, and keep your windows open in your house. Don't eat pork because your 'nature' doesn't like it. Don't eat blood cake that they sell in the market. Don't eat at other Beninese people's houses because your ancestors don't like that either. It's fine if you eat at a restaurant however. Don't have a Beninese girlfriend, because your ancestors are racist and won't like you going out with an African girl. If you do have a Beninese girlfriend, she may cut a small piece of your hair and give it to her parents. They will take the hair to a Vodun priest, and he will put a spell on you to make you stay in Benin and marry their daughter. Then her family will take all your wealth. Your family won't accept it either if you marry a Beninese girl. She can also put a magic powder on your bed that will make you give her whatever she wants."

"I thought I was immune to curses and magic?" I interject.

"Yes" he replies, "but not if you make yourself vulnerable. You need to keep your hygiene habits the same here in Benin as you did in America. Use cologne, use a tooth brush and not tooth sticks" (people in Benin often chew on wooden sticks to clean their teeth). "Use a toilet and not a latrine, because your spirits don't like the smell, plus the gas gives tuberculosis." I wonder if the Peace Corps would honor a prescription for a flush toilet from him . . . ?

"How long will it take before I notice a difference in my hearing?" I ask.

"After three months your ear will start getting better, but it won't be completely cured until you repatriate your travel weary guardian spirits and rejoin them with the ones you left at home."

"So when would you like to start the remedy?" he asks . . ."

"Uh . . . I need to think about it. I'll get back to you," I reply. I thank him, pay him the 1500 CFA ($3.00) for the consultation, and, for obvious reasons, I don't go back for the treatment.

Although I did not let him try to cure me, I was at least able to get what I really came for: a better understanding of traditional medicine, and an interesting story to tell. Mr. Hihonvi seems normal to me, except for the fact that he has an overactive imagination, which is a good filler for the hard scientific knowledge that is scarce in a country as impoverished and undereducated as Benin. I thought he did a very good job of mixing his limited knowledge of Western medicine with traditional African animist beliefs, common sense, and knowledge he has of Westerners. I realize how lucky I am to have the luxury of having access to modern scientific medicine. However, for a poor Beninese person who does not, Mr. Hihonvi is the next best thing.

# ON THE ROAD TO AGADEZ

## Preparations:

I have been in Benin now for a year and a half, and I am about to take my first real vacation from my post. I have only left Benin once since I arrived when I was medevaced to the U.S. due to the sudden and permanent hearing loss in my left ear, which I acquired just a three weeks after arriving here. That was a year ago, but I don't really consider it a vacation since I was only home for four days, and the other two weeks I was running around Washington, DC seeing doctors in the middle of winter just after a blizzard. Now that my Peace Corps service is more than half over, I am ready for a getaway to discover some of Benin's neighboring countries.

I have been saving up my vacation days so I can take an extended vacation to Niger and Burkina Faso. Because travel by bush taxi is very slow and arduous in West Africa, anything less than two weeks would be too short. I have budgeted three weeks for this trip, and I am betting I will spend about two weeks of it either in a bush taxi or waiting for one! Even though we are called "volunteers," we have jobs to do, and we are required to stay at our posts during the week, unless we have work related business elsewhere. We accumulate two vacation days per month. We can travel within Benin, or go out of the country with Peace Corps' approval, as they need to know where we are in case of emergencies.

I have taken several trips away from Allada on weekends and holidays to attend parties thrown by other Peace Corps Volunteers. I have gone to Cotonou every 4-6 weeks for a day or two to see other volunteers and to buy groceries I can't find in Allada. I have also left to pick up my living allowance from Peace Corps headquarters every three months, and to attend Peace Corps meetings and conferences. While in Cotonou, we PCV's always take advantage of modern services not available "*au village*," such as restaurants, nightclubs and shopping for the "*bonnes choses*" (good things) as the Beninese say. However, we cannot indulge too much, since we are on such meager budgets (only $6 a day). I have visited other PCV's around Benin on shorter trips, but now I am ready for a longer break to Niger and Burkina Faso.

I have spoken to volunteers who have traveled outside of Benin, I have studied some maps, and I have also done some reading. Both Niger and Burkina Faso sound like very interesting places to visit. Where I am in southern Benin, it is very green and tropical. However, I want to see the desert and experience an entirely different part of West Africa. It's easy to think all of Africa is very similar, but I know that is not true, and I want to explore West Africa's geographical and cultural diversity. I also want to go to Togo, Ivory Coast, and Ghana, but I will have to wait a few more months to take that trip.

I did some mileage calculations, and if I make it as far as the Sahara desert in Niger, it will be about 1,300 miles, or the distance from New York City to Miami! If I make it to Ouagadougou, the capital of Burkina Faso, my return trip will be a few hundred miles longer than the first leg. Driving such a long distance in a nice car on well-maintained roads in the United States can be long and tiring. I can only imagine what it will be like in overcrowded, beat up bush taxis, driving over horrible roads and dealing with the bureaucracy of police stops and border crossings. I hope to God I don't have any bush taxi rides from hell like the one I had from Djougou to Allada. I have heard many stories, and I expect the worst, as I have learned from experience. I considered flying to Niger from Cotonou, but flights are too expensive and infrequent. Besides, I would miss a lot of things in between, so bush taxis will be my primary means of transport.

My next step is to find travel partners, as I would rather not travel alone. After talking to many volunteers about my trip, I find two other Benin PCV's, Chris and Suzie, who want to go with me, and we agree on a date when we will leave. Our next step is to get our passports from the safe at the Peace Corps Office, and hand deliver them to the Niger and Burkina Faso embassies, along with the hefty fees required to get our visas. Each visa takes a day, so we have an excuse to hang around Cotonou for two days and have some fun enjoying modern amenities in the big city.

**February 24<sup>th</sup>, 1997 (Cotonou to Malanville)** We are finally on the road! Suzie, Chris and I arranged for a taxi to pick us up at the Peace Corps office at 7:00 AM, and we are shocked when the driver shows up right on time. I barely slept last night because I was so excited about this trip. We rent an extra seat in the back of the taxi with the goal of making it to the Nigerien border at the northern most tip of Benin by nighttime. We are not sure if it can be done, but since we're leaving so early, we think we may have a chance. It's a five-seater, and the driver already has two other people in the front who are going as far as Parakou, the fourth largest city in Benin (150,000 people), so there should be no stopping to let people out and pick up more passengers until we arrive there. The extra seat we're renting makes a big difference in terms of comfort, because we actually have space between our hips, instead of cramming a fourth person into a back seat made for three. I am glad we can move our legs a little to maintain circulation.

We have been on the road a few hours, and suddenly the driver swerves off the road onto a detour. We are on a very bumpy dirt road that parallels the paved road for a mile. It's annoying because the road construction at this spot has been going on for a year and a half, and it still doesn't seem anywhere near complete. As I try to write in my journal, my pen jogs back and forth across the page with every bump, and the sentences I write resemble a Richter scale printout during a powerful earthquake. Luckily it is over fairly quickly, and we are soon back on the pavement. As we pass Bohicon, about two hours north of Cotonou, the air becomes noticeably drier and cooler, which is a relief from the heat and humidity of the south. Although I am keeping my fingers crossed, so far this has been a bush taxi ride from heaven!

Cotton is one of Benin's cash crops, and I can tell cotton is in season, as I notice a continuous trail of cotton on both sides of the road from Bohicon north that has blown off the trucks taking it to Cotonou. From there, it will eventually be exported by boat. Unfortunately there are only a few textile factories in Benin, so they have to export most of it. We pass an amazing number of trucks that are overloaded with cotton. I have seen at least five or six that have tipped over on curves in the road and were left there.

As usual, riding in a bush taxi on these roads is a hair-raising experience. We are on an undivided road with almost no break down lane, we're doing 60-70 mph, and our driver passes cars near the crests of hills, and before blind curves. There are a lot of obstacles to avoid such as goats, pigs, dogs, pedestrians, people on bicycles, slow moving vehicles, and broken down vehicles. Since we departed from Cotonou, I swear I have seen 50 wrecked cars and trucks that were left on the side of the road, and I certainly hope we don't become one of them. We make record time to Parakou as it takes us only five hours! The only stops were for police, gendarmes, food, and gas. We averaged 52 mph! I believe this is one for the record books. However, we are now stuck in a taxi station, waiting for the driver to find two people to fill the two spots in the front seat, as the two passengers from Cotonou got out here. We sit here waiting for an hour and a half, until our driver fills the seats. Shortly after, we leave Parakou and we're on our way to Malanville, which is a small town on Benin's northern border with Niger.

Chris and Suzie at a taxi station. Notice the taxis are very old Peugeot 504's from France and the larger Peugeot station wagons.

We are cruising along making good time when the driver unexpectedly pulls over. He gets out of the car, and looks under the hood. I get out to look as well, and I discover that we have a broken fan belt! The driver waves down a zemidjan driver, and leaves all of us on the side of the road while he goes looking for a mechanic in the next town. A half hour later, he comes back with a mechanic and his toolbox. God knows how long it will take to get it fixed. They are working now, and I hear banging. They're probably using a hammer to do what normally requires a box wrench.

I check to see if they're making progress, and just as I thought, they're using a hammer to loosen a big nut. It turns out the pulley coming off the crankshaft broke. Unfortunately, we prepaid the driver, so if we want to get another taxi, we will have to fight with him to get our money back. Then of course, we will have the hassle of finding another taxi. I decide I will give him another hour (until 4:30 PM) before I start making a fuss.

Luckily at about 4:15 PM, they fix the pulley and we are once again on our way. As we pass the town of N'Dali, I notice the ground is very brown, as the climate is becoming drier the farther north we travel. In addition, many farmers have intentionally burned their fields to clear them of brush, which adds to the bareness of the land. Already the landscape appears much different from the landscape in southern Benin. The trees are becoming sparser, and the brush is not as tall, although there is more tall grass. I am seeing cattle that I don't see in the south, because the land is too thickly vegetated there to allow for animals to graze. As usual, we have to stop many times for the gendarme's roadblocks, where they inevitably extort money from the driver. The driver willingly pays the usual 200F bribe, as he knows the gendarme will throw the book at him if he does not pay, possibly holding us up for hours.

Thankfully, we arrive at the Malanville taxi station at 8 PM safe and sound. When we get out of the taxi, the usual chaos ensues. All of the other drivers who are waiting there for more passengers swarm us yelling out different destinations to jockey for our business in case we are going on to another destination. We thought our driver was going to take us across the Niger border to Gaya, but he announces to us at the last minute that he is going no farther than Malanville. We quickly find another driver to take us across the border, but we soon realize he is the only taxi going in that direction, and he still needs two more passengers before he will leave. He responds with the obligatory *"toute de suite"* line when we ask him when we will be leaving. We know very well that "right a way" can mean anywhere from 30 minutes to five hours, so we decide to find a hotel here in Malanville, and deal with the border crossing tomorrow morning. All totaled, today's trip from Cotonou took us about 15 hours to go 390 miles, or about 26 mph!—Not quite the pace we had established getting to Parakou.

We find a taxi to take us to the hotel on the outskirts of Malanville, and we feel the driver is giving us the "Yovo price," so we bargain hard to get him to charge us what we feel is a more reasonable price. We spend at least five minutes haggling over the equivalent of 40 cents! When I first arrived in Benin, I never understood why volunteers spend so much time and energy bargaining over such small amounts of money. Now I understand that it is a matter of pride, and not so much about the money. Paying a fair price by local standards makes us feel accepted and respected, and not like an outsider tourist. Besides, we are on a very tight budget, and small amounts of money add up over time. Unfortunately, we do not have our helmets, so we can't take Zemidjans, and have to resort to the pricier car taxis.

Our "hotel" is nowhere near the standards of the even cheapest American hotel. In fact, this particular hotel does not even have electricity or running water. We have to use a shared latrine, and take bucket showers at the end of the hall. Our room has one queen-sized bed with a mosquito net. We get all of these "amenities" for a mere 2,500 F ($5.00)! To save money, we will share the room and the bed. It seems odd, but we have no issue with sharing the bed, as Benin PCV's are used to platonically sharing beds with volunteers of the opposite sex. Often, when we go to Cotonou for a getaway from our posts, or for official business, we sleep on the few full size beds in the PC office. Sometimes we stay in hotels in Cotonou, but they are too expensive to stay in every time. Bed space is at such a premium in the PC office that we go to bed alone and wake up with another volunteer in it the next morning, either male or female. Generally, if volunteers stay out too late partying, they have to sleep on the dirty couch in the lounge or on a mat on the floor.

We get a laugh when the hotel owner asks if we are going to stay all night, or pay by the hour! We eat dinner at the buvette in the hotel, and a gendarme who is also eating there jokes that I will have a long night with my two wives. He also jokes that since it is cold (70 degrees), one of my wives will be jealous. After dinner we go to bed early, and by chance we all wake up at 4AM and talk about our trip for an hour before falling back asleep.

**February 25th, 1997: (Malanville to Niamey)** We get breakfast at a roadside stand, and we order omelet sandwiches and instant coffee. The French style bread is as fantastic here as it is in Cotonou. It is one of the lasting gifts from French colonization. While we are eating, we hear a loud "poof" sound behind us. We look back and see a large cloud of billowing black smoke rising above the taxi station. Seconds later taxis and a large crowd of people come pouring out onto the road to escape a car fire that erupted. It reminded me of the idiot our taxi driver bought gas from on the way up here. He was smoking a cigarette while he poured the gas into our car from a glass bottle and we were sitting in the car. I would not be surprised if something like that just caused the explosion. We quickly finish eating, and walk down the road along with a mass of other curious people to investigate. We see a car fully engulfed in flames. Moments later the wind kicks up and the flames move towards us. The group starts to run back the other away from the flames. As far as I can tell, there are no fire trucks here, so they will probably just let it burn itself out.

Because of the chaos, we have a hard time finding a taxi to cross the border and drive on to Niamey, but after looking for half an hour, we find one. At the Benin exit point we have to fill out forms and wait to get our passports stamped. We cross the Niger River, and then have to do it all over again on the Niger side.

In Gaya we have to wait for 20 minutes for the driver to have his papers inspected by the police. Unfortunately, the police officer comes out to the car and announces to us that the driver's insurance is not valid, so we have to find another taxi. We quickly find one, and now we are sitting in a "death van" waiting for it to fill up. We call it a "death van" because it holds so many people. Several children are staring at us. I give them my evil eye to try to show them what it's like to be stared at, to have some fun, and perhaps if I'm lucky, scare them away.

This is the "death van" we had to wait four hours to fill up before it left.

While we are waiting, street vendors parade past the car with their goods on their heads. I buy some *brochettes* (meat kabobs), *beignets* (fried dough balls), some nasty tasting nuts, and a mango for lunch. It has been entertaining just sitting here watching all the people and sellers and goings on. We arrived here at 10:00 AM, and we wind up waiting and waiting and waiting. Then we wait some more . . . . We finally leave at 2:00 PM. That is four hours of waiting!

There are 22 people plus one baby in this van, which has only 15 seats. The luggage on the roof is as high as the van, and I wonder if the driver knows anything about physics and the concept of center of gravity. Just as we depart, the driver stops to pick up one more person, so there are now 23 people and a baby in the van. I have one butt cheek on two seats with a space between the seats. I feel lucky because the guy next to me has only one cheek on a seat. Three people are sitting on someone's lap, two people are hanging off the back of the van, and one is on the roof! Now you know why we call it a "death van." Unbelievably, no one is complaining because this is simply how public transportation works here.

The Nigerien (Not "Nigerian" as in Nigeria) countryside is very different from the countryside in Benin. The landscape is very dry and desert-like. In addition, the architecture of the houses is different from those in northern Benin. The villager's grain silos are also different from those in Benin. There are vast empty spaces and lots of scrub brush, and I see camels crossing the road occasionally. We are driving fairly slowly, so I'm not as afraid as yesterday when we were doing 60 mph. I have to keep reminding myself that travelling is half the fun on a trip in West Africa, and the suffering will give me some good stories to tell. There is no adventure without fear, danger, and discomfort. In addition, adventures like these build character, or at least that's what we volunteers like to say to make ourselves feel better during trying experiences.

A few times we have to stop for gendarmes. The driver must not be paying enough bribes, because two times the gendarmes make the driver take the baggage off the car to inspect it. The driver gets some of the passengers to do it. The gendarmes do not even look at the baggage, and luckily, before all of it is removed from the van, they signal to put it back on. At other stops, the gendarmes want to check everyone's papers, so we all have to get out of the van and then get back in. To rush the stragglers, the driver starts driving off before everyone is in, so they have to run to catch the van!

We pull into Niamey before dark, and we walk to the Peace Corps hostel where we spend the next few nights. Today's trip from when we left our hotel in Malanville to Niamey took nine hours to travel for 170 miles. That's a woeful 19 mph average speed!

Fortunately, we don't have to worry about exchanging money, because Niger is part of the *Communauté Financaire Africaine* (African Financial Community), which has a common currency (the CFA). The members are all former French colonies except for Guinea-Bissau. The worrisome part about money when travelling in West Africa, however, is that no one here accepts traveler's checks or credit cards, so I am carrying about $600 cash in a pouch around my neck under my shirt. It is all the money I will spend for this three-week trip. I have never carried more than $200 cash in the U.S., and it is unnerving because others can so easily identify me as a tourist. I do have some traveler's checks with me, but they are only for emergencies, since I can only exchange them at banks, and I am not counting on them being easy to find or open when I need them.

Niamey is the capital of Niger. It is so much less crowded than Cotonou, and I love it already. The streets feel wider, and there is much less traffic, pollution, noise, and garbage. The sidewalks are uncluttered, unlike in Cotonou, where often one has to walk in the road because vendors and construction materials block them. There is hardly anyone riding motorcycles here in contrast to Cotonou, where it seems there are more motorcycles than cars. The resulting clouds of pollution from many two-stroke engines are suffocating. Here the air is much cleaner. I see a few camels and donkeys in the city. In Cotonou, the only animals I have ever seen were a herd of goats one time. There are some mud buildings in Niamey, but in Cotonou, they are all made of cement. Here we are not *Yovos,* but "*Anisaras*" or "*Batoures.*" We've heard these terms a few times, but we are not taunted with them the way we are with Yovo in Benin. I am surprised that there are so many paved roads in Niamey because Niger is much poorer than Benin. According to the CIA's World Factbook in 2011, Benin is ranked as #199 in poverty out of 230 nations, while Niger is ranked at #228! (www.cia.gov) Only Afghanistan and Angola are considered poorer than Niger. Benin's GDP per capita income is $1600 per person, and sadly Niger's is only $700.

Often the populations of capital cities reflect the ethnic make up of the country, and Niamey is no exception. Niger is very ethnically diverse, and the ethnic groups are often very distinct from one another. Walking around I see many people I can tell are from varying ethnic groups because of their skin color, facial features, body types, their style of dress, jewelry, as well as their accents when they speak French. In addition, some ethnic groups have noticeable facial scars and tattoos. Some of the well-known ethnic groups in Niger are the Songhai, Tuaregs, Djerma, Hausa, Fulani and the Gourmanché. It is fun learning about them, and trying to identify them by their dress and physical characteristics. I know that Fulani are distinct because they usually tattoo designs on their faces, and the Fulani farmers often wear very large brimmed pointed hats that they decorate with ostrich feathers. They are very tall, and the Arabs are very light skinned. The Tuaregs often wear indigo turbans and ornate jewelry.

The Peace Corps hostel is very nice, and feels like a youth hostel in Europe or the U.S. It's too bad we don't have one in Benin. That is why we're forced to share the few beds in the Peace Corps office with any volunteer who needs a place to sleep. I can tell the experiences of Niger PCV's are different from those of Benin PCV's. First of all, their program is bigger than Benin's. Peace Corps Benin has 80 volunteers, while Niger has 130. Niger is a much bigger country, and most volunteers are posted in very remote, small villages. They start learning a local language from day one in training. They all learn their local language very well, and some do not even learn to speak French because French is not as important as it is in Benin. They work in teams, and they have trucks and regional hostels.

While staying at the hostel, we meet three Togo Volunteers who by chance are also on vacation in Niger. Coincidentally, they were in Philadelphia for three days with my training group for our staging. I got to know them a little those three days, but we have not spoken since then, which was over a year ago.

After a few days of sightseeing in Niamey, the six of us decide to travel east together to the town of Zinder, and are we are excited to continue east to the Tahl desert after Zinder.

**February 28th, 1997: (Niamey to Zinder)** The six of us: Pam, Shefali, Chris, Suzie, Rick and myself, are in a nine seater taxi with 12 people crammed into it, on our way east to Zinder. Niger volunteers told us that it is a 12-14 hour ride, so traveling with a group makes it more fun. We are having a dream ride on straight paved roads, and we are almost half way there when I smell something burning. I point it out to the driver, so he stops the car and checks under the hood. It turns out the wiring is overheating and melting! The driver waves down another taxi and goes to find a mechanic. We are sitting under a tree on the side of the road waiting.

After a half hour, we decide to go for a walk in a tiny nearby village. The air is very hazy due to the Harmattan winds and the dust they bring from the north. It is very dry, and my lips feel chapped. We see fields of onions, millet, and sorghum around the village. They are the staple crops here that are well adapted to the dry climate. I am surprised to see that some farmers using irrigation systems, and that they're growing onions now during the dry season. I have not seen irrigation in Benin.

It's amazing to me that they can grow anything here, as the soil seems to be nothing more than sand.

The driver returns with a mechanic, and he is trying to tape up the melted wires. However, we all doubt that we will make it to Zinder tonight. After an hour, the mechanic somehow works his magic, and the taxi is running again! Amazing! We arrive in Zinder at 10:30 PM The trip door to door was about 490 miles, and took us 14 hours, so we had an average speed of 35 mph. We are all dead tired, and the driver is nice enough to take us to the door of the Peace Corps hostel. The Niger volunteers staying there are friendly. We go to the local buvette to get a drink before bed. I sleep like a rock, because I am so tired from spending so much time on the road.

**March 2ⁿᵈ, 1997: (In the Sahara—Zinder to Aderbissinat)** We spent yesterday recovering from our long trip and investigating Zinder. It is in south central Niger, in the Sahel, a semi-arid region just below the Sahara Desert. We are not far from sand dunes, which stretch as far as the eye can see, and we are all very anxious to see this stereotypical feature of the desert. Since it rains occasionally in this part of the desert, there are sparse amounts of trees, bushes, and grass. Zinder is a small town with not a lot to see or do. It's no big deal though, as we knew this already, and it is just a stop over.

I cannot believe we have been travelling for about a week now. Today we need to decide where we're going to head next, and we're at an impasse. We cannot decide whether we should go to the Thal desert to the east of here near the Chad border and offers nothing more than sand dunes, or visit Niger volunteers' posts around Zinder. We discuss the pros and cons of each option for what seems like hours, and I am getting tired of so much indecision. Shefali then jokingly says, "Why don't we go to Agadez?" Agadez is a small city, a little over 300 miles north of here. It is 300 miles through the Sahara Desert, which may not sound far, but it is at least a two-day trip; that is, if we are lucky.

We think it would be out of the question, as the Niger Peace Corps administration prohibits its volunteers from going there. However, the Benin Peace Corps administration has no such a rule for Benin volunteers. It is off limits because of the Tuareg rebellion from 1990-1995. There was sporadic fighting between Niger troops and the Tuaregs in the Aïr Mountains near Agadez. Tourists were evacuated for their own safety during the fighting so we will probably be some of the first tourists back there since the peace accord was just signed a year ago.

There has been a long-standing conflict between the Tuaregs and the Nigerien government. The Tuaregs were angry because many of them are nomadic herders, and have no land rights provided by the Nigerien government. They travel the Sahel on camels with their cattle constantly searching for grass to graze on. They have clashed with the sedentary farmers over land use and rights to the sparse watering holes. They feel that they are not given a fair share of profits from Niger's lucrative uranium mines and are underrepresented in the Niger government. To the north of Agadez is the town of Arlit, where the uranium mines[1] are located. When the Nigerien government discovered uranium on the land that the Tuaregs call home, they shared little revenue with the Tuaregs, while reaping substantial profits (Morrison, Jessica).

We speak to some Niger volunteers here at the Peace Corps hostel, and they all tell us that the Tuaregs have not attacked anyone in a long time, and that the situation is calm. They say the only people at risk are Europeans who rent expensive four-wheel drive vehicles and venture out into Tuareg rebel territory on their own. Besides, an armed military caravan escorts the bus we will take to Agadez, so there should be no worry. In our quest for adventure and lack of a better idea, we decide to go to Agadez. We have heard and read much about it, and we are very excited to see it ourselves. Christine and Rick are not feeling as adventurous as the rest of us, so they decide to stay in Zinder a few days before heading back to Niamey.

It's 8:30 AM and Pam, Shefali, Suzie and I are at the bus station. The bus is big, solid and new, so I am confident that there won't be any mechanical problems. We are used to very old and dilapidated bush taxis, so it is comforting to see a new-looking vehicle, especially considering the terrain we will have to cross. The bus to Agadez leaves only twice a week because it can only go with a military caravan. I'm told an army jeep with

---

[1]   *Those uranium mines are the same ones that President George Bush spoke of in his 2003 State of the Union speech. He claimed that Saddam Hussein was attempting to acquire yellow cake uranium for his weapons of mass destruction (WMD) program. Bush used this "intelligence," which later turned out to be false, as an important reason for going to war with Iraq.*

a large machine gun mounted on the back will be riding in front of the caravan, with another flanking the rear. However, it remains to be seen if this will actually happen. I have learned to be skeptical of what people tell me in West Africa, as information is usually not very reliable.

Because of the caravan, we are not going to get to Agadez this evening. We don't understand why we can't go directly to Agadez today because it's not that far. The trip could easily be done in one day, but we are told that we are going to have to spend the night in an oasis village called Aderbissinat, around the halfway point. It is a very small village, so there is zero chance of there being a hotel. We are planning to sleep outside if need be. What begins to worry us is that everyone boarding the bus is equipped with a thick warm blanket and a mat to sleep on. Upon seeing this, Suzie says, "Maybe they know something that we don't." "I think you're right," I say. We have nothing along the lines of a blanket or a sleeping bag, and barely any warm clothes. I don't even have any warm clothes in Benin, since it is always so hot.

We leave Zinder around 9:00 AM, and we seem to be making good time. We see many interesting villages along the way. It was really cool this morning, but it is pretty warm now, probably the high 80's or so. The landscape is desert. Although there are a few low trees and bushes, the majority of the landscape is just sand. My glasses are covered with dust kicked up from the road that blows through the window. I have to wipe them off at least every ten minutes. The sky is very hazy from the dust, and we see many cattle and camel caravans alongside the road. The bus is quite comfortable compared to the bush taxis we are used to taking in Benin. We have the space one would expect on a normal bus. The only difference with this bus is that there is no aisle. The aisle is occupied by passengers sitting on seats that fold out from the left row of seats. We have seen the jeeps with machine guns off and on, but for the most part, they ride up ahead of us and stay out of sight. We must not be in a dangerous area now, because they tell us that the caravan will not form until tomorrow. We are excited about Agadez. It should be fun and interesting.

Looking out the window, I see nothing but vast expanses of flat sand. We must be in the Sahara or very close to it! At this point I discover first hand what a mirage is. I used to think, "How could anyone see imaginary ponds of water in the middle of the desert?" The heat you see rising off hot pavement looks similar to water from a distance, but it is much more convincing when all you can see to the edge of the horizon is sand. Because the hot rippling air rising off the sand is so far away, it truly looks like a large body of water, and I'm not even thirsty! You can't get close to it because it is on the horizon, and it is always moving away from you as you move closer to it. It's no wonder why dehydrated, delirious people lost in the desert are duped and ultimately lured to their deaths by this cruel trick of nature.

There is a Beninese woman sitting next to us who has been living in Zinder with her Nigerian husband. She is going to Agadez to sell rice. I speak Fon with her a little, and she is surprised that I can speak her language, just as I am surprised to meet a Beninese person in Niger. We speak a little in French about the differences between Benin and Niger, and how she misses being in Benin. If you have lived in only one country in Africa, it is easy to imagine that all of Africa is the same, which indeed it is not. Traveling to another African country, and meeting an African who is also a foreigner like myself, reminds me that cultures vary greatly within Africa.

The bus has sand ladders on the roof. They are heavy perforated strips of metal about 10 feet long and two feet wide, which are put under the wheels of the bus in case it gets stuck in the sand. So far, the roads have been paved. I wonder what the road will be like up ahead, and if we will need the sand ladders. For the most part, every truck I've seen on this road has them strapped on the side. I suppose that even on paved roads, you may need a sand ladder because of the sand drifts.

12:53 PM—Oh no! . . . the pavement just ended. We are bouncing up and down and hitting bumps, washboard, and potholes, while the bus is moving at an incredible speed for these road conditions. I hope the road is not this bad the entire way!

We stop in a small village to let some air out of the tires, so we will get better traction in the sand. While the driver does that, we get out to explore a little. This place is really interesting! We are in the middle of the desert! We see many beautifully dressed Tuaregs riding their camels. They wear dark blue indigo turbans and long robes. They look so graceful and at ease on their camels. I cannot imagine how I would look trying to do the same. Riding camels is a way of life for them, so it is understandable that they are so adept at it. As I look around, I see nothing but sand for 360 degrees. It is desolate and exotic at the same time.

Pam, Suzie, and me in front of our bus when it stopped to let some air out of the tires to improve traction in the deep sand we were driving on.

A proud Tuareg perched on his camel that he uses for transportation. Notice the fur is rubbed off the back of the camel's neck because they control it by rubbing their bare feet on that spot.

We're now back on the road. Looking behind me, I see two men wearing turbans with their entire faces covered, and they are each holding a big machine gun. I cannot help but wonder whether I should I feel threatened or protected by these guys. I assume that they are part of the military escort. Had there been two men wearing turbans and toting machine guns in the U.S., or anywhere else for that matter, it would certainly feel different, but I guess it's OK here. At this point, the thought strikes me, if there is no danger from Tuareg rebels at this time as we were told, then why do we need a military escort?

Whoa! The bus suddenly veers off the road and into the sand. My heart jumps, and I grip the rail in front of my seat tightly preparing for the worst. Surprisingly enough, the bus only slows down a little, rocks to one side, and does not tip over. I can hear the engine struggling to keep the bus moving through the deep sand, and we slow down considerably, but we keep moving, running parallel to the road. Several times the bus fishtails, and I have the sensation that we are going to tip over. We weave our way through gullies, large bushes, and small sand drifts. Why in God's name did we veer off the road like that? Is this bus driver trying to scare the hell out of us? Seconds later we pass a huge sand drift about five feet tall that blew over the road, and the bus suddenly swerves back onto the hard packed dirt road. I underestimated both the experience level of our driver and the power of the bus. At any rate, it would have been interesting to see them use the sand ladders to extricate the bus from a sand drift. Several more times the driver swerves off the road, bushwhacking our way parallel to the road to avoid sand drifts covering the road. It is as thrilling as an amusement park ride.

A little while later, we roar into a small desert village called "Aderbissinat." There is sand everywhere. It looks like there was a sand blizzard because all the streets and houses are surrounded by sand, and some houses are even buried up to their roofs by sand drifts! The wind is blowing, so there is sand in the air too. Now I know why almost everyone wears a turban. They do so to cover their mouths and faces from the blowing sand, as well as to keep the hot sun of their heads.

We are ready to search for a place to stay in the village, and as we are getting off the bus, I start talking to a nice guy named Muhad. He wears a bright yellow turban, and has a light Arab complexion, as opposed to the very dark skin of the non-Arabs in West Africa. He is very friendly, and says he will help us find a place to stay for the night. We get our bags off the top of the bus, and follow Muhad and his friends Abdu, Mustapha, Mustaph, and Aïsha through a maze of mud huts. We pass some camels, cattle, and sand drifts on the way. We arrive at a small mud hut with a flat mud roof and a mud wall surrounding it. This hut is typical for the village. We go inside, and it is surprising how much cooler it is inside than outside. The floor and walls are cemented, and plastic prayer mats that Muslims usually kneel on at prayer time cover the floor. What is striking is there is no furniture at all! We sit down and chat with our new friends. It turns out they are returning from a wedding in Zinder and they are all related. Luckily they speak French well, so we have no problem communicating with them.

They kindly invite us to spend the night there with them. We are a little skeptical, but after a little discussion amongst ourselves, we decide to accept their invitation seeing that we do not have any other option, and they seem very nice. On our way to Aderbissinat, we envisioned sleeping outside on the sand, freezing our butts off, so this is an offer we cannot refuse. They are not asking us for money either, as we are used to in Benin, so this is a pleasant surprise.

Our new friends have made this trip before, so they are prepared. They brought a lot of food that they generously share with us. We are blown away by their generosity. Often Africans make me feel stingy, greedy, and aloof because they are so gregarious, giving, and welcoming of strangers. I have a hard time feeling equally generous, outgoing, laid back, and trusting of strangers here. I rationalize by reminding myself that it is not totally my fault, as we are all products of the society we are brought up in.

We eat sitting on the floor with them. They treat us to a delicious lunch of stewed mutton, bread, and fruit. For desert, they have a tasty Arab cake and fried dough. We finish the meal with tea, as is the custom among Arabs. It is a strong mint tea that they drink several times a day. They use the same tea leaves to make tea three times. The first batch is the strongest, and it gets progressively weaker the second and third time they brew it. After lunch they pray, and we take a short nap. They rented the house, but since it is too small for all of us, they go to look for a bigger one. A little while later they come back and lead us to the bigger house. It is three rooms, and resembles the first one in construction style: mud walls with a flat roof that is also made of mud. Where I live in Benin, most houses have straw roofs, but here there isn't enough vegetation to provide for straw roofs. Surprisingly, both this house and the other one have pit latrines. In Beninese villages there are rarely latrines so most people just go to the bathroom in the bush.

We drop our backpacks off at the new house, and our friends offer to show us around the village. It is advantageous to sightsee with locals, because they can negotiate picture taking and ward off people looking to take advantage of us. Picture taking here can be very awkward, as people in West Africa are generally very sensitive about it. Some of the more superstitious people believe you can use a picture to put a curse on them, and other people feel that you are taking something from them. Our friends ward off people who want to pester us, and they know where the most interesting spots are. We walk around for about two hours. The village seems very sleepy, as there are few people in the roads. There are no paved roads of course, nor are there any dirt roads. There is just sand. Many of the huts are dilapidated, buried in sand, and abandoned. Muhad says that because it is the dry season, many people have left Aderbissinat to look for grass for their cattle.

I am standing at the doorway of a house that is almost completely buried in sand from many sandstorms.

Aderbissinat is ethnically diverse. There are Fulani, Tuareg, Hausa, and Arabs here. The Tuaregs are the most impressive by far. They are very proud looking. The men dress in dark blue indigo Turbans that cover their entire heads and most of their faces. They ride huge camels with very ornate and colorful camel saddles. They are a sight to see. Tuaregs are known as warriors, and they carry ornate swords and knives on their sides, as well as colorful leather pouches around their necks. They are also renowned for their jewelry and Agadez crosses.

"Where am I!?," I think to myself. It feels so different and exotic. It reminds me again of how far I am from the United States, and how far I am from my new home in Benin. I am sure that if I spent a long enough time here, it would become home to me just as Benin feels like home to me now. Adapting to life in Benin convinced me that I could adapt to almost anything. Being out of Benin and being in an unfamiliar environment again makes me realize how much I have adapted to living there.

Technically, we are in the northern Sahel, just south of the true Sahara, because there remains some sparse vegetation. However, as far as I am concerned, we are in the Sahara. Walking around we see a Koran school, and we are able to peek in through the open door. We see an old man whipping the students who aren't reciting their passages correctly. They are reciting all at once, creating a din, so I don't know how he can tell who is reciting properly and who isn't. The "school" is a small room made of a wooden frame, and the walls are made of plastic bags and grain sacs tied together. On our way back, we see that more trucks have arrived for the caravan to Agadez tomorrow. We go back to the house and hang out. At dinner we all sit on the ground outside the small mud hut we will call home for tonight. We eat macaroni with a tasty sauce, and meat that our new friends prepare for us over a fire. After eating, we have the requisite three cups of tea and dates that I brought from Niamey. We chat a lot and enjoy each other's company. These people are really nice and Suzie, Shefali, Pam, and I can't quite understand how anyone can be so kind. Initially we were suspicious that they had ulterior motives, but quickly we are becoming trustful of them and realize that they expect nothing in return.

We go to bed around 9:00 PM. I luck out and get to sleep on a foam pad. Today it was very hazy, dusty and breezy. It has not been very hot, but damn, it gets cold at night! Luckily, I am sleeping in the back room away from the door and windows. I realize how cold it is when I get up at 3 AM to go to the bathroom. I bet it is only 55 or 60 degrees. I am used to a minimum temperature of 75 degrees in Benin, so anything less is cold for me. I think I may be getting sick, which is always a worry when you are several days away from the nearest doctor. I am worried about my digestive system, and wondering if I am going to have another bout of diarrhea. Diarrhea is a nuisance at home, but a crisis when travelling by bus or bush taxi, so I have to keep my fingers crossed.

**March 3rd, 1997: (The Sandstorm)** We wake up at 6 AM and have a quick breakfast consisting of some sort of local cake, fried dough, and tea. At 7:30 we are all on the bus ready to go! There is a flurry of activity as people load up the trucks that are preparing to leave. There are at least 15 large trucks, each loaded to the hilt with sacs of grain and boxes of who knows what. On top of all the trucks sit dozens of turbaned men. It appears that several more trucks arrived last night. As we are getting on the bus, a fierce sandstorm quickly picks up and visibility is now only 30 feet or so. My teeth are gritty from breathing the sandy air. When we get on the bus, the seats are covered with fine sand that blew in over night through the gaps in the windows. The bus and caravan pull out of the village, but after only five minutes, we stop to wait out the sandstorm. My guess is that the wind is blowing at 40-50 mph. It seems like a blizzard because of the wind, low visibility, cold, and drifting sand. I have to wipe the sand off my glasses every few minutes, even though all the windows are closed! Very fine sand is falling on the paper I am writing on, and it is clogging the tip of my pen.

This is one of the trucks of the caravan and me during the sandstorm. You can see how cold it was. The men on top of the truck travel the whole trip up there. Notice the sand ladders on the side of the truck.

Our Arab friends are incredible. They took us in, fed us, and now they are saying that they will get guides for us in Agadez to take us into the desert on camels. I would not be surprised if they even offer to put us up in Agadez. They are very interesting because they're educated and have knowledge of the West.

Whoa! Someone just opened the door of the bus and a cloud of sand and cold wind blows in our faces. Sometimes the gusts are so strong, the bus rocks back and forth. Suzie, Pam, Shefali, and I are all excited about getting turbans. We want to have that "desert look," and protect our faces from the sand.

The bus is more full than yesterday, as people got on in Aderbissinat. Wow, is it windy! It is funny to see people get out and go to the bathroom, because there is no place for them to hide, and that includes us. You have to aim carefully—in accordance with the wind. Today the machine gun toting, turban wearing, military guys are sitting right behind us. Whoopee!! The jeeps ride ahead past the bus, and on the back of them, just as I was told, are huge machine guns so I don't imagine we will have any problems with Tuareg rebels today. I have a guy on the bus help me tie my bed sheet around my head to act as a makeshift turban. It keeps my head warm, and acts as an air filter to keep me from inhaling airborne sand. They tell us that we are waiting for the gendarmes to check the trucks in the caravan . . . for what I do not know. He says that we should be able to travel in this sandstorm.

Pam, Shefali, Suzie and I are bored so we decide to write a collective poem to pass the time:

### "Sandstorm"

Big Bird flying across the sky
Drops some sandy poop in your eye

Yellow blizzards of frosting desert
Lost camels wandering in my head
If you're stuck in the desert you'll be dead

Sand in every orifice of your body
Silicon fragments of an expansive voyage
On the horizon lies the promise land: Agadez

Little red riding kid bares his extremities for the desert winds
Tea in the Sahel with you
Pouring libations for the desert

Rocking to and fro
In the cool desert snow
We sit idly waiting to know
Whether we'll be buried or if we'll ever go.

We'll be food for the camels
Yea, hurray, what a way to go
All we are is dust in the wind.

Damn! It is 9:30 AM and we are back in Aderbissinat because of the sandstorm. Abdu said this sandstorm is strong, and it should be over in a few hours (maybe). He thinks we will leave by about 2 PM. I heard that all the food in the village will be gritty for the next few days due to the blowing sand, and I have already had the chance to experience some crunchy bread myself. Half of the people get out of the bus, and we are waiting it out here in the bus with the other half.

11:30 AM—We are still sitting here, and now we are ready to go! All of the drivers get in their trucks, as does our bus driver. They start up their engines and honk to let the passengers know that we are going to leave shortly. "Hurrah!" we think, but I am slightly concerned at the same time, as the wind is still blowing and visibility is still low. Everyone piles into the bus and on top of the trucks. I sarcastically say to Suzie, "We should be leaving any hour now," and we both chuckle hoping that I am wrong. Unfortunately, I was right, because now it is 1:00 PM, and we are still here! It was a false alarm and we have not moved an inch! Many people got off the bus again. We are still sitting here on the bus, and I just came back from a short walk to keep from going crazy. I ask a gendarme why we have not left, and he says that the visibility is still bad, but they hope to leave today (if we're lucky). I am now covered from head to toe in very fine sand. My clothes and skin are caked with it. The wind has died down somewhat, but the visibility is still very poor.

3:20 PM—@#$%^&*!! We are still sitting on this damned, God-forsaken bus! The wind eased up hours ago, and it is quite clear now. Not long ago, we had another disappointing false alarm. All the drivers got in their trucks, started their engines, and honked their horns, All the people got in, but we didn't go anywhere! An argument ensued between the truck and bus drivers, and the gendarmes leading the military escort. It seems that the drivers did not want to go, and the escort did, but I am not quite sure. No one can tell us whether we will go today or not. We are all getting very frustrated. Why in the name of God can't we leave! I really have no idea, except that Africa is a place beyond my comprehension, constantly testing the limits of our patience.

The drivers, after arguing amongst themselves, and with the gendarmes for a few hours, finally decide that it is still too windy, and visibility is still too poor to depart. We get the final word at about 3:30 PM. We are pretty aggravated and disappointed, but at the same time, we are happy to get off the bus where we languished in cold, windy, sandy impatience for eight hours. I am grateful that they are concerned with our safety, as safety is seldom a concern in West Africa. I have heard news stories on the Radio France about convoys getting lost in the Sahara due to sandstorms, and the dead bodies of passengers were found several weeks later.

We all march back to the house where we stayed last night and we get cleaned up and relax. As usual, our hosts surprise us by the food they conjure up and the meal they prepare. We eat spaghetti with meat, carrots, tomatoes, and tea. After eating, we relax around the fire in front of the hut, talking and enjoying each other's company. The next morning, they make us stewed lamb and some really good bread. We are in a tiny village in the middle of the desert, and I have no idea where they find things such as carrots, bread, mattresses, eating utensils, mats, etc. It definitely helps being a local.

**March 4th, 1997: (On the Road to Agadez)** We get up at 6:30 and this morning it is crystal clear outside. There is no wind whatsoever. The calm after the storm always seems so peaceful and pristine, and it is much appreciated. Yesterday people said that the sandstorm could last days, and we were worried that we would be stuck here forever. I am relieved to see clear blue skies. It is 7:17 AM and we're off!! It is for real this time, I hope.

The landscape is quite remarkable, driving through a sea of drifting sand. When we left Aderbissinat, there was no wind and the sky was clear, but now that we are out some distance into the desert, the wind is picking up and the sand is starting to blow. We often turn off the dirt road because sand has drifted on it. The bus rocks back and forth, bumps up and down, and fishtails in the deep sand. But we never get stuck. Sometimes we can see nothing but sand in all directions. I see now why it is a good idea to travel in a caravan, not only for protection from rebels, but also in case of mechanical difficulties. If you are alone out here and you break down, you probably will not live to tell about it. Just contemplating that scenario makes this quite an exciting trip.

We finally pull into Agadez at 11:30 AM. We thank our Arab friends profusely, and say good-bye. We find a cheap hotel made of mud of course, for $8.00 a night, and we go off to explore the town. We research a guided camel trip into the Aïr Mountains. We find Agadez to be very interesting due to its unique mud architecture, and the impressive mud mosque in the center of town. We visit the *grand marché* (central market) and shop for some Tuareg crafts which are sold all over town, such as jewelry, knives, swords, leather pouches, and blankets. The people are friendly, but we can tell they are tourist starved because they never leave us alone. There is always someone following us, trying to talk to us and either sell us something or try to be our guide. We find if very odd when we see downhill skis and snowboards in front of some stores. We inquire about them, and we find out that tourists rent them for skiing down sand dunes in the desert farther north!

So far, Pam, Shefali, Suzie and I have been getting along and enjoying each other's company, but lately we are starting to get on each other's nerves. We have been travelling together for a long time now, but we know it will be for only a few more days. Pam and Shefali will be heading back to Togo. I am going to Ouagadougou in Burkina Faso, on my own, and Suzie will be heading back to Benin. Before we head back, our goal is to take a camel trip into the desert.

We find Tuareg guides to take us out for two days. We head out on a dry riverbed north of Agadez, and explore a few sedentary Tuareg villages. We are a little disappointed, because we thought we would be riding the camels on our own. In fact, our guides walk and guide the camels while we ride them, so we go very slowly. Nonetheless, it is a very interesting and new experience. The scenery of the Aïr Mountains is beautiful. We take a three-hour break for lunch, walk a few more miles, and set up camp on the riverbed. For dinner, they make us *"pain de sable"* (sand bread). At first it sounds paradoxical and inedible, but in fact it is delicious. They make a fire and then dig a hole. In the hole they put the hot coals from the fire, and then pour in a pasty mixture of semolina, the kind of wheat flour used to make pasta, and water. They cover the semolina and water mix with sand and let it cook. After 30 minutes they dig up a large sand covered dough ball. We were all very incredulous as to how this could possibly be edible. They let it cool and then remove the outer layer that is caked with sand. They then break apart the center, and we eat the balls of unleavened bread in a meat sauce. Surprisingly, the meal is sooooo . . . good. We are all very impressed at their resourcefulness, and how they are so well adapted to life in the desert. We would not last two days out here alone.

After dinner we sit around a fire and they tell us Tuareg stories under the stars, which are brighter than any I have ever seen. There is absolutely no light pollution here and the air is dry, so the sky is dazzling. It is the dry season, so they don't have tents for us. We go to sleep in the open air, enjoying the stars and fresh air.

On our last day in Agadez, we get together with Abdu, Mustapha, Mustaph, and Aïsha in their home to see them one last time before our 16 hour bush taxi ride back to Niamey. We take a different and more direct route back to Niamey. Luckily, the road is paved the whole way, and we have no mechanical breakdowns (only psychological ones), so we are able to make it back in one VERY long day. I know Pam, Shefali, Suzie and I will always remember the kindness that was offered to us, and the adventure we had on the road to Agadez. This trip made me realize that the joy of traveling in West Africa is as much, if not more, the adventure of getting to your destination and who you meet along the way, than the destination itself.

# STORIES FROM BENIN:

## Adapting to Life in Benin:

### My Social Life in Benin

Because there is no priority placed on efficiency and professionalism in Benin, every encounter with people is social. Life in Benin is very social in almost any situation, so obviously there is no distinction between one's "work life" and one's "social life." Whenever I went into town to do errands, it took me forever because everyone was so friendly, and they expected me to talk to them. They loved to chat, joke, and laugh with me. One afternoon I went into town to do a few simple errands, but it took two hours because I had to socialize with so many people. I first went to the electronics repair shop to get my desk light fixed. The owner wasn't in his shop, so I went ahead and returned my bottles to the beverage depot. Of course no one was there, so I had to come back later. I stopped by my postmate's house. He wasn't home. I stopped by the bank to get some money, and ended up talking with a person while I waited. I then went to the CARDER office to talk to my counterpart about work related matters. Then I bumped into Jean, the new French Jehovah's Witness missionary, and chatted with him for a while. I went to buy flour at the boutique, and I chatted with Cirafin, the clerk who I was friendly with. While I was there, I flirted with the cute hairdressers that worked next door. I then stopped to buy some peanut brittle from Ferdinand across the street, and we chatted a little in Fon. As I was riding by the bar called "La Détente," Sylveste called me in. Marius, a person who I was working with, left me a message with Sylveste saying he had to cancel an appointment. Sylveste took the opportunity to ask me why I hadn't been stopping by to say "hi" to him, or why I hadn't at least waved to him as I often rode my bike by the open doorway to the bar. I promised him that from then on I would yell "Salut, Sylveste," as I was passing by on my bike, and I would try to stop in to talk from time to time. The head of the CLCAM bank and his friend who were both sitting at the bar, started talking to me, so we chatted for a few minutes.

After leaving I bumped into a Beninese friend and we spoke for a few minutes. I then went back to the beverage depot to drop off my empties and pick up a new case of soda. On my way back, I saw my neighbor sitting out in front of his shoe repair workshop, and he waved me down so we could chat a little. Then I bought some bread from the bread seller who sat on the side of the road, and she made some smalltalk with me in Fon. I went back to the electronics repairman to get my desk lamp fixed. Luckily he was there, and I chatted with him a little. On my way home, I ran into my postmate, and we spoke a little.

The funny thing was whenever I was riding my bike from place to place, people were constantly calling out my Beninese name, "Gandaho," or my French name, "Christophe," calling me "*Yovo*," or just hissing to get my attention because they had nothing better to do. They probably wanted to chat with the white guy (surprise!) and probably wanted to ask me for a *cadeau* (present). If I had stopped to talk to everyone who was calling me, I wouldn't have returned home until midnight, and I ultimately would have accomplished nothing! All of this socializing was very tiring. I felt like a celebrity because I was always being pestered and given so much attention. I took advantage of it and flirted with the cute girls, spoke Fon whenever I could to practice, and had some laughs. I talked to everyone, as long as I was in the mood, and if I had the time and energy. If I had not taken the time to speak to at least the people I saw on a regular basis, they most certainly would have found me aloof. Besides, my days were never so busy that I didn't appreciate socializing to kill time. I guess they felt the same way, and that was why they were so eager to chat. Had I been in a hurry, I would have been frustrated by the constant expectation to socialize.

## Peace Corps Psychovac Legends

Being a Peace Corps Volunteer is supremely difficult, and we endure many hardships over our two years away from the comforts of the United States. We are usually sent to poor countries, and we are given a living allowance that is only enough to support a standard of living on par with the local people ($6 a day for Benin PCV's). We endure relative poverty, culture shock, homesickness, cultural isolation, health problems, major climate changes, linguistic barriers, eating food we're not used to, and living in less than luxurious conditions, just to name a few. In fact, it is so difficult that some volunteers lose their psychological fortitude (i.e., they "lose it").

Legends abound about these people among Peace Corps Volunteers, which are passed on to new volunteers in the traditional African manner of story telling. Usually these stories are told at Peace Corps Volunteer gatherings over several beers, and I doubt they have more than a grain of truth to them, which is I why I call them "legends."

"Psychovac" is an informal term that means a volunteer must be evacuated (i.e., sent home) due to psychological or emotional distress. I have heard three legends about three infamous PCV psycho-evacuees, each from different sources. I wouldn't be surprised if the same stories are told from the Philippines, to Benin, to Mongolia.

The first story was about a PCV who made donuts. Lots and lots of donuts. She kept making more and more. She made many more donuts than she could eat, so she hung them on strings from the ceiling around her house.

Another legend was about a volunteer who put a sock on his hand, and communicated solely through his hand puppet. As legend has it, the villagers didn't think anything of it, and thought that was what all Americans did.

The last legend was about a hapless PCV who was in his latrine when the floor collapsed under him. He was trapped in a soup of excrement for days, until he was finally discovered and pulled out of the muck.

## Playing Doctor

Peace Corps gives all the volunteers a first aid kit in a big blue plastic box, and a few hours of basic first aid training. It was necessary, as healthcare was very sparse, and where it was available, it was almost always very primitive at best. The kit contained all sorts of first aid items. If we were not able to make it down to Cotonou in case of a serious emergency and we needed to get injections at a local hospital, it also contained rubber gloves, hypodermic needles, and syringes. They were put in the kit because hospitals in Benin had a reputation for cleaning hypodermic needles and syringes and reusing them! The kit is intended for the volunteers only, and we were told not to tell anyone we had it, but somehow my neighbors knew to come see me when they had a problem. Sometimes I felt like I was playing doctor, despite that fact that I had virtually no medical training. My neighbor Felix came over once with an infected wound on his finger. I had him soak it in iodine, and I re-bandaged it for him a few days in a row. Luckily it healed soon after, and he was extremely grateful. It is sad to think that a simple cut like that could have become dangerously infected because he could not afford iodine and bandages. He also did not have the basic medical knowledge to know how to prevent a simple infection.

Oftentimes I would give the children band-aids for cuts and scrapes. I felt very sorry when my neighbors came to me with more serious health problems but I couldn't do anything for them. Sometimes I gave them money, but I was afraid that I would create more dependence, and they would start coming to me for money every time they got a sniffle, bump, or ache. I worried they would even fabricate illnesses to get me to give them money. When it was more than a cut or scrape, I had to tell them to go to the doctor in town. Sometimes they got toothaches, but as far as I knew, there was no dentist in the area.

## Electricity in the Bush

I loved where I lived during my two years of service because my house was located on a remote bush path across from a housing compound where at least 40 people lived. I felt like I was living in a typical African village, but I was only 2 km away from the town of Allada, where I could get a lot of products and services not available in a village, so I had the best of both worlds. To get to my house, I had to ride my bike 1 km from the center of Allada on a dirt road, and then another kilometer down a narrow dirt bush path. It was surrounded by corn and pineapple fields and large expanses of extremely thick vegetation.

Because I was 1 km from the dirt road, I was just out of reach of the power company. My only choice was to get the electricity informally from my landlord's house who lived on the dirt road at the end of the bush path. This was not my idea, as the volunteer who lived in my house before me had obtained electricity this way, and my landlord suggested that I do the same since there was still a separate electric meter there just for my house. I was lucky because my landlord still had the wire that my predecessor used, and most of the support poles were still in place. The landlord had taken the wire down, because he was afraid someone would steal it, as my predecessor had been gone for over a year before I arrived. I had to pay an electrician to install wire to carry the electricity the 1 km from my landlord's house. Getting electricity connected to my house and maintaining it was a major task.

When I first got to post, I found an electrician who would run the wire from my landlord's house to my house. At that time, The Peace Corps was providing volunteers with refrigerators, and I asked the electrician if he was sure that the wire would carry enough current make it run properly. He assured me that if I bought some new wire, it would work fine. "No problem, not to worry," he confidently told me, so I paid him about 20,000 CFA ($40 USD) to go to Cotonou to buy a roll of wire to add to the existing wire. The problem with the wire that I had was that it was a collection of pieces that varied in thickness and quality, and they were all spliced together. I was a little leery, because he said that with the money I gave him, he could buy a few hundred meters of wire, and that would be just enough to ensure that the refrigerator would work. I figured that if only a portion of the wire was thick enough, the rest of the thinner wire would prevent enough power from getting to my house. He assured me that this was not the case, and because I did not have enough money to buy a thousand meters of new wire, I had no choice but to trust him.

He said he would have everything hooked up in a week or so. I waited and waited and waited. I got very frustrated because I did not want to keep using kerosene lanterns at night, as they were inconvenient, they smelled, and they put out a lot of heat. It was also very frustrating having a fan sitting in my bedroom that didn't work while I was sweating to death, and the refrigerator was sitting idle in the kitchen. I had to go to his house on several occasions to find out what was taking him so long. Each time I did, I either could not find him, or he had a different excuse as to why he had not been able to do the work. Ultimately, it took him a month before he was able to string the wire up on the poles along the side of the bush path and connect it to my house.

When he finally finished the job, I was excited to get the refrigerator working. However, when I turned it on for the first time, the light in my kitchen grew very dim, and I could tell that the refrigerator was not working. Crap!! I was furious at the electrician, because he swore up and down that it would work and I had just spent 20,000 CFA for nothing! Obviously there was not enough power getting to my house to make the refrigerator work, and I didn't want to spend a ton of money to buy 800 more meters of wire. I was very lucky, however, because my postmate, who lived in the center of town, had the luxury of electricity provided directly by the SBEE power company. By chance he had a kerosene powered refrigerator. I hadn't asked the Peace Corps for a kerosene powered refrigerator because I thought that I would have electricity, and by now it was too late to get a kerosene powered one from them. My postmate was nice enough to swap with me. In return, he had the luxury of not having to buy kerosene, fill the tank, and keep the wick adjusted. I on the other hand, was very grateful just to have a working refrigerator.

As you can imagine, relying on 1 km of old spliced wires strung along wooden poles in the ground was problematic. Over the two years that I lived in Benin, I had 12 power outages due to wire problems! On average, that worked out to an outage every two months. The first time the wire shorted out, it took me three days to get the electrician to fix it. The second time, it was another short circuit, and it took me two days. The third time, the outage occurred after a strong thunderstorm, and the roof of an adjacent house blew off, cutting the wire. It took me a week to get it fixed that time. The fourth time a wall collapsed from the same house whose roof had blown off, and it cut my wire again. That was when I learned how to fix the wire myself. The fifth time a tall truck backed under the wire and broke it. The sixth time one of the poles fell. The seventh time someone lit a brush fire under the wire and melted it. The eighth time mice chewed through the wire in my ceiling while I was on vacation. The ninth time the circuit breaker tripped. The tenth time, a screw came loose in the fuse at my landlord's house. The eleventh time the wires shorted out once again, and the twelfth time lightening shorted out the wire. Arrgghh! I was not able to fix it myself every time, and when I needed the electrician, it took him at least a few days to come and fix the problem. As you can imagine, I found the constant outages very annoying, and it was better I had a kerosene refrigerator because it kept working even when the power was out.

Besides the outage problems, my electricity had some other peculiarities. The amount of power that was getting to my house was so low that when I had more than one light turned on, and then I turned my boom box up loud, the light would flicker with the beat of the music. I think this was because the radio drew more power during the drumbeats. Another scary symptom of this shoddy electrical hook up was that whenever there was a lightening strike nearby, blue sparks would fly out of my wall sockets! I had a feeling the entire hook-up was not grounded properly. I should have known better, but one time I was listening to music with headphones during a thunderstorm, and I got a shock in my ear! I had termites eating the thin wood poles holding up the wire, and I wondered if they would need to be replaced before I left. Luckily they held out. The last thing I had to worry about was the vines and brush growing alongside the lines, and I had to trim them back a few times.

During my two years, I did have electricity most of the time, but it came at the price of a lot of aggravation. I was very grateful for the two florescent lights and four light bulbs I had. The only appliances I used where my radio and my fan; ahh, my beloved fan. I would have given an arm or leg for it had someone tried to take it away from me, as it got me through many sweltering days and nights. I was lucky because many volunteers in Benin didn't have electricity or the luxury of a fan. Sometimes they slept outside during the hotter months, as it was so hot in their houses that candles would warp! When I got home to the U.S., I felt very relieved knowing that when I turned on a light, I could rest assured that it would work and stay on.

## Allada has a Library!?

I had been living in Allada for over a year, when I discovered by chance that there was a library in Allada! I found out about it by asking in the town hall. It really aggravated me because I would have taken advantage of it much sooner. I didn't feel so bad though because my postmate, the "*doyen*" (the experienced one) who had been here two and a half years, and claimed to know everything, did not even know it was there. The most annoying fact was that it was right under my nose, and I passed it every day! There was no sign at all, and looking at the building, it was not evident that it was a library. When I first got here, I asked a few people if there was a library near by, and everyone said "no." Since I never saw a library nor heard anyone talking about it, I assumed that there wasn't one. Nestor, my Beninese friend, who was in high school, knew about it, but he had not been there. It was very small, and there were books on Vodun, so I was very excited. It was sad that most people in Allada could not read, and the ones who could, did not. The fact that this library was right under my nose while I had been buying expensive books in Cotonou bookstores on Vodun was annoying.

At the town hall they told me that the library "should have been open" from 9 am to 11:30 am, and from 2 pm to 5 pm on Monday, Tuesday and Thursday. I kept track, and for a week I saw that the library was closed when it should have been open on four different occasions. It wasn't until the second week of checking that I finally found it open. Evidently the caretaker showed up only when he felt like it, and the sad thing was that he could barely read himself.

He told me that the library was funded by La Cooperation Française (a French NGO), and not by the Beninese. The building was built with American funding and the Cooperation Française furnished the books. However, the maintenance was the responsibility of the community.

In order to take books out, one had to pay a small membership fee. Adults paid 1,000 F each (about 2$ USD), and students only had to pay 200 F (about 40 cents) for a yearly membership. Since there were only three adults signed up, and less than a dozen students, there was no money to buy a sign indicating that it was a library, or to even pay the electric bills. As a result, the electricity was shut off. There were four or five shelves of books and a reading room. There were 20-25 copies of student textbooks and a few big piles of magazines. There were also books about Vodun, history books on Benin, France, and Haiti, as well as some works of French literature. The selection was definitely limited, but offered enough to make the library a valuable resource.

The caretaker told me that he suspended the borrowing privileges for most students, and teachers, because they often did not return books they borrowed. He only lent books to people he knew personally and trusted. He gave magazines to the high school students who weeded around the walkway to the building, since there was no money to pay someone to do it. There was no bathroom or a latrine in the library either. He said that he was going on vacation in August, so the library would be closed all month. I could not help feeling sad about the state of this library and about how little anyone seemed to care about it. It was a clear indication of the dismally low literacy rate here.

## Life in an Information Vacuum

In the West people must deal with information overload. In Benin the opposite was true, and there was an "information vacuum," Because so few people could read or write in Benin, putting posters up to inform the public of events, or publishing them in a newspaper was very uncommon in small towns, and unheard of in villages. In their place, people who needed to make public announcements paid a *crieur publique*, or a public crier. He was also called a *gongonneur*, which literally means "bell ringer" because he walked around from neighborhood to neighborhood tapping on a cowbell before yelling out his announcement.

For me it was paradoxical that I could get information on what was going on in the U.S. or in the Middle East on my short wave radio much faster than I could get information about what was going on in Benin. One example was when I heard about the bombing at the Atlanta Olympics in 1996 before my mom in Connecticut did. It happened after she went to bed, but since Benin is six hours ahead of Eastern Standard Time, I heard about it on my short wave radio in the morning before she had woken up. When I spoke to her on the phone that day day, she told me about it and was surprised that I already knew.

Local news was very slow to travel in Benin. For example, a gas tanker truck blew up only a few miles from my town and killed several people. My neighbors and I didn't hear about it until several days later. There were no local radio stations or local newspapers. The only newspapers were from Cotonou and other big cities, so they did not cover local news. Even if there were a newspaper there, it would not have done very well, since so few Beninese are literate, and so few can even afford such a non-essential expense. The result was that most news traveled by word of mouth, by public criers, and occasionally by posters or large banners announcing a significant event.

Since almost no one had a phone, I usually had to show up at people's homes unannounced. The result was that I rarely found the person on my first attempt, and I had to leave messages, either oral or written, depending on whether the recipient was literate. If I made an appointment to meet someone, and I needed to change my plans, I had to go through the same process to inform them that I wasn't coming. Growing up I was always taught that being reliable is a very important quality, and that you must do what you say you will do, such as showing up on time for meetings. At first I went out of my way to tell people I wasn't going to make a meeting if something else came up, but after being stood up so many times myself, I eventually lost my desire to do so. This is just another example of how I adapted to the local culture, and adjusted my values to the realities of my environment.

The fact that there was a library in my town, and I found it after being there a year, is a perfect example of how little information was disseminated in Benin. Few people had a T.V. and there was only one Beninese T.V. station. It broadcasted only from 5 pm to midnight, so it was not a sure way to communicate to the Beninese public. Radio was the predominant way that people received news. Even so, there were only a few radio stations that broadcasted out of the bigger cities, and they broadcasted primarily in French. For the many people who didn't speak French, they had broadcasts in local languages, but they were for only a few hours a day.

There was very little statistical information available about Benin such as divorce rates, suicide rates, crime rates, inflation, growth of the economy, consumer spending, etc. that we are so accustomed to hearing, because there were few agencies to collect, analyze and disseminate that information. In short, information, and especially reliable information, was very hard to come by in Benin.

## Botched Haircuts

Since I was one of only four or five white people living in a town of 10,000, I had no choice but to get my hair cut by barbers who had never cut a white man's hair before. Considering how different white and black people's hair is, I was not surprised that the first few haircuts I received were terrible. I made sure to go to the same barber so he would learn, and after a few attempts, I was getting pretty good haircuts for about 75 cents including the tip.

## Skiing in Benin

Of course skiing is impossible in Benin, but so is trying to get the average Beninese person to understand what it is. How do you explain what skiing is to someone who thinks frigid is 70 degrees, and the only time they've seen ice is when they bought it to put in a drink? How do you explain what a mountain is when the tallest thing they have ever seen is a hill a few hundred feet high that's only a few kilometers away? How do you explain what snow is when the only thing they've ever seen fall from the sky is rain? Strapping boards to your feet? Ski lifts? All of this . . . for sport and enjoyment? Believe me, explaining the concept of skiing to a Beninese person is not an easy task!

## Dropping the Fan Milk Man

I am an avid road cyclist have ridden as much as 105 miles in day, and when I was racing, I rode as much as 5,000 miles in a year. I like to think that I can ride pretty fast. In Benin Peace Corps gave all volunteers a fairly nice Trek mountain bike to use to get around since we didn't have a motorcycle or a car. It was so hot in Benin that I couldn't really enjoy riding for exercise, so I was a little out of shape. I was still riding a lot for transportation purposes, so I thought that I was fast by Beninese standards.

One day I was riding down the paved road returning from a village where I was working, and I passed a Fan Milk man. Fan Milk is a brand of ice cream, and men would sell it from their specially made bicycles that had a large cooler welded to the front of the bike. They traveled from village to village, and this particular Fan Milk Man must have been returning to Allada from a day's work at the Ouegbo market, about five miles north. With a cooler full of ice cream, his bike probably weighed three or four times as much as my bike did, so I was sure that when I passed him, I would look back and he would be way behind. However, a minute or two after I passed him, I looked back and he was right on my wheel! I couldn't believe it! I proceeded to ride harder, and a few minutes later when I was sure that he had tired out and was way behind, he was still hanging on! I was dumbfounded!

I had a fairly light mountain bike with 18 speeds, and his bike had one speed and weighed a ton. I was wearing thick soled shoes with toe clips on the pedals. He was wearing flip flops. I rode even harder until my legs were screaming, and I was breathing as hard as I could. It took me about two miles before I dropped him (i.e. I opened a gap between him and me), but by that time I was almost to Allada. When I got to Allada, he was still close behind. I figured he must have sold all his ice cream and his cooler was empty, so his bike probably was not that heavy (which was really just wishful thinking). I stopped to tell him how impressed I was that he was able to ride so fast with such a heavy bike. I looked in the cooler hoping to see it empty, but it was not! It was still a quarter full, and I felt like a real loser. The reality is that the Beninese are very fit because they eat very low calorie, low fat diets. They get a lot of exercise walking, riding heavy bicycles if they can afford one, and doing household chores such as fetching water, carrying food home from the markets, and of course working in the fields with only hand tools. Although there have been few African cyclists in the Tour de France, I bet the Fan Milk man would have been a good candidate. Unfortunately, very few Beninese have the resources to get involved in cycling, as it is an expensive sport. As for me, I felt humbled and I gained a greater respect for the physical strength that the average Beninese person must exert every day just to survive.

The Fan Milk man and his bike.

## Feeding Frenzy in my House

Rule of thumb—If you invite Beninese villagers to your house, DO NOT have a buffet or self service. After I got settled into my house in Allada, I threw a house warming party. I invited about 20 of my neighbors over for popcorn, beer, and some cookies that I made. When I brought the food into the living room, and put it down in front of them, I couldn't believe what I saw. They started pushing and shoving each other and they started grabbing the food as fast as they could. I swear they ate everything in less than ten minutes, and after about 30 minutes they left. I had several parties at my house, but after that, they were all outside, and I let my neighbors cook and distribute the food according to their traditions. The women would always serve everyone, and there were no feeding frenzies, because everyone knew that they would get their share without a fight.

## "Fun" with Beninese Banking

**Piggybanks:** I was at a seminar for different types of savings and loan organizations, both traditional and modern. They gathered to discuss how to get the Beninese to save more money, to invest more, and to encourage banks to make loans to small businesses as a way to promote economic development in Benin. Present was a small manufacturer of clay piggybanks because he too played a role in encouraging the Beninese to save money. Also present was a representative from CLCAM (the most prominent savings and loan bank in Benin). I thought it was hilarious when the representative from CLCAM got defensive in a conversation with the piggybank manufacturer because he felt that piggybanks would be a threat to his business! The sad part was that he may have been right!

**Getting a Loan in Benin:** An organization named CBIDIBA runs a traditional savings and loan organization for women only. They make micro loans to its members. The way it worked was that the members paid a contribution every week of about 200 CFA (about 40 cents) that went into a general pool of money, and each contributor had a book showing how much she contributed. When enough money was collected, each woman could apply for a loan. The loan had to be for an income generating activity. An executive committee decided if the plan the applicant proposed was acceptable for receiving a loan. This type of micro finance organization is also called a "tontine." The sad thing about this organization was that in order for a woman to get a loan, she had to be on good terms with her husband! This was because CIBADIBA knew that the husband could sabotage the woman's plans for using the money, and if he did, she would not be able to pay the loan back. Therefore, in order to prove that the woman was on good terms with her husband, she needed her husband's approval and she needed someone who knew her to attest that she was indeed getting along with him!

**The Change Game Revisited**: I once went to a CLCAM bank and asked them for change for a 5,000 CFA note (about $10), and they told me that they didn't have change! I knew that was not true, and I had to beg and plead. They finally gave in. Can you imagine that happening in the U.S.?

**Piles of Cash**: Because the banking system was so primitive in Benin, I had to rely heavily on cash for all financial transactions. I could not use a credit card unless I was staying in the best hotel in Cotonou (which never happened), and almost no one accepted checks. On many occasions when I was in the bank in Cotonou, I saw business owners walk into the bank and deposit stacks of cash ten inches high and worth the equivalent of thousands of U.S. dollars. In the U.S., the police would probably investigate for drug dealing or other illegal activities. In Benin this practice was perfectly normal.

When I was a volunteer, the Peace Corps paid my living allowance every three months. It was only $600, but that was a very large sum of money in Benin. Even in the U.S., I never have that much cash on hand. I had to withdraw the entire $600 at once so I could bring the money to my bank in Allada. I did not want to have to make a trip to Cotonou every time I needed money because there were, of course, no ATM's. The problem was that the bank in Cotonou couldn't wire the money to my bank in Allada. I also could not write a check from the bank in Cotonou to the bank in Allada, because practically no one accepted checks, including my bank! My only choice was to carry $600 cash from Cotonou to my bank every three months. I always felt uncomfortable doing it, but luckily, I was never robbed and I never lost it.

**The Money Changer:** One day I was doing some shopping at Dantokpa, the huge outdoor market in Cotonou. The market was fascinating because of its sheer enormity and because there were so many different products sold there. Every section of the market specialized in a certain product. For example, all the cloth sellers were situated in one section, all the radio sellers in another, the sellers of cooking utensils in another, etc. Because Benin is close to Nigeria, there were a lot of people who came to Benin from Nigeria to buy and sell goods. Nigerians use the Naira currency, and the Beninese use the CFA, so the money must be converted. In one section of the market, the moneychangers sat on benches with huge stacks of money and a calculator ready to make a currency exchange for a fee. As I was walking by them, they hissed at me trying to get my attention in hopes that I would need to convert some money. I was amazed at the large stack of money he had that must have been eight inches high, so I went over to him and asked him how things were going. I asked if I could look at the money. I knew the Nigerian Naira wasn't worth a lot, but a stack of money that large must have been worth a small fortune. He handed the stack to me to look at it, and I thought I would play a joke on him by slowly walking away with it to see how he reacted. I walked away slowly and maintained eye contact to see how far I could go before he made a move. I kept walking, and walking, and walking, until he was almost out of sight. He did not even flinch! I didn't want him to accuse me of stealing, so before he was out of my sight I returned the money to him. I could not believe that he let me get that far so I asked him why. His response was, "White people don't steal!" His attitude was common in Benin, because the only white people that are in West Africa are missionaries, international aid agency workers, and embassy employees, so we have a solid reputation. Walking away with a stack of cash was certainly proof of that!

**Lack of Confidentiality:** In Benin street food is ubiquitous. Women, and sometimes men, set up small tables on the side of the road and sell all types of hot and cold food to passers by. In Cotonou, the capital city, one woman sold sandwiches near an open sewer, so we Peace Corps Volunteers called her outfit "Sewer Sandwiches." One day I got a sewer sandwich, and I found that the wrapping she handed me my sandwich in was an internal bank statement from the bank across the street! The statement had a list of local businesses, amounts that they deposited, and their account balances! I recognized the names of many of the businesses, because they were restaurants, stores, and hotels that I had frequented! I guess the bank could not afford a shredder, and the sewer sandwich lady found the bank's garbage can a good source of food wrapping paper. Perhaps she ran out of cement bags or discarded school papers to use that food sellers often used.

## Meeting the King of Allada

**November 11<sup>th</sup>, 1995** Today we are meeting the King of Allada in the small village of Togudo, about one km from Allada. We are on an excursion as part of our Peace Corps pre-training. I am here with the seven other trainees in my group, a few current volunteers, and a few Peace Corps trainers, so we are a group of about 13. We arrive at the palace at about 10 am, and we are told that the king is not ready to see us yet and that we have to wait outside. We wait at least two hours outside the Royal Palace before we are even let in! It seems odd to me that they make us wait so long because they knew that we were coming. Perhaps the king is concerned that if he does not make us wait, we will think that he is not busy, and therefore not important. I suppose the waiting creates suspense, as well.

The palace is a compound of mud huts with tin roofs surrounded by a high mud wall. The buildings have a layer of cement over the mud to make it look nicer as is commonly done in Benin. The outside is nicely painted and decorated with the symbols of the past kings of Allada. When the king is ready to see us, one of the king's servants takes us through the entrance vestibule that leads into the compound. We pass several small mud huts as we walk over the dirt courtyard until we arrive at the room where the King, Kpodegbe Toyi Djigla, receives his guests. From the looks of his accommodations, it seems as if he is living a more or less traditional lifestyle, probably very much like the previous kings of long ago, except he has electricity and a car. His job as king of the Allada Kingdom is essentially to preserve tradition, so his living conditions are very appropriate.

We are led into a small room that is decorated simply with pictures of previous kings. There are straw mats on the floor. Before entering the room we have to take our shoes off. We sit down on the mats in front of a large wooden chair with thick cushions. We wait another 20 minutes until some of the king's servants bring us all soft drinks. Ten minutes later they tell us to hurry up and finish our drinks because the king is now ready to enter. Before he enters, we are told that it is customary for men and women to remove their shirts when in the presence of the king. As we are Yovos, the king will make an exception. There are at least a dozen Beninese men among us and they all have their shirts removed. As the king makes his entrance, everyone bows down from their sitting position on the floor, touching their foreheads to the ground as a sign of deference. We Yovos are not sure what to do, so we just do as everyone else does and we bow down as well.

The king is very well dressed in a black robe and pants made of expensive looking velvet, embossed with gold designs. He carries two elaborate scepters and wears traditional African necklaces and bracelets. He speaks French very well with an affected tone, but considering his status, I suppose his demeanor is appropriate. On one side, he has a woman fanning him, and on the other side, a woman is holding a colorful umbrella over his head. When he is outside, an umbrella makes sense to shield him from the hot sun and rain. Considering we are indoors, the umbrella is merely a symbol of his importance.

He greets us and then he asks if we have any questions for him. I ask him what his role is as king. He explains that he is responsible for the upkeep of the Vodun traditions and morals because he is a messenger of God. He explains how he can have up to 500 wives if he so desires, but he has less than 20, so as not to be ostentatious. He then explains how he is very busy preparing for an important festival and how lucky we are that he has made time for us. He says that before leaving he will bless us. We are then instructed to come and hold his scepter while one of his servants chants blessings. The 20 of us on our knees in a semi-circle, all trying to hold on to his scepter, creates somewhat of a pig pile, and becomes uncomfortable very quickly. He does the blessing in Fon so I do not understand it. It goes on for at least five minutes and after each blessing, we all respond "*Eda.*" I start getting cramps in my arms and we are all trying hard not to laugh. I have the misfortune of being at the bottom of the pile and it is very hot and uncomfortable. When it is finally over, and we are finally excused from the huddle, we all gasp for air and let out a sigh of relief.

After the blessing ceremony, the king calls us up individually to be touched on the back of our head with his scepter to grant us each an additional blessing. He then invites us to take a group photo. Before we leave, our Peace Corps trainers, who are Beninese, and therefore know the customs, give an envelope with 2,500 CFA (about $5 USD) to the king's servants and another envelope for the king with 10,000 CFA (about $20 USD). We all bow down, touching our foreheads to the ground as the king exits the room.

After training was over, I met the king a few more times at traditional ceremonies, and he was always in full regalia surrounded by pomp and circumstance, as well as a full entourage of servants. He is truly a sight to see.

## It's a Small World

I was in a small village in the middle of nowhere. I had to ride on the back of a motorcycle for 45 minutes on narrow, remote, dirt bush paths to get here. There were no signs of Western civilization such as electricity, telephones, or modern construction anywhere. There were just mud huts and thick bush. I felt like I was truly in the depths of Africa when a villager handed me a Watchtower publication in French! He was a Jehovah's Witness spreading the word. He then tried to get me to attend one of their services! It was then that I realized that there is no escaping Western influence, no matter where you are in the world!

Another experience that reminded me of the pervasiveness of Western culture was when I was in a similar small remote village as I described above. I went out to the village to work with a farming cooperative and one of the members invited me into his hut while I was waiting for the other members to arrive. He happened to have his radio on. Immediately, I noticed the station was playing a Michael Bolton song! Like Michael Bolton, I am from Connecticut, and it was funny because he had spoken at my graduation ceremony at UCONN just a few months prior!

As I described in "Market Day in Allada," I often saw people wearing T-shirts from the U.S. Seeing the Beninese wearing college fraternity T-shirts, Michael Jordan T-shirts, Levis, American sports team T-shirts and the like on a regular basis also reminded me of the influence of the U.S. here.

## "Professionalism" in Benin

So many times I felt that even the professionals in Benin were amateurs. However, I cannot really blame them, as they are all working with very limited resources. They cannot afford to produce quality work and usually their customers cannot afford to pay for it. Some workers not only lack materials, tools, and parts, but they also lack the training to do the job correctly.

For example, I paid a mason to cement my patio floor. When I got home, the patio floor was cemented, but there were goat hoof prints all over it! He didn't have any temporary fencing to put up around it to prevent the neighbor's goats from walking on it, even if he knew that this could happen. Another example was when I paid my neighbor to put a straw roof over my patio, and he swore that it would be waterproof. It turned out that it was not waterproof after all because the pitch was not steep enough. I had a carpenter make me some furniture, and the handles soon fell off the drawers. I bought a cheap radio, and it broke within months. I had it fixed in town by a repairman, but the same problem kept occurring because he did not have the proper parts to fix it correctly. If I did really want him to fix it correctly, I would have had to pay his transportation costs to go to Cotonou and look all over to get the right parts. The radio was so cheap that it wasn't worth it for me to spend the money. Another time I had my ceiling white washed. The ceiling flaked white dust when it was dry out, and when it was humid, the white became semitransparent. I could have had it painted, but paint was too expensive. I had numerous problems with my electricity and electrician, as I described above. I also found that mechanics cannot fix cars properly, because they do not have the proper tools or parts, which results in frequent breakdowns.

## Urban Planning Woes

In Cotonou they had been working for months building a new brick sidewalk down one of the main avenues. Only a week after it was done, numerous vendors, parked taxis, and people selling a myriad of goods crowded the sidewalk so badly that the pedestrians had to walk in the street, just as they did before the sidewalk was improved! These people had operated on the sidewalk before when it was only dirt, so the fact that it was paved in brick didn't bother them one bit! It was too bad for the pedestrians.

There were very few paved roads in Cotonou. Before I left they paved several streets near the Peace Corps office, which also happened to be in the middle of the red light district. Sadly, only months after the streets were paved, they became covered in sand from the side streets that were not paved.

## Should I Send My Wife Away?

Often the Beninese have very large families, despite the fact that they cannot afford them. When I was teaching small business development skills to a farming cooperative, I was trying to explain that one way to have more money is to have fewer children. Someone then asked, "How do you have less kids?" I explained what condoms were, as some had never heard of them before. In Benin, polygamy is fairly common, so I addressed the men saying that having only one wife is a way to save money too.

An old man who was usually very quiet put up his hand and said, "I've got three wives, does that mean I should send two away?" I replied through my interpreter, "No, of course not. It's too late, you've got to take care of all of them." Suddenly all 20 women in the room roared with delight. They jumped out of their seats screaming, and ran up to me to shake my hand vigorously and thanked me for what I had just said. They were so happy and surprised a man would actually stick up for them, especially a white guy, which is a strong endorsement for their side. The Beninese men have a habit of mistreating their women, and because of polygamy many women are neglected.

## Is There Romantic Love in Benin?

One day Vivino, the mother of Vivi, was yelling and screaming to absolutely no one in particular in front of her house. I was in my house several hundred feet away making lunch when I heard all the commotion. She was hysterical and she was ranting, raving, and waving her fists in the air. There were some children nearby who were laughing at her. I could not understand a word she said because it was all in Fon, and she was speaking so quickly. Obviously she was very angry. I could tell that she was airing her anger publicly, and looking for pity and compassion from anyone in an earshot as the Beninese often do. She went on for at least ten minutes, and I was very curious why she was acting this way.

After she settled down, I asked some of my neighbors what all the brouhaha was about. They told me that her husband recently took on a second wife and Vivino was extremely jealous. She was insulting the woman and her family who she had never met. This did not stop Pierre, her husband, from taking on his second wife. In most polygamist households, all of the wives live in the same housing compound, but they each have separate huts where they care for their own children. In this case, due to Vivino's strong character and resulting tirade, Pierre had to build the new wife a house away from the compound and close to town to keep her away from Vivino.

I observed that male-female relationships in Benin differ much from those in more developed countries. Since I lived in a rural village setting and near a medium sized town, my observations were based on very traditional relationships of mostly uneducated people. I did not observe romance between couples and wondered if it is luxury that requires a certain level of wealth. Women in Benin are much less empowered than women in the West. They are more dependent on men and are subservient to them. It seems when a woman looks for a mate in Benin, finding a man who can provide for her and her children is paramount. Romantic feelings are second, or even a distant third priority.

It is possible that men and women in rural settings are romantic toward each other, but I never saw or heard of it. I never saw any public display of affection among couples, not even handholding. I never saw men give their wives special gifts or do anything special just to please them. However, I have heard that men occasionally buy their wives fabric so they can have clothing made or the men give gifts to their in-laws.

In general, having children is very important for both men and women and is crucial to any marriage. Childless couples by choice in Benin are almost unheard of. If a couple is barren, the woman is usually blamed, and she is shunned. In fact, one of my neighbors, the wife of Antoine, was unable to have a baby, and the rest of the family ostracized her. They made fun of her so much that she decided to leave, and Antoine had to build her a house in another part of town.

In Benin, the men tend to be very sexist and often have many mistresses on the side. It is so common that it is called "having a second office." If you are a healthy married man, and you don't have a few girlfriends on the side, you would probably be considered weird, or even undesirable. One exception is men who are devout Christians. Christianity teaches that infidelity is a sin, so some Christian men follow this teaching, but by no means is it the norm. On the other hand, a woman who cheats on her husband would probably be beaten and severely punished, if not sent back to her parents, the equivalent of divorce.

Traditionally men rarely help with household chores or with raising the children. The men's job is to work in the fields to produce food for the family and take care of the animals. Women take care of the children and do all the food preparation. They also have to earn money by buying and reselling goods in the markets. They sometimes produce cottage industry goods such as palm oil, soap and other food items.

It seemed to me that men and women aren't really friends, but are more domestic partners. For friendship, they turn to family and friends of the same sex. I have also never heard of platonic relationships between men and women. If a man is "friends" with a woman, then sex will be part of that "friendship." For that reason Peace Corps made it clear that female volunteers should never invite a Beninese male to her house alone or he will certainly get the wrong idea.

Dowries are an essential part of a traditional marriage. Before a man can take his new wife home to live with him, he has to negotiate a dowry that he gives to her parents depending on his resources. If he divorces her, he can ask the family for the money back. If a woman cheats on her husband, the husband can divorce her by demanding that her new husband reimburse him for the dowry.

Some of the more traditional roles of women are changing today as the government and NGO's are supporting and encouraging girls to stay in school. Some women are even going to the University. I saw some women working in more formal jobs in cities such as in banks, and some are even police officers. As anywhere, education and birth control are the most important tools to empower women. Outside of the cities families are less interested in educating their daughters and there are fewer accessible schools. Uneducated men are seldom willing to use condoms. The result is that uneducated women are relegated to very traditional roles with little power to control their future.

Relationships of the wealthier, educated, middle and upper class couples in the cities are more like Western couples. In Cotonou men and women go to the beach, they go on vacations together, and sometimes go shopping together. If the woman is educated and works outside the home in a professional role, many of the above observations about uneducated couples do not apply.

## Stories about Children:

### The Perfect Photo Op

One time when I was riding my bike down the road, I spotted a perfect photo opportunity. It was a group of young children, probably six to twelve years old, all walking in a straight line up a steep dirt path with metal basins full of water on their heads. I thought it would be a great picture that would capture something uniquely African and show Beninese children fulfilling one of their important roles. I quickly stopped, got off my bike, opened my bike bag, and removed my camera so I could take the picture before the kids got to the top of the hill. They must not have known what I was taking out of my bag, because suddenly they all threw their basins of water on the ground and ran as fast as they could back down the hill. I felt bad, as they were probably all going to get in trouble and possibly hit by their mothers for spilling the water, which I'm sure they worked hard to fetch from a spring at the bottom of the hill. I was going to ask their permission before taking their picture, but they didn't give me the chance!

### Bringing Machetes and Razor Blades to School

This sounds like a recipe for disaster or gang violence, right? It probably would be if it were in an American school, but in Benin all school children from elementary school to high school bring razor blades and machetes to school every day for quite innocent and non-violent reasons. The machetes are for weeding the schoolyard, and the razor blades are for sharpening pencils. The schools are too poor to be able to hire groundskeepers to cut the grass, and they don't want any grass to grow because they fear it will harbor snakes, many of which are venomous in Benin. They can't afford pencil sharpeners, so they use razor blades instead.

## The Name Game

After I had been back in the U.S. for a year, I started to date a woman named Cara. I wrote a letter to a friend in Benin telling him about her, and not long after sending the letter, Cara and I broke up. Low and behold, I got a letter back from my friend in Benin saying that his wife had a baby girl, and that they had named her Cara! Had it been a boy, he would have named it Chris. I wrote him a letter back explaining that Cara and I had broken up, and that she was only a girlfriend, not my wife as he had thought. A month later I received another letter from him saying that he changed his baby daughter's name from Cara to Amélie! It was easy for him to change, as he did not have a birth certificate for her yet, and he did so without me even asking him to. The funny thing is that soon after I received his last letter telling me that his daughter's name was no longer Cara, Cara and I got back together. Today we are married. Fortunately, he had another daughter, and of course, he named her Cara.

## Garbage Day

I found it funny to see how much the neighborhood kids cherished my garbage. I had a routine of taking my garbage out on Saturday mornings, and they were quick to pick up on that. The second I opened my front door, and they saw that I had the garbage basket in my hand, they came running like bats out of hell from across the dirt path. They practically attacked me to get it, and when I dumped it on the ground, they dove for it and fought tooth and nail to get what they wanted. One time a kid left bleeding! They loved to play with everything, so anything that I did not want them to get, such as used tissues and razor blades, I had to throw down my latrine. Any paper that I didn't want them to have, such as personal letters, I had to burn at night. One time I tried burning my agenda book that I didn't want them to have, but I made the mistake of doing it during the day. Despite the fact it was on fire, they descended upon it, plucked the burning book out of the fire, and ran away with it before I could catch them!

My trash was like gold to them. I threw away interesting things that I had brought from the U.S. and had worn out as well as various imported items I bought and used. My garbage offered them hours of fun because they had no toys other than what they made themselves from what they could find.

Anything that I did not throw down my latrine, burn, or give to the kids, I wound up burying in my yard. After two years, the only items I had buried were batteries and tin cans that amounted to a few small holes in my yard. That's proof of how little waste I created in two years.

## Animal Stories:

### The One-Week Death Defying Chicken

**March 10<sup>th</sup>, 1996** Dead meat is hard to find in Benin. In fact, the only way you can buy a chicken in my town is when it is alive. Because almost no one can afford a refrigerator, and most people don't have electricity, everyone cooks and eats their food the same day. There are bush rat sellers on the side of the road in the center of town who sell cooked bush rat, but I must admit I am not too crazy about it. There is a guy who slaughters a pig a few times a week in town, but he does it on random days, and the meat is available only in the morning. By the time I get there, it is usually gone. I did see a guy selling beef in the Allada market for a while, but the market takes place only every five days and he has not been showing up for a long time now. I can get cooked meat in the sauces that the women prepare and sell on the side of the road in town, but it is often full of gristle and bone fragments since they usually chop meat haphazardly with a machete. They serve the sauces and stewed meat chunks with rice and beans, or with pâte. Usually it's not bad, but this time I want to cook my own meat, and my only option is to buy it live.

I've been having gastrointestinal problems as of late, and I'm guessing it is due to the bad hygiene practices of the street food sellers. That is another reason why I want to do some cooking at home. As for meat, chicken is my only option because I'm cooking for only myself, and it is relatively inexpensive.

The last time I bought a live chicken, my neighbors made fun of me because they said it was small and skinny, and I paid too much for it. In order to avoid the haggling and usual price discrimination for being a Yovo, I ask my neighbor, Bernadette, to buy the next chicken for me. The only place where I know to get a chicken is in the market, and it won't happen for another four days. However, each day Bernadette walks to nearby villages to buy and sell goods to make money and she can get me a chicken sooner. I give her 500 F ($1 USD) to buy me a live African chicken (I will explain what an "African Chicken" is later). Today is **Friday**, and I told her that I would like to have the chicken for Sunday. She agrees to help me and says it won't be a problem.

That evening while I am in their housing compound socializing with them, they tell me that Bernadette bought the chicken today. Since I am not going to kill it for two more days, she had to let it run free to find food. They usually run free and forage for whatever they can find. That is how the Beninese raise chickens, goats and pigs. I never understood how they don't get lost or run away, but they assure me that my chicken will return. I suppose the owners create enough compost and food scraps from dishwater to keep them around since very few people actually feed their animals. Sometimes animals get stolen, but they rarely run away. I am not too concerned about the chicken since it is commonplace to let the animals run free.

**Sunday** rolls around and I am now ready to cook! I go over to Bernadette's house and ask her for my chicken. "No, I'm sorry. I don't know where your chicken is," she tells me. "It's running around somewhere, but we'll find it for you by tomorrow." A little disappointed, I go home and cook something else.

**Monday night**: I again ask for the chicken. My neighbors tell me that they have not been able to catch my chicken yet, but they know that it is sleeping in the tree next to Antoine's hut, so not to worry. "Come back tomorrow and you will have your chicken," they assure me. No wonder I don't eat meat very often, I think to myself!

**Tuesday**: Today I am hopeful that I will finally get my blasted chicken! I go back to claim it, but I find that they still have not caught it! They can see that I am getting impatient, so they get some corn and throw it on the ground below the tree where the chicken is sleeping to entice it to come down. It doesn't work and must not be hungry. I can't believe this! I insist that they do something to catch it, as this is getting ridiculous! Tineto then gets his homemade crossbow, aims at the sleeping chicken, and shoots it right out of the tree! Finally—I will have chicken for dinner! . . . But the bird quickly runs into the thick brush as soon as it hits the ground. It appears that he hit the bird in the leg and only wounded it. We rummage through the bush for at least a half-hour, but to no avail. Damn it!! They promise me that if I come back tomorrow, they will have the chicken for me.

**Wednesday**: On day 5 (Good Lord!) I return to claim what I have dubbed the "Death Defying Chicken." Tineto and his son Nestor rummage through the bush across from their hut, and after 20 minutes they catch the elusive bird. Finally! Hurray!

Nestor and I bring the bird to my house to kill it. I want to chop its head off so it will die quickly and not suffer, but Nestor will not hear anything of it. According to Beninese tradition, animals must be bled to death by cutting their necks after giving them some water to drink. "Don't you want the animal to suffer the least?" I ask Nestor. "Yes" he replies. "Well then, which way do you think it will suffer the least? Would you rather it die slowly by bleeding to death, or die quickly after we chop its head off?" I ask him. "By chopping its head off," he replies. "OK then," I say, "let me chop its head off." "No," he says, "Our ancestors didn't do it that way. We must cut its neck." I give in and we do it his way. How can I argue with hundreds, or perhaps thousands of years of tradition? He pulls the bird's neck back, and I cut it with a machete. The blood pours out, and a few minutes later, the bird expires. We soak it in boiling water to loosen the feathers, and pluck them. Nestor then cuts the chicken open and guts it, which takes at least a half-hour and it makes quite a mess. Once all the feathers are removed, I am shocked at how scrawny and bony it is. All that grief for such a skinny little bag of bones!? I give the head, feet and organs to Nestor for helping me pluck it. He is grateful, as the Beninese consider the head the most delectable part! By now it is late, and I am too tired to cook it for dinner, so I end up making spaghetti. Luckily I have my Peace Corps issued kerosene refrigerator that I can keep the bird in until tomorrow.

On **Thursday** (Day 6), Tineto comes over my house and asks me whether I want to bring the chicken over to his house to eat it with him, or if he should come over my house with Antoine to eat it with me! Knowing how small my wounded chicken is, and how much grief I went through to get it, I politely refuse his "kind invitation." That evening, I finally cook it, and eat the whole thing in one sitting because it is so tiny. On top of that, the meat is tough and rubbery, and not very flavorful. It is so chewy that my jaw gets tired from chewing! It is so small that after eating it, I am still hungry!

Suddenly I begin hallucinating about eating a fat and tender American chicken, where a single leg is almost enough for a whole meal. The problem here is that chickens are not bred for consumption and are rarely even fed! The only food they get is what they find rummaging around. After this incident, I will not be buying chickens very often. When I do, I will buy it myself and I will kill it the same day. I will certainly NOT let it run free!

## More Chicken Stories

When you live in a Beninese village, or even a small town, people almost always have chickens and roosters running around that will eventually be sold or eaten. It was annoying as hell for me because the roosters always crowed at some God-awful hour, between 4 and 6 AM, and woke me up. When I was staying in a hotel in Cotonou, a rooster started crowing at 5 AM and I could not get back to sleep! I could not believe that they were waking me up even in a city of a million people, while I was staying in a hotel for that matter! On second thought, I actually saw cattle being herded on Cotonou streets, so I suppose it's not that surprising that people had roosters there too.

I once heard that a Peace Corps Volunteer trainee was living with a Beninese family, and a rooster crowing every morning was disturbing her. She told the family it was waking her up, and the rooster ended up on the dinner table the next evening! On many occasions I wished I could have exacted such revenge on those extremely annoying birds.

## Humphrey the Turkey

**November 28th, 1996 (Thanksgiving Day)** Cindy, a Peace Corps Volunteer who lives in Dassa, was nice enough to organize a Thanksgiving dinner at her house for any volunteer who wanted to come. Holidays in

Benin are difficult for PCV's because we cannot be with our families. When we are in Benin, the Peace Corps Volunteer group is our family, so someone always has a party and it makes the holidays enjoyable.

Cindy bought a live turkey last week in Porto-Novo for 16,000 CFA (about $35 USD). She brought it back to Dassa in a wicker basket, and the trip took her about three hours in a bush taxi. She kept the turkey in her walled in backyard last week, and she named the turkey "Humphrey." Being cautious, she clipped the bird's wings and chased it around to make sure that he could not fly over the wall. She fed Humphrey every day and had to put up with its annoying "gobble gobble" every morning at 5AM.

Two days before Thanksgiving, she discovered that the Humphrey was gone!! Cindy did not know if it was stolen or if he had somehow escaped. Upset, she told the neighbors about it, but the party had to go on. Since she lives in Dassa, a bigger town than Allada, she has a small grocery store, and was able to buy two frozen chickens and a live duck. Oddly enough, her dog attacked and killed the duck last night, so we wondered if he also killed and ate Humphrey, feathers and all, but that seemed very unlikely.

Today about 20 PCV's are here for the Thanksgiving party. It's going well, but everyone is a little disappointed about not having turkey, and puzzled at the same time about what happened to it. Just as we are finishing our Thanksgiving meal of roasted chicken and duck at about 9 PM, there is a knock on the door. Cindy's neighbor came over to tell us that the police had her turkey, and the two thieves who stole it! We all start laughing hysterically, as we cannot believe what a crazy story this is turning out to be! The neighbors tell us that the thieves climbed the wall at night and grabbed it.

The next day a group of us goes to the police station to claim Humphrey. When we arrive, we find the long lost turkey unharmed and standing on a chair in the office with one leg tied to the arm of the chair. An officer shows us the thieves in the holding cell. They did not fare as well as Humphrey. They have fresh cuts and bruises all over their arms and faces from the beating they received from the civilians who caught them, as well anyone else who may have passed the scene before they were taken to the police. In Benin people tend to get violent towards thieves and usually practice vigilante justice. The police often have to save the criminals from the public!

Cindy gives a statement saying what happened. I ask the officer what punishment the thieves will likely receive, and he says they will probably get a year in prison! We put Humphrey in the basket, and I carry it back to Cindy's house on my head. Cindy has a dilemma as to what to do with Humphrey. Sell him? Eat him? Keep him until next Thanksgiving? Have another party? Ultimately, I think she ended up selling him.

## Pig on the Loose

In 1996 I threw a New Year's party for my neighbors at my house. For the party I gave money to my neighbors to buy a pig, and I made them responsible for taking care of it before the party. I also put them in charge of slaughtering it and cooking it. Lo and behold, on the day of the party, the pig got loose and they could not catch it! There is no such thing as a vegetarian party in Benin, so we had to find a way of catching it soon. After chasing it around for several hours, my neighbors said that they couldn't catch it, but they could shoot it. They knew someone in the area who had a rifle would do the job, but he would charge a fee. They asked me if I would pay it. I was outraged because I was already paying a substantial sum of money to feed a lot of people. Due to their negligence, I would have to pay even more, so I firmly responded "no." Being resourceful, they negotiated with the gun owner that in return for his services, he would get the best part of the pig

I was pleasantly surprised because he came over quickly and shot the pig in front of Antoine's house in no time. He walked away with the pig's head that I had absolutely no use for anyway, so in my opinion, his services were free. Despite the "pig on the loose," the party was a success.

## Goats

Just after arriving to Benin, I was walking down a city street in Porto-Novo with another Peace Corps Volunteer. A car passed us, and I could swear that I heard a screaming baby coming from the car. I asked Jude what it was, and he said that they routinely tied them up and put them in the trunk. "Wow!" I thought. "That is terrible!" I was so aghast I didn't pursue the topic until later. When I finally asked Jude how and why they tie up babies, and put them in the trunks of cars, he laughed at my ignorance and said, "You thought those were babies in the trunk!?"

"Well . . . yea . . . I guess . . . They sure sounded like babies," I replied. "Those were goats, not babies!" he explained, to my embarrassment. I quickly found out how much a small goat sounds like a human baby crying when they bleat. Perhaps that is why they call baby goats "kids?"

### Scary Snake Encounter #1

I was walking into my kitchen to get a snack one day, when I saw a green snake slithering through a small opening in the kitchen window. It quickly made its way to the very same spot on my kitchen shelf where I was going to reach for a snack. Had I reached ten seconds later, it may have been waiting there to bite my hand. When I realized what I was up against, I started screaming "*serpent!, serpent!, serpent!,*" until my neighbors came running over with sticks. The Beninese have no mercy for snakes, aside from the sacred Python which is not venomous, so they hunted the snake down in my kitchen and they killed it with a stick. I was glad, as I later found out that it was an extremely venomous Green Mamba.

"Serpent" is a battle cry in Benin, as there are many venomous snakes and many people die from snakebites. Because people live surrounded by woods, and because most people work in the fields, they run into snakes quite often. My neighbor Tineto was actually a priest of a Vodun cult called Ja, which protects its initiates from snakebites and from curses. He performed healing ceremonies for people who had been bitten by snakes by cutting them above the bite location and rubbing in a magic powder he created by burning a secret mixture of medicinal leaves. Feeling more vulnerable after this encounter, I asked Tinto to initiate me. I spent three days in the woods, performing many secret elaborate rituals with several other initiates and existing members to become a *Javi* (a son of Ja). To this day I still wear my protective Vodun ring we prepared in the woods, and I have never been bitten by a snake!

### Really Scary Snake Encounter #2

One night at about 10 PM, I was sitting in my latrine doing my business when out of the corner of my eye, I saw a black slithery object. All I had was a flashlight to see with, so initially I thought it was a bug or a stick. I then realized it was a snake that had slithered between my feet! My shorts were around my ankles, so I had to leapfrog out of my latrine door very quickly. I wanted to scream for my neighbors to kill it, as I had when the Green Mamba got in my kitchen. However, everyone was asleep, so I grabbed a stick and killed it myself. As I was standing in my front yard with my shorts around my ankles, I realized that I was lucky this did not happen during the day, as my neighbors would have come running in response to my distress call, and seen me in a rather compromising and hilarious situation.

## Tastes like Chicken

One time, my neighbors caught a spitting cobra in one of their traps. They killed it and ate it. They invited me to try some and it was good. There was not too much meat, but yes (you guessed it), it tasted like chicken.

## Mice

Over the two years that I lived in Allada, I killed 45 mice and 3 rats in my house. I know this because I kept a tally. My house was surrounded by a cornfield, so I was in a bad spot with regards to mice. I used three methods to kill them: traps, my shoe, and my dog. It was fun chasing them around the house, or watching my dog do the same. They were annoying, as they would run around in the ceiling of my house at night and make noise. They scared the hell out of me my first night there because I didn't know what the noise was, and I thought someone was trying to break in.

Once I set traps for them and went away for a week. When I returned I was almost knocked over by the stench of dead rat. After this, I made sure that I didn't set the traps when I was away for more than a few days. When I went away for a three-week vacation, I (the cat) was away, and the mice certainly played. They got into everything! They chewed into my electric wire, causing my power to short out! They ate the chalk from my chalkboard, they ate through my plastic food containers, and they ate the string holding up my drop ceiling in the kitchen, causing it to partially fall down. They got into my salt, garlic, corn flour, cookies, powdered soap,

Alfredo sauce mix, beans, flower, and vegetable seeds. They made a nest in my straw sleeping mat, and of course they crapped all over the place. They ate holes in my socks, ate half a candle, and they even ate some hot pepper! They left almost nothing unscathed! They sure have strange appetites. That was an act of war, and I was seriously P.O.'d. After this, I had no mercy, and I killed as many as I could. In fact, when I was cleaning up the mess with the help of a few neighborhood kids, we killed six mice with flip-flops. My dog got in on the action and killed a few on his own too.

## Lizards

There were always tons of lizards around my house. One time a lizard was crawling up the wall in my bedroom, and it fell on my head, scaring the daylights out of me! At night, they would run around in my ceiling along with the mice making noise, and they would crap all over the place. One time I opened the window shutter and found at least 50 lizards clinging to the exterior wall of my house! My dog loved chasing them around, and that was always fun to watch.

## Termites

There are tall castle-like termite mounds all around southern Benin. The funny thing is that you never see the termites unless there's a termite storm. Termite storms usually happen after the first rain at the end of the dry season. I believe this is when they mate. It usually happened for a few days, and they swarmed around any light source at night. They didn't sting, but if you got between them and a light source, you would be bombarded by thousands of bugs. The next day you would see their wings all over the ground, and you wouldn't see them again until the next year.

## Ants

One night I went out my back door to take a bucket shower, and immediately after stepping outside, my feet were repetitively bitten. "Youch!!" I yelled, while backing up and slapping my feet. Ants! What had happened was that thousands of trooper ants invaded my back walkway to feast on my dog's food that he hadn't eaten the night before. I had to jump over them to get into my bucket shower area. Sometimes I saw trooper ants crossing the road. They traveled in formation, in lines and with purpose. I always wondered where they were going, and after that I knew to stay out of their way.

Once I sat down on a fallen tree by the side of the road, and I learned what it feels like to have "ants in your pants" (and yes . . . . I danced!)

## Vodun Stories:

### Yovo Dances

I was watching a public Vodun ceremony in the center of Allada one afternoon. It had been going on every afternoon until dark for a week or so. The ceremony took place in front of the Agasu Vodun convent, and consisted mainly of the Agasu Vodun initiates dancing around the sacred tree. There was a large crowd of at least several hundred people gathered there listening to the drumming music watching the Vodun initiates in their regalia dancing. I found I could see what was going on best by standing on a bench as everyone else was doing around me. I watched from the back of the crowd for a while, and I found the dancing interesting and the drumbeat captivating. As captivating as it was, I could not sit still, so I started dancing in place in what I thought was an inconspicuous manner. I then noticed one of the drummers pointing at me. The next thing I knew, there were hundreds of people pointing, laughing, and screaming in delight, while simultaneously cheering me on! The Vodun ceremony suddenly stopped, and I was not only embarrassed, but also afraid that the Vodun priests would be angry with me for disrupting their ceremony. The damage had already been done and I wanted to have a little fun, so I continued dancing for a few more seconds to please the crowd.

I am sure they had never seen a Yovo do their African style dance before, and I am sure they thought it was a gas. The ceremony had been going on for several days so it was getting a little monotonous for everyone, and they were looking for some diversion and levity (à la "Yovo"). The Vodun priest came over to me and he invited me to dance in front of the whole crowd. I was both flattered and happy that he wasn't angry, and I was confident the crowd would love it, so I took him up on his offer. I am usually a pretty reserved person, but being a Yovo in Benin for a year taught me to be very outgoing. I learned the best way to deal with the constant attention here was to ham it up a little and have some fun. The Beninese always got a kick out of it, and we always had some laughs. I stepped off the bench and did a quick little Beninese style dance for a few minutes and the crowd went absolutely nuts. Everyone immediately surrounded me and they egged me on by clapping, screaming, and yelling in delight. They yelled so loud I thought my eardrums would burst. When I stopped, it took the crowd a few minutes to settle down before they could continue with their ceremony. I heard about my dancing at the Agasu ceremony for the rest of my two-year stay in Benin, and they even invited me back a few times to dance again at their other ceremonies! I'm sure that it wasn't because I danced well, but instead because they found it such a novelty to see a Yovo trying to do a Beninese dance.

## Kluito Ceremony

Taking pictures in Benin was very tricky because I never knew what kind of reaction I would get. When I went to a Vodun ceremony, and I wanted to take pictures, I was always prepared to pay. On one occasion, I negotiated with the Vodun priest a price of 1,000 CFA (about $2 USD) to take pictures, and a discussion ensued between the priest and the dancers over who would get the money. They stopped the ceremony, and they all went into the convent to argue over how they would divide the money. After ten minutes they returned and continued the ceremony. I am not sure how they ended up dividing my donation.

## Wrong Place at the Wrong Time

A Peace Corps Volunteer in Benin was out walking one night when he happened to pass an exorcism ceremony at the wrong time. The ceremony was being performed to cure a person of an illness that they believed to be caused by an evil spirit. In order to cure the person, they had to drive the evil spirit away. Just as they were driving the spirit away, the volunteer happened to walk by. This was bad news for the volunteer. The Vodun priest suggested he too should be purified to make sure that the evil spirit did not take up residence in him so he agreed to also be exorcised. In order to drive the spirit away, they had him strip and bathe in a special leaf infusion. In order to inoculate him against evil spirits, they made two small cuts on his chest, sides, and back, and rubbed a specially prepared black charcoal powder in them, which had spiritual powers. The black marks stay after the cuts heal, as the charcoal powder essentially forms a tattoo. The Beninese equate this procedure to vaccinations, as they frequently have it done to their children to protect them from illnesses. If you ever see a Beninese person with his or her shirt off, you will likely see these marks. Western style vaccinations are offered at village social centers from time to time, but unfortunately, many people believe their children do not need them because they are already protected by using this traditional manner.

# Interesting Cultural Differences

It is an understatement to say that the Beninese culture is different from American and Western Culture. Because Benin is a very poor country, the people are forced to be quite resourceful to get by and survive. Here are some of the more interesting differences that I noted during my two years living in Benin:

**Food:** When it comes to food, nothing gets wasted. The Beninese eat every part of the animal including the skin, head, marrow, guts and feet. They eat snakes, guinea pigs, and bush rat. I even saw children cook and eat rats!

**Post Office:** The post office reuses old stamps that were never sold. They cross out the old denominations, and print new denominations over the old ones. For example, in 1996 I bought some stamps that were originally printed in the 1970's or 1980's! When the scales were broken, the clerk "guesstimated" how much a package or letter weighed by picking it up and moving her hand up and down!

**Painters:** When painters paint the inside of houses, they throw sand on the floor to catch paint drops and spills instead of using drop cloths, because they cannot afford them. Remember, time is always more plentiful than money in Benin, so spending a few hours sweeping up sand is preferable to spending money on drop cloths. Most people have tile or cement floors, so this is no problem. Imagine my dismay when I paid painters to whitewash my house and they started emptying buckets of sand all over my floor!

**Toys:** Parents can almost never afford to buy their children toys, so the children make their own, usually out of garbage. Of course the *Yovo*'s garbage is the best garbage of all. They play hoop and stick from old tires or bike rims that they find. They tie strings to beetles and lizards and play with them. They hunt birds with handmade slingshots, and they play with them until they die.

**Curiosity about the Yovo:** I rarely let anyone in my house because when I did, they always scrutinized everything I owned, asked what it was, where I got it, what it was for, and then they'd ask if I'd give it to them. For this reason, I entertained all of my guests on the porch.

**Birth Dates:** Many older people do not know their date of birth, as they were not born in a hospital. Even if they were born in a hospital, they may not know how to read, they may have lost their birth certificate, or they may have never been given one in the first place. Many hospitals do not keep records, and don't even issue birth certificates. In fact, patients have to keep their own health record cards at home, and they must bring them to the hospital each time they go to be treated. Due to the lack of record keeping, people who do not know their own birthday become a year older on New Year's Day. If they don't have a birth certificate, and they need official identification that shows their date of birth, they can simply guess on the application.

**Sex:** People are very forward and open about sex. To the Beninese, sex is as natural as eating and breathing, and they are not at all shy about it. They have no problem asking you if you are having it, with whom you are having it, how often you are having it, and whether or not it is good.

**Where Yovos are From:** Many illiterate Beninese villagers have received little or no education and have limited knowledge about history and geography. Some do not know about the history of slavery. As a result they do not know there are black people in the West and are surprised to see African American volunteers. Some people think that all white people come from the same place, which they call in Fon, "*Yovotome*" (the land of the white people).

**An Alternate View of History:** Many of the people I met who knew about slavery and the slave trade, felt that their ancestors were as much to blame, if not more to blame, as the white slave traders. I found that very surprising, as that is not a common or politically correct point of view in the West.

**Commemorative Clothing:** The Beninese love very loud, colorful clothing, and the concept of "gaudy" is incomprehensible to them. When an important event takes place in Benin, they often print fabric that marks the occasion. People then make clothing out of it. For example, Pope John Paul II came to Benin, and they made cloth with his picture, the date of his visit, and some other designs to commemorate the occasion. Another time, they made a *pagne* (cloth) for the *Fracophonie* conference; one for president Kérékou, and one for the King of Allada, which had his picture on it along with the names of his predecessors. This cloth was sold everywhere, so I often saw people wearing it. People use the cloth to make all sorts of clothes, including pants. Depending on how the tailor cuts the fabric, the person's picture that the cloth commemorates can end up on the derriere. I was surprised no one seemed to feel bad about having the Pope's picture on his butt.

**Funeral Processions:** Despite the fact that most Beninese people live in mud huts with no running water or electricity and survive on only a dollar a day, they pull out all the stops for funerals. Funerals are very showy, provided the family can scrounge up the money, and they tend to mimic Western funerals. I have seen people riding on top of the cars in the procession playing drums. They sometimes use a hearse, and I have even seen someone in the funeral procession hanging out of a car window videotaping the procession! They believe that if they do not send off their deceased relatives in style, no matter how poor they are, the deceased relative will get angry and will seek revenge upon the family.

Ultimately, any type of misfortune can be interpreted as a form of revenge by angry ancestors or evil spirits. If they have a proper ceremony, they believe that their deceased relative's spirit will be appeased, and will therefore cause them no harm. Unfortunately, many people who have no money have to borrow to finance funerals, and they wind up spending all of their savings for these elaborate ceremonies. It really holds them back from progressing financially.

Oftentimes the ceremonies last for several days. They kill animals to eat, and the family pays large sums of money to feed anyone who comes to pay their respects, which can be an entire village. They buy caskets, pay for hearses, pay drummers, and rent audio equipment for music and dancing, as funerals are considered celebrations of the person's life unless they were very young and died tragically. They also spend a lot on their clothing. The entire family buys the same patterned cloth, and they have it made into matching clothing for the ceremony. This is a way for them to show their solidarity on the day of the funeral, and in the future, as they wear the clothing long after the ceremony is over.

Believe it or not, traditionally the Beninese bury their relatives inside their houses! Many Beninese are Christians and they bury their dead in cemeteries. Non-Christians usually only bury relatives in their houses if they live in mud huts where the floor is dirt and is easily dug up. An important aspect of the Vodun religion is the proximity between the living and the dead. They worship their ancestors' spirits and burying their relatives beneath their feet is a symbolic way of maintaining this proximity.

**Investing in Benin:** The most common way of saving and investing money in Benin is to build a house very, very slowly. They cannot invest in stocks because there is no stock market in Benin as there are so few private companies. People often do not put their money in the bank because there are very few banks in Benin, and people often have to travel out of their way to get to one. Banks charge high fees and often do not pay interest on savings. Many people were burned in 1994 when the government devalued the CFA currency by 50% to help increase exports, so many Beninese are distrustful of saving their money as cash. They risk losing money to vermin like termites and mice if they hide it in their houses. In addition, most people house their families in one or two small rooms, so it is hard to hide money anywhere that is safe.

There is a lot of pressure to share resources with family members in need. If a relatives knows that another relative has money saved, they pressure that person into sharing it during emergencies, such as when a family member is sick or if there is a death in the family. In times of emergencies, the whole family is expected to contribute what they can, and if a person has a stash of money either at home or in the bank, he will be ostracized if he does not share a large portion of it. In order to avoid having to share a large amount of their savings, the Beninese often invest extra money into building houses made of cinderblocks or cement. If they have a few extra CFA, they may have a mason make a stack of bricks, or add a few sheets of tin to a partially constructed roof. For this reason I have seen many half built houses. As far as I know, mortgages are only for the rich in Benin, so the average person may spend 5-10 years building his house!

**Lice:** Lice is a very common problem, especially among Beninese children. In order to cure it, people shave their heads bald. They resort to this because they cannot afford the medicated shampoos that kill lice.

**Beninese Hospitality:** In Benin hospitality is extremely important. They try to make guests at their houses as comfortable as possible, no matter how poor they are. When guests arrive the host immediately offers them a seat in the shade and something to drink. If the family has money, they may offer beer or soft drinks. Usually they offer water without asking if you are thirsty. If you are not thirsty, instead of drinking the water given to you, it is perfectly acceptable to pour some on the floor as an offering to the ancestors. Most floors are made of either cement or dirt, so doing so causes no harm.

**Garbage at Home:** In mud huts in Beninese villages, people never have garbage cans. They either throw garbage on the floor of their huts or outside on the ground. Since they sweep in and around their huts every day, they always know the mess will be cleaned up soon. After they sweep, they throw the garbage (most of it is biodegradable) in a garbage pile near their house. Animals come to eat from it, and children pick out anything interesting to play with, while the rest of it decomposes. If the pile gets too big, the villagers may burn it or use it as compost. They consume so little, that the garbage piles remain very small even though no one carries it away.

**The Definition of Dirty:** Their huts are always surrounded by dirt because they cannot afford cement, pavement, or a lawn. They cut down all of the grass to keep the snakes away. I always found it funny that they sweep their dirt yards and the dirt floors in their huts to keep the dirt clean. After all, they don't want dirty dirt. This makes perfect sense in Benin, but by Western standards, there is no such thing as "clean dirt." It is a paradox to us, like "dehydrated water," because we define that which is not clean as having dirt or being dirty. You can only find "clean dirt" in Benin.

**Poverty at the Municipal Level:** The town hall of Allada (the county seat) had their electricity turned off because they did not have the money to pay the electric bill! The same thing happened at the national museum in Ouidah!

**Lack of Mechanization:** In central Benin (around Dassa) it is very rocky. There, people, usually women and children, break rocks into gravel to be used in concrete for a living! They sit on the ground and hit the rocks with a heavy piece of metal. It seemed like a horrible way to make a living, and I am sure there are machines that could do the work of 20 people in a tenth of the time. The same is true of their farming techniques as most people in Benin are subsistence farmers, and only use hand tools.

**The Beninese Want the Opposite of What Yovos Want:** In Benin women want to be fat, white and have small breasts. Being heavy is a sign of wealth as you have enough money to feed your family and yourself beyond your basic needs. Being light skinned probably has something to do with wanting to have an exotic look and be more like "modern" Europeans. Breasts are not sexually attractive to men so women would prefer to have less weight to carry around on their chests. The Beninese also prefer cloudy and cool days because it is always so hot. The sun is very intense so cloud cover is always welcome.

**Menus:** When you go to a Beninese restaurant and order meat, they usually kill the animal shortly after taking your order, and sometimes they even go to the market to buy it. For this reason it often takes a long time to get your food, sometimes over an hour! This is because they cannot afford to keep a large supply of ingredients on hand. Another result of this is that they have few things they have printed on the menu. Before I learned to ask what they have the conversation sounded something like: "I will have this." Then they say, "Sorry, we don't have that." I say, "OK then, I will have this instead." "Sorry, we don't have that either." "OK, then I'll have this." "Sorry, we don't have that either." "Then what do you have!?" "Well, we have only this, this, this and this . . . ." So, when going to a restaurant, remember to ask them what items on the menu they actually have before ordering, and by no means should you go to a sit down restaurant if you are very hungry. In that case your best bet is to buy street food because it is always ready to be served.

**Lack of Toilets:** Some bars and restaurants in the cities only have pit latrines and no bathrooms with running water. To wash your hands, most restaurants bring you a small bowl of water and a little bit of blue powdered Omo soap, which everyone at the table uses to wash their hands just before eating. Considering many Beninese foods are eaten without utensils, it is a very good idea to wash your hands thoroughly.

**Service:** Good service is very rare in Beninese restaurants and wherever you go for that matter. In the West we have grown to appreciate a refined level of professional service in all sectors of our economy. Benin does not have a tradition of professional service, so it is best to have low expectations.

Benin is not a hotspot for tourism, so they have not adapted to the needs and desires of tourists either. If you receive bad service, it is likely the person will at least be friendly toward you, and this will generally quell your frustration somewhat. Bad service is usually a symptom of inefficiency or a lack of resources. It is almost never because of bad attitude.

**Beef:** The art of butchering has not reached Benin, so meat is usually hacked off the animal and not removed in any specific way. When buying beef in the market, you can get filet mignon and brisket in the same order for the same price. Often beef contains bone fragments, and it is as tough as shoe leather.

**Fire Fighting in Benin:** From a Beninese newspaper article I read in 1997, Benin had only 157 firefighters and 16 fire trucks, of which seven were broken down. I'm not sure where those firehouses were, but I am confident that most of them were in the major cities such as Cotonou, Porto-Novo, Abomey, and Parakou. As for all of the other towns and villages, if there is a fire, the people have no recourse other than to let it burn itself out.

**Handshaking:** When greeting someone, the handshake is crucial in Benin. It is so important that if your hand is dirty, or you are carrying something, you should put out your wrist, and the person will shake it instead of your hand. If you do not, people will think you're aloof.

After informal handshakes, both people slide their middle fingers together and they perform simultaneous snaps with their thumbs. It takes a while to get used to, and to do properly. Once you have mastered it, however, people will know you're an old pro at living in West Africa. This is a very informal maneuver and should not be used in formal situations.

Men and women usually shake hands too. If a man is romantically interested in a woman, after the handshake, but before releasing her hand, he quickly tickles her palm with his middle finger so only she knows his intentions.

**Homosexuality in Benin:** Homosexuality is still completely in the closet in Benin. It is not openly discussed and to me, it seemed that it didn't even exist there. During my two years, I only met one Beninese man who was overtly gay. Knowing this, it may seem odd that men who are close friends, sometimes hold hands and even give each other pecks on the lips as a greeting or departure. Men usually hold hands when they are trying to lead a friend somewhere, or if they are talking and are trying to make a point.

**When is Three Days From Now?:** In Benin they count days like money because they count the current day. For example, three days from today is, today, tomorrow and the next day. So if today is Monday, three days from now is Wednesday and not Thursday, as it would be in the West.

*"Il faut me donner"* **Mentality:** *"Il faut me donner"* means, "You must give me." I heard this thousands of times in Benin. *"Yovo il faut me donner ton vélo, Yovo il faut me donner de l'argent, Yovo, il faut me donner 500F . . ."* ("You must give me your bike, you must give me money, you must give me 500 Francs") . . . I felt like a walking dollar sign! I was always hounded for gifts, money, an American pen pal, or a visa to the U.S. When I did give them something, they usually just asked for more, stating their other unmet needs. Or they would point out how my gift was insufficient in some way. Friends and neigbors often gave me an attitude along the lines of "It's about time you came around and gave me something," especially once they realized they were not getting anything else. They pushed me to my threshold of coerced generosity, but in the end, they always thanked me and generally showed appreciation. They just wanted to make sure they couldn't squeeze anything else out from me before thanking

me. Sometimes I felt like I was Santa Claus and every day for them was Christmas.

**Gastro-intestinal distress:** As a Yovo in Benin, I suffered from this problem on a regular basis. A few times it resulted in the unfortunate problem of "partial momentary loss of sphincter control" as well as "Involuntary Mutual Simultaneous Excretion." One time, I heard a volunteer yell "Sphincter, don't fail me now!" as she lifted her leg to get on the back of a zemidjan. Luckily for her, it did not.

# Rich and Famous on $6.00 a Day

**June 8ᵗʰ, 1997** Being rich and famous while earning only $6.00 a day seems like a fantasy, doesn't it? For me it is a reality. My daily living allowance that Peace Corps pays me is indeed only the equivalent of $6.00 a day, yet I feel as if I am rich and famous. In Benin, government employees earn on average the equivalent of $120 a month, or $4 a day, and they are considered middle class! The average hired farm or store worker earns only the equivalent of one dollar a day! By American standards I am considered a volunteer because I am not paid a "real" salary, yet I make more than most government employees in Benin, so I've got to be careful not to offend anyone when I explain what it means to be a "volunteer."

Despite their meager pay, government employees often have large families of five to ten children, sometimes with more than one wife, and they are able to feed and clothe them on their salaries. I, on the other hand, make the equivalent of $180 a month, and I have limited living expenses with only myself and my dog to feed. The cost of living here is very low. For example, my rent is only $12 a month, but it is paid by the community. I can get a huge meal on the side of the road in town consisting of rice, beans, and pasta for only fifty cents! If I splurge and get meat to go with it, it may cost $1. After the basic necessities, I usually have enough money left over to take short weekend trips to visit other volunteers in Benin, and to buy expensive imported foods like cheese, butter, and chocolate once in a while when I go to Cotonou. The Beninese can rarely afford such luxuries.

The unique concept behind Peace Corps is to live at or near the same economic level of the local people, so the volunteer can better understand the culture and lives of the people they're trying to help. I live in a small three-room cement house with a tin roof, which is down a long narrow dirt path on the outskirts of town. I have electricity and a fan, thank the Lord, but no running water. I pay my neighbor to fetch me water every day out of the cistern in front of my house. I take refreshingly cool bucket showers, and do my business in a pit latrine in my front yard. I don't have a TV or phone, and I get news from my short wave radio. My sole means of transportation is my Peace Corps issued Trek mountain bike, which I use for short trips, and I must take bush taxis for out of town trips. By American standards, these are very austere living conditions, but I've adapted to them out of necessity. Believe it or not, I've made myself very comfortable, and I genuinely want for nothing, except American junk food and pizza!

Most people would probably ask, "How can he feel rich without a car? Without a TV? Without a phone? Without running water? Without a computer? On only $6.00 a day!?" Being here has made me realize how materialistic we Americans are, and how much we base, or try to base, our happiness on material objects. I have discovered that being rich is truly nothing more than a state of mind. It is a matter of having enough money to take care of your basic needs, and then some. It is also a relative state in which you have more than most everyone else around you, and when there aren't many things available that you don't already have or want. All of these conditions apply to my situation. I don't have many things, but then again, there aren't many goods or services available here in my little town. There are no fancy restaurants, no concerts, no computer stores or supermarkets selling expensive gourmet ice cream and 50 different varieties of breakfast cereal. I have realized that what one wants is a function of exposure to marketing and seeing others with enviable goods. Here in Benin, there is not only a lack of products, but marketing is practically nonexistent. There are very few people with enough wealth to buy luxury items, so I am not pressured to feel that I need anything that I don't already have. In Benin stores don't have sales to get me to buy things I don't really need. There is no "keeping up with the Joneses," and there is no planned obsoletion of products to consistently entice me want more and better products.

I feel rich here in Benin because people perceive me as such, and they always ask me for money. If I had a penny for every time someone asked me for money, or a "*cadeau*" (gift), I would be a millionaire! People here equate white skin with money and handouts because the French colonized them for 61 years, ending in 1960. Strangers, children, adults, women, men, old and young, educated, and uneducated, all walks of life aren't too proud to ask the Yovo for a *cadeau* at any moment. Often as I'm riding my bike down the dirt roads, I hear kids yelling out "Whitey, give me money!" or "Whitey, give me a gift!" I refuse to give gifts to strangers unless they are crippled or missing a limb. It is more difficult to refuse my neighbors because they are my friends. They often ask for gifts and loans, and it's especially difficult when they come to me for money when they're sick or need money to pay their school fees so as not to be kicked out. I sometimes hesitate to help them, considering there are 40 of them. I am afraid that if I show too much generosity, I will be besieged with requests, and I will perpetuate their dependence on outsider's charity as colonization did. When I do give them handouts, I make them promise to keep quiet about it. After all, I came to Benin to teach people how to help themselves and to be independent. I did not come to give handouts. Nonetheless, I often feel like a walking dollar sign which can be very unnerving at times.

Buying things is always an ordeal in Benin because sellers double their prices when they see white skin. They believe that those who have more should pay more. It is effectively a tax on being rich. Being rich and from the developed world makes it difficult to have real friends, as it can be so hard to tell who really wants to be my friend for who I am, and who wants to be my friend for a chance at monetary gain or a free trip to the U.S.

I am famous here not because I have money. I am famous because my white skin makes me stand out, because I am different and because I'm from a far away and exotic land. Coming here from a lily-white town in Connecticut was a real eye opener. The fact that I am one of five white people living in a town of 10,000 certainly gets me a lot of attention. People are curious and always want to talk to the Yovo. No matter where I go, I can never go unnoticed. I am used to always being stared at, talked about, and pointed at, as well as being singled out in a crowd. At times it's flattering to get so much attention, but often it's annoying to never be left alone and to never fit in. While I was living in Dagleta during training, I hadn't seen a fellow white person in several days, and I had to remind myself that it was normal to be white in some parts of the world. I had to remind myself that I wasn't the freak of nature that the people were making me out to be.

Because I am different and interesting, everyone knows me, yet I know relatively few. When I ride my bike home through town and down the dirt path leading to my house, many people call out my name. I often wave without even looking to see who it is because I rarely know the person. Usually, this is because I had either talked to them briefly one time and forgot who they were, or I had never met them and they had learned my name by word of mouth. Often people are disappointed when

I can't remember their name, but that's what happens when you are a celebrity. I know people will remember me and talk about me for many years after I leave, because I still hear stories about the other Peace Corps Yovos who were posted here and left several years ago. I talked to a Peace Corps Volunteer who after finishing her service, returned to her village in Benin several years later. She was shocked to learn that the current Peace Corps Volunteer living in her old village knew so much about her, even though they had never met each other before!

Despite the fact that we are often overcharged, white people are sometimes given special treatment. It is flattering but not healthy for the Beninese people's self-esteem and national pride. Many people look up to me and give me special treatment because I am white. They often feel inferior to whites because they know that western nations are wealthier, more educated, and more powerful than their small impoverished country. In conversation I have heard them say that they believe whites are more intelligent than Africans. Their inferiority complex stems from being colonized by the French, and seeing many manufactured products they buy coming from western nations. Sometimes I get better service at the post office or bank than Beninese people do because they perceive me as being more important. I went to the King of Allada's public ceremony without an invitation, and found myself sitting next to other regional kings, government ministers, and local dignitaries, because my presence was seen as an endorsement for the ceremony being I was the only white person there. Whenever I go to public gatherings, I am often given the best seat without even asking. For example, people believe that sitting in the front passenger seat of a taxi is more comfortable than the back, and often the driver asks a passenger sitting there to move to the back to let me sit up front just because I am white.

I love Benin. I love being rich, and I often enjoy getting special attention and privileges because I am white. When I return to the U.S., I surely won't miss constantly being singled out, stared at, being called "Yovo," always being hounded for money, and getting ripped off whenever I buy anything. On the other hand, when I am finally back home in the U.S., I won't enjoy the feeling of being "poor." Unless I'm a millionaire, I will be made to feel that no matter how much money I have, I will still need more.

In addition, when I return to the U.S., I will return to relative anonymity. I will lose my celebrity status, which I am sure I will miss at times. I will certainly possess a new found sensitivity towards minorities of any type. I will certainly do my best not to single them out despite my curiosity about what makes them different. Now I know what it's like to be constantly noticed for the one trait that makes me different from everyone else.

# A Stranger in My Old Life

## My Departure:

I had worked for over two years as a small business development volunteer in the Peace Corps, and the time was finally at hand for me to return home to the United States for good. I prepared for my departure from Benin for several months, and I had been saying good-bye to everyone for the past two weeks. I attended going away parties my Beninese friends threw for me, and I had one for myself at my house as a way to say good-bye to my friends and neighbors. My last few months in Benin were the most gratifying because when people realized that I was leaving for good, they came out of the woodwork to show their appreciation for my efforts to help them. I thought many people who I tried to help over the two years were indifferent about the efforts I had made. Instead I was very flattered and gratified, as many people went out of their way to thank me, give me presents, and express their sadness that I was leaving. It was extremely sad having to say good-bye, and it was stressful trying to get everything wrapped up before my departure date. It was a great feeling to finally feel that people were grateful for my efforts. I did receive some signs of appreciation over the two years, but sometimes it wasn't enough to keep me from getting discouraged. It was too bad most of their gratitude came at the end of my stay, and not sooner. It is a common problem for Peace Corps Volunteers to wonder if all the work they have done made any difference at all. I knew when I left that I made at least a small difference in some people's lives, so I left Benin with a warm glow and a sense of accomplishment.

On my last day in Allada, I was waiting on my front porch with many of my Beninese friends and neighbors. We were waiting for the Peace Corps vehicle to pick me and my belongings up to bring me to Cotonou. I was leaving, and I didn't know if I'd ever come back or see my friends again. Despite all the good-byes and preparations I had made to leave, the emotional reality didn't hit me until the Peace Corps vehicle pulled up in front of my house. Seeing it was a symbol of the definitive end of my Peace Corps experience and it caused my sadness to boil over. In the movie "Goodwill Hunting" Robin Williams said, "You know you're really going to cry when you feel it start in your toes," and that is exactly the way I felt. I was suddenly overcome with emotion, and I cried uncontrollably even after we were several miles from Allada. The sadness over leaving Benin had been simmering deep inside me for quite some time, but I had been repressing it, denying it, and ignoring it. I felt like a big baby, but once I calmed down, Mathieu, our stoic and trusty Peace Corps driver, assured me that this was a common occurrence when he picked up volunteers to bring them to Cotonou for the last time. This alone is a strong statement as to the personal impact the Peace Corps experience has on volunteers. I know I had a strong influence on my Beninese friends too, because they were crying as well, although they are normally very stoic.

As I was saying good-bye I thought about the innumerable experiences I had and all the people I had met. It had been an incredible adventure and the most stimulating two years of my life. I experienced so many new and exotic things, met so many interesting people, faced so many challenges and I had grown from these experiences in so many ways. Often it was very trying, frustrating, and even depressing, but it was equally thrilling, rewarding, invigorating, and downright fun. In Benin, I endured many hardships. However, the hardships and difficulties were what made the experience so worthwhile, and forced me to grow and change so much. I had been pushed to my limits and as a result, I had become a better person. I had become very close to many Beninese people. I learned the Fon language fairly well, and I delved into their culture and religion to learn as much about Benin as I could. All along I knew my time in Benin was limited so I tried hard not to take it for granted. In some ways I felt as if I had become part Beninese, and now I had to leave that part of me behind in order to move on with my life in the U.S.

Two years was a lot of time to get to know my Beninese neighbors very well. We shared many experiences together, and I felt strong ties to them. They became a surrogate family to me and were a support network for me. Nestor was a good friend who I paid to fetch water from my cistern every day. He hung out at my house quite often and we would chat about all sorts of things. Nestor was like a little brother to me because he was fourteen at the time. He and his older brother Angelo helped me with my Fon. I paid Céléstine, and Léandrine to do my laundry (by hand of course) every week, and they also swept my house. They would tease me, I'd tease them, and we'd have some good laughs. I was constantly surrounded by the neighborhood children such as Niclesse, Narcisse, Aubain, Alès, Bernadette, and Joachim, just to name a few. There were so many children I could never keep their names straight. I also became close with Tineto and Tineno, Nestor's parents. In addition, Nestor's aunts, uncles, cousins, grand-parents, and great aunts and uncles also lived in the housing compounds across the path from my house. I hung out at their houses every day, and they came over to see me often too. Everyone accepted me and explained to me aspects of their culture that I didn't understand. They helped me with my Fon every day and were very patient with me as I learned. I had several parties at my house for them. They invited me to their family events, such as a funeral, and a naming ceremony for Antoine's baby. Tineto even accepted me into his Vodun cult called "Ja," and initiated me as a full-fledged member during a three-day ceremony in the woods, which was very flattering. With their help I had become part Beninese.

Tinto and Nestor at my going away party.

Some of my neighbors at my going away party.

One day when I was taking an afternoon nap, I woke up and found all these children on my front porch waiting for me to come out and hang out with them.

I realized that if I did come back to Benin, it would never be the same again. I would return as a tourist and not a resident. Many of my friends and neighbors cried too. They helped me load my bags into the van, and after many difficult and heartfelt goodbyes, I was on my way to Cotonou to fly back to the U.S. a few days later. I had mixed feelings about returning to the U.S. I was very sad to leave Benin. At the same time, I was very happy to return home, because I had been gone for two years, and I missed my family, friends, and country greatly. I was also glad to be going home because I had grown weary of the inconveniences of Benin, as well as the cultural frustrations and the difficult living conditions. I felt that I had achieved the goals that I had set for myself in the Peace Corps, and I was ready to move on to the next stage in my life. I was very much looking forward to the luxuries and amenities of America and being back home again.

Before we left Benin, Peace Corps did a good job of preparing us to return to the United States. They gave us booklets that got us thinking about career options, as well as preparing us for "re-entry shock" or "reverse culture shock." They even had a two-day seminar to help us prepare for these issues, as well as deal with the administrative tasks we had to complete before getting on the plane to go home. Many people said that it is harder re-adjusting to your own culture when you go home than it is adjusting to the foreign culture because you expect the foreign culture to be different. You expect it to be difficult and frustrating, so you are better prepared to deal with it. You know you will have to change and adapt to it, but it is not obvious that you are faced with the same problem when you go home after having lived abroad so long. I heard that it takes Peace Corps Volunteers as long as they were away to completely re-adjust to American culture when they come home. I think it took me a little more than two years. This probably isn't the case for non Peace Corps types such as American ex-pats who work for American companies, NGO's (nongovernmental organizations), or the U.S. government. Often they live on an American salary, have most of the luxuries they have in the U.S. or more, and they often socialize with other Americans. They isolate themselves from the Beninese culture to a certain extent and they do not have to adapt to it as much as PCV's. Some PCV's who are unhappy with their situations at their posts in Benin sometimes find excuses to be somewhere else. They spend as much time as possible with other Peace Corps Volunteers or with other American or European ex-pats. My guess is that it is easier for the people who live with the Beninese culture at an arm's length to leave and re-adjust to the U.S. when they come home.

I valued my time in Benin, and over the two years I made a concerted effort to integrate myself into the Beninese culture the best I could. I got tired and frustrated at times. When I did, I looked for reprieves by hanging out with other Americans or Europeans from time to time, but I spent the vast majority of time at my post with the Beninese. This of course made it that much more difficult for me to leave and re-integrate into American culture. Beyond living in a small town, working directly with the Beninese, and living near their economic level, I learned as much Fon as I could. I learned as much as I could about the culture, and I made a lot of Beninese friends. By the time I left, in our Peace Corps *franglais* (combining French and English), I would call myself *bien intégré'd* or "well adapted" to the Beninese culture. Volunteers would often tease each other as they observed one another doing something uniquely Beninese with skill, confidence and panache. They would say, "Wow, you're *bien intégré'd!*" One example is hissing or shouting "*Tanti*" at a bar or restaurant in order to get the waitress's attention. It is something all Beninese do, but since we would never do that in the U.S., it takes us time to overcome our ingrained inhibitions. Bargaining and maneuvering through a market while quickly deterring Beninese who try to prey on Yovos new to the country is another set of skills that often earns a volunteer the *bien intégré'd* label. Killing your own chicken and speaking the local language well are also examples. Having made such strong relationships with the people and becoming so intimate with the Beninese culture, made it that much more difficult for me to leave.

In our close of service seminar, we learned about the several phases of reverse culture shock that everyone goes through to one degree or another. I will describe those phases as I experienced them.

## My Arrival Back in the U.S:

As I passed through the gates of the JFK international arrivals building, I was overcome with emotion again. I felt overwhelmed and had the urge to cry when I saw the American flag because I was so happy to be back in my own country. When I saw a police officer, I felt a sense of pride regarding our relatively strict standards and ethics. In Benin corruption is rampant, and the police commonly take bribes. I was proud that our system is very effective, and that there is relatively little corruption compared to West Africa. I spent two very long years in a place that couldn't possibly be more different from the United States. I loved many aspects of Benin, but many aspects drove me crazy, and I longed for many things in the U.S. I know it sounds corny, but I was so happy that I kissed the ground (i.e., the floor in the airport). I felt truly proud to be an American because of all that we have accomplished and continue to accomplish as a nation technologically, economically, and culturally. Returning home from such a small, poor, unrecognized country that has little influence in the world made me feel more proud to be an American than before I left. I felt happy to be in a place that I knew and understood well, a place where I could feel comfortable, and where I wouldn't always feel strange and like an outsider.

I had feared returning to the U.S. long before actually coming home. I feared it so much that I had nightmares from time to time while I was still in Benin. I had heard stories about how hard re-adjustment was for volunteers who I knew in Benin and had returned home before me. We changed dramatically from living in a country like Benin. When I was in Benin, I knew I was changing, but I did not know for sure how I had changed until I was back in the U.S. and could make comparisons with my old self. I was afraid to come to grips with the new person I had become after spending over two years in Benin. When I went to Benin, I was just out of college, and before going home I feared all the major life decisions that I had before me such as getting a job, finding a place to live, and getting on my feet again. Life in Benin was fairly simple for me, and I feared going back to all the complexities of life in the U.S.

As I walked through the airport I felt so many different feelings. It felt as if I could see a fourth dimension that I could not see before I had left two years prior. It is easy and normal to take your own culture for granted, but after living in such a different place for so long, and then coming back, I was able to compare everything with what I became used to in Benin. I could see all the differences between the U.S. and Benin and the values that underlie them. I call this a "fourth dimension," otherwise known as culture. Our culture is around us all the time, and our perspective either allows us to see our culture or be blind to it if we have nothing to compare it to. An American astronaut, Sandy Magnus, after returning from outer space said, "When I came home I was appalled at the level of force squishing us like bugs into the Earth. Once you've escaped gravity, you realize how overpowering it is" (Brown, Mike). We experience gravity every day, but we rarely think about it until we've lived in a zero gravity environment. The same is true for culture. We don't think much about our own culture until we've left it, experienced another and then returned. As I was walking through the airport, I realized that I was acutely aware of my own culture, and I was constantly comparing everything American to its Beninese equivalent.

I thought, "Wow! There are white people everywhere and hardly any black people!" I wondered, "Where are all the black people?" because I was so used to being one of five white people in a town of 10,000. I noticed how everyone was in such a hurry because I was used to everyone being so laid back. The floors were so clean! Where was all the dirt? I was used to living in a place where everything was dirty because the only pavement was on the three paved roads in the whole country.

I was in my country but it all seemed so strange and disturbingly foreign! I remembered how things were in the U.S., but I could not help feeling these emotional reactions as I wasn't used to it anymore. It was November and it was so cold. I wanted a blanket. I was used to cold weather being 70 degrees. And all the food! I was used to having very limited choices of food in Benin, and I hadn't eaten a bagel with cream cheese in two years! I said to the cashier, "I'm sorry, but I only have a $50 bill. I don't imagine you would have change?" And she did!! I was amazed that she had change for such a large bill and for such a small purchase. If I had the U.S. equivalent of a $20 bill in Benin, it was almost worthless, because almost no one would have change for it.

While I was in Benin, I had to adapt to so many things that sometimes I felt like I was becoming a different person. I had to change many of my values, habits, and behaviors in order to adapt to the way things worked in Benin, and adapt to the way people interacted with me. I adapted to being a "celebrity," as the Beninese give white people so much attention. I adapted to the heat, the food, not having running water, and the many inefficiencies of a developing West African country. Above all, I adapted to the people, who are very nice, but are also very direct and extremely outgoing. Privacy in general is a foreign concept to the Beninese. They can seem very intrusive to Westerners, who are used to people being standoffish toward anyone that they consider a "stranger." They would ask me all sorts of personal questions like, "Where are you going?" "Why are you here?" "How many kids do you have?" "Why don't you have kids?" "Do you have a wife?" "No . . . . Why aren't you married?" and "Why don't you take a Beninese wife?" I also had to learn how to deal with people always asking me for money because I was perceived as rich, and people always wanting to chat with me. I had to adapt to the Beninese laid-back way of life where nothing ever gets done quickly, and everyone is always late. I adapted to speaking two foreign languages (French and Fon), to being on my own, to constantly being sick, as well as being away from friends and family, etc. I eventually learned to enjoy most of these differences, and in doing so I had to change myself.

My challenge upon returning was to re-adapt to life in the U.S. I wondered what would happen to my Beninese identity "Gandaho." I worried that Gandaho would cease to exist because I wasn't in Benin any more. "Gandaho" *was* my alter ego, and I had to leave him back in Benin. I wondered, was he dormant and waiting for me to return to Africa to be re-awakened, or was he gone forever? Who would I be in the U.S? Would I be my old self, would I be Gandaho, or would I be someone in between the two? I was disoriented and I felt like a stranger in my old life.


## The Euphoric Stage:

When I initially got home, it was great to be united with my family and friends. I was ecstatic to get caught up on all the things I had missed over the last two plus years, and to share with them as much as they cared to hear about my experiences in Benin. Unfortunately their attention spans were not as great as my desire to talk about Benin. I was so happy to be back among the luxuries of the modern world. The first thing I did when I got home was go out for a pizza with my family. I got tons of toppings and ended it with a huge hot fudge sundae. I felt like I was in heaven! It was funny to think how I took such a simple pleasure for granted before I left, and how much I enjoyed it after not having it for two years. I could get pizza and ice cream in Benin, but it was nowhere near as good, and I could only get it in Cotonou. It was expensive, so I only had it a few times.

I spent my first three months living at home with my parents trying to re-adjust, and the first month was a time of euphoria. I spent a lot of time doing all the things that I wasn't able to do in Benin that I missed. First and foremost was eating all the foods I craved, and visiting or calling all my friends and family. In Benin there are a few really good dishes, but over all, the food is plain and there is very little variety. Essentially, their cooking is based on rice, beans, corn flour, and starchy tubers such as African yams and manioc. The starches are always served with a hot sauce of some sort, and they sometimes include small chunks of stewed meat. You can get fruit easily in Benin, but besides these foods, there isn't much else available. All meat and dairy products are expensive and hard to find. I always got enough to eat in Benin but my diet was monotonous, and it lacked comfort foods except on rare occasions.

In Benin I ate Beninese food and anything I could cook myself from scratch using very limited, locally available ingredients. An exception was when I went to Cotonou about once a month. I would go to restaurants and come home with a large bag of imported foods from the French supermarket, Prix Unique. Because the trip to Cotonou was expensive and arduous, I would go at most once a month. When I was there I bought cheese, butter, vegetables, and chocolate that were imported from France. Preparing food based on recipes from the U.S. was always a feat, as it was hard to get the ingredients, and I didn't have any fancy cooking implements. I only had a few things I brought from the U.S., the basics I could buy in Benin and a Peace Corps issued camping stove. Often I would have to omit or substitute many ingredients that were not available in my town. Luckily past PCV's collaborated to write a Peace Corps Benin cookbook that adapted American recipes to locally available ingredients and cooking implements. My most proud moment was when I made a carrot cake with cream cheese frosting. I used a Dutch oven, which entails putting a cake pan in a larger pot on top of small tomato paste cans over the camp stove. It came out surprisingly well. While in Benin I often dreamed about American food, and I had many cravings that I could only satisfy by getting these luxury items in Cotonou once a month.

My comfort foods like Doritos, Hostess Cupcakes, and Kool-Aid were definitely nowhere to be found unless a care package arrived from the U.S. When a care package did arrive, it was the highlight of the month! I remember when I finally received a care package that my aunt and uncle sent me by surface mail. It took nine months, and surface mail is only supposed to take three! In the package there were Ring Dings and other junk food. The Ring Dings had mold on them because they were so old, but I did not care one iota. I scraped off the mold and I gobbled them up without a second thought. They were good nonetheless! As volunteers we spent many hours discussing all the foods that we missed and craved (the third "S" of the three S's), so I know I was not the only one who felt this way.

When I got home I was suddenly faced with an almost infinite variety of food, which was overwhelming at times. I ate so much that during the first month back that I gained ten pounds! I wanted to eat everything, and it all tasted sooo good since I hadn't eaten any of those things in two years, especially the junk food. The meat and chicken is so tender and so fat here! I was used to not eating meat very often in Benin, and when I did, it was always as tough as shoe leather. I remember going to the food court in the local shopping mall, and I devoured everything there with my eyes. Then I bought my lunch. I bet the people working there thought I was pretty weird when they observed me wandering around staring longingly at all the different foods wishing I had a limitless appetite. I went into supermarkets a few times just to look at all the interesting foods but did not buy a thing.

During my first few months back in the U.S., I missed Benin, but I was too distracted by all the wonders of the modern world, so it didn't bother me too much. Some of the things I missed while in Benin were TV, shopping, computers, movies, the freedom and luxury of being able to get in my car and drive anywhere I wanted to go. I missed hot showers, being comfortable, not sweating all the time, not sticking out like a sore thumb, having so much choice for everything that I needed or wanted, and of course the ease, efficiency, and speed that things get done. My stereo sounded so nice, as I was used to using a small low quality boom box in Benin. At home I went bike riding on roads that seemed as smooth as ice since I was used to riding on bumpy, dusty, or muddy dirt bush paths in Benin. I had so many movies to get caught up on, as well as much TV watching, which I quickly got sick of. I took hot showers with water that seemed to fall from the sky as opposed to my cold bucket showers in Benin. The only time that I could take a hot shower with running water in Benin was when I was staying in a nice hotel in Cotonou once or twice a year, so I surely appreciated it when I got home.

I remember having goose bumps as I was in my parents' living room sipping a tall glass of orange juice in one hand while flipping channels with the T.V. remote control in the other. This simple pleasure made me feel like I was on top of the world! I realized that I was able to watch over 80 channels, and I had the portable phone on the coffee table in case I happened to need it. All I could think at this point was how if I were in Benin, I would be hot and sweaty, and if I wanted to use the phone, I would have to ride my bike one mile into town. I would have to pay a lot to use it, the connection would invariably be bad, and I would probably get cut off a few times. I would have to take a one-hour bush taxi ride to go to the American Recreation Center in the capital city if I wanted to watch American T.V., and I would have only a few channels to watch. If I wanted orange juice, I would have to squeeze it by hand and it wouldn't even be cold.

I occupied myself with many other things besides eating and seeing friends and family those first few months after arriving home. I got caught up on local news, revisited local places that I missed, and of course I went shopping. There were so many things to buy! My desire to consume had been stifled for two years since I had so little money in Benin, and there were so few goods and services available. When I was in Benin, I was very poor by American standards. Here I had a bit more money at my disposal, and I had plastic! It was amazing! All I had to do was give the cashiers a plastic card, and they gave me whatever I wanted without giving them any money! I didn't even have to bargain or dicker over change, which was such a relief. I found it amazing that I hardly ever needed to use cash. I had a whole jar of change at home but I never needed it. I could tell that cashiers preferred that I give them inexact change, as did the people standing behind me in line, because cashiers can make change faster than I can search through my pockets for it. In Benin however, it was the exact opposite. One time I remember on a taxi ride that a woman had a 10,000 CFA bill (worth about $20), and we all had to wait at least ten minutes while the taxi driver looked for change so she could pay him.

It was a lot of fun going through my old belongings that I hadn't seen in over two years. When I went to Benin, I only brought two suitcases with me, so most of my belongings stayed in the U.S. Items such as my clothes, music, books, computer, bike, etc., all seemed new to me again, which was an odd feeling. It was a similar feeling to when you are looking through your attic and you find things that you haven't seen in many years. After living in Benin without all these items, I realized that I didn't really need any of them, despite the fact that I had so much stuff! In Benin I realized that having few belongings simplified my life and gave me a lot more free time to do things such as read, socialize, cook, and sleep. Personal belongings take up time, because you have to learn about them, shop for them, buy them, pay for them, talk about them, use them, clean them, organize them, worry about them, maintain them, repair them, protect them, insure them, sell them, discard them, and replace them! What was quite strange to me was that I had to re-acquaint myself with a lot of the things that I hadn't used in so long, such as the car. I had to get used to driving again, as I had not driven in over two years. I had to refresh my memory on how to use my CD player, computer, VCR, washing machine, and dishwasher. I was amazed at how the internet exploded during my absence, and how much I had to learn about it in order to get caught up.

I had to deal with the many other complicated aspects of living in the modern world that I was comfortable with before going to Benin, but I had to reacquaint myself with them after returning. Examples are credit card terms, banking rules and fees, how to use the ATM, trying to remember the hours that businesses are open, and getting auto and health insurance. One time, in my laid back Beninese style, I stopped to smell the roses after I withdrew some cash from the ATM. All I was doing was inspecting the receipt it spit out before I took my cash and all of a sudden, *wallumph*, the ATM swallowed up my money!! I was beside myself. What a ridiculous machine! It took me about two weeks of calling the bank to finally get it back, and their explanation was that it is a safety measure put in place to protect users in case they forget to take their money from the machine. I don't know how anyone could forget a $100 that they just withdrew, unless they had Alzheimer's or some similar degenerative brain disease! Are people here really in that much of a hurry that they would forget money they just withdrew? These were just a few of the small challenges of readjustment that I faced, but of course the big questions were looming on the horizon. Questions such as: "What do I want to do for a living?" "How will I find a job and how long will it take? "Where do I want to live?" "When will I buy my own car?" And of course, "when will I move out of my parents' house and make it on my own?"

I enjoyed the speed and ease of using ATM's despite the problem I had the first time I used one after returning from Benin. I could withdraw money in less than two minutes from an ATM, and did not need to wait in line in a bank! In contrast, it took me about a half hour to withdraw or deposit money in Benin on a good day! Outside of Cotonou there were no checks, credit cards, wire transfers, or ATM's, so everything had to be paid in cash. Peace Corps paid us every three months. I had to take $600 cash (a small fortune in Benin) from the bank in Cotonou to my local savings bank in Allada. To make any deposit or withdraw, it was a four-step process. First I had to put my bankbook on the counter and sit on the wooden benches with all the other people who were waiting.

Then the teller called me up when he got to my bankbook and asked me the details of my transaction. I then had to sit down again. After a few minutes, when the teller had finished entering the transaction into the computer, he called me back up to the counter to sign the receipt. Of course I had to sit down again and wait. After the teller gave the bankbook and the signed receipt to the cashier, the cashier finally called me up and gave me the money along with my bankbook and receipt. I was shocked because one time the teller after seeing how much I had in my account, said "Why don't you give me a little money since you have so much?" I kindly refused and he proceeded to call me stingy!

In Benin people are almost never in a hurry and they are seldom concerned with time. As a result people are almost always late, and they often do not show up for appointments at all. This was something I never got used to in Benin. I always felt like they were being inconsiderate to me and were wasting my time, even though I knew that was part of their culture. No matter how hard I tried to be late, often I would still show up near the appointed time, and I would always be left waiting. When I got back to the U.S., I was surprised at how precise everything works here. It's like clockwork! If you have an appointment at a certain time, and you show up more than ten minutes late, you feel obligated to apologize. School schedules, busses, trains, movies, meetings with friends, etc. seem to always be on time, or very close to it. I was certainly relieved to be back home and to have schedules that people adhere to, and not always be left waiting.

I was completely shocked at how efficient we are in the U.S. I went to the post office to send five packages, and the woman worked so fast I got tired just watching her! It took her only about four minutes. In Benin it would have taken a half-hour on a good day. First I would have had to wait for the postal clerk to show up, and then socialize a little with her. Then she would have worked very slowly with a scale that uses small metal weights. Sometimes the scale was broken so she would have to pick up the item and guess its weight! She would then have had to figure out the price and would have had to do all sorts of math to figure out how to reach the required amount of postage with the stamps that she had in her drawer. It sounds easy, but when you need 1585 CFA of postage and all you have are 500 F stamps, 65 F stamps and 50 F stamps, it can get tricky. Sometimes I would have to put ten or more stamps on a package in order to reach the correct postage, and if she didn't have the correct stamps, I'd have to overpay since underpaying was not an option. One time she didn't have enough stamps, and I had to come back the next day! They surely don't have electronic postage scales that just spit out a postage label.

I can get so much done in one day in the U.S. because I have two things: a car and a phone. One time, while I was in a department store, I had to stop and ask myself "How did I get here?" Then I remembered, I had driven there on the highway in the car, but because it was so fast and effortless, I had nearly forgotten. When I thought back to how arduous most bush taxi rides were, it seemed like I had been teleported there like in Star Trek.

One time, after arriving back in the U.S., I went to see an old friend who lived about an hour away, so we met in a shopping mall half way between our two houses. The whole outing took four hours total, from the time I left to the time that I returned. In Benin it would have taken days. First we would have had to correspond by mail, and when we finally arranged a time and meeting place, the bush taxi ride could have easily taken half the day in each direction. Here all I had to do was call her on the phone and jump in my car, and we were there. The day I went to meet her it rained. Had I been in Benin we would have stayed home because rain is a perfectly acceptable reason for not venturing out due to the muddy dirt roads. Here the rain was not even a consideration.

In Benin the lack of a phone made life very difficult when I was trying to get anything done. Arranging to meet with someone locally meant that I would have to ride my bike to the person's house, sometimes several miles away, and hoped that he was home. If the person wasn't home, I had to leave a message with a family member or neighbor, and then go back in hopes of finding him. If I was trying to set up a meeting with a cooperative, I would have to set up an appointment for a week or two later, and often the person would not remember since they almost never write anything down. This was extremely frustrating and time consuming to say the least. Nowadays, many people in Benin have pre-paid cell phones, so I imagine communications are a lot easier for Peace Corps Volunteers.

The fact that stores in the U.S. abide by the business hours they post on the door seemed nothing short of a wonder to me. I cannot tell you how many times I went to a place of business that I frequented in Benin, only to find that the shop owner was not there, forcing me to come back another day. All businesses close for the lunchtime siesta from about noon to three to eat and take a nap to escape the intense heat and humidity. Almost no businesses post official hours, so their siesta can last from noon until as late as five PM. They also don't take keeping regular business hours seriously. Many shop owners work alone, so if they are sick, if they have to travel, or if they have other matters to attend to, their shop will be closed, and there is never a sign on the door with an explanation as to why.

While I was in Benin, I felt exhausted by noon every day and I frequently took a two to three hour nap. In Connecticut, it's not hot most of the year, and I only feel sleepy in the afternoon if I have a big lunch. The result is that I have a lot more time and I feel much more productive.

I heard from other returned volunteers that the first trip to the supermarket was a traumatic experience, and this certainly proved to be the case for me. I made the mistake of going to a Super Stop & Shop for my maiden voyage, instead of a smaller local grocery store. I had a medium size list, but it took me almost three hours! I looked at and studied everything just like a foreign visitor would because it all seemed so new and interesting. I had the desire to eat everything that I liked, missed and dreamed about while I was in Benin. Here the oranges are orange and not green! The green peppers are as big as softballs, and so are the tomatoes! A package of two chicken thighs have more meat than an entire chicken in Benin! There are 50 types of breakfast cereal . . . a whole aisle full! I couldn't believe it. In Benin the only items that have a large selection are cloth and beans. There choice is usually very limited. I had about 20 items on my list, and every item had at least five different products on the shelf that qualified. That meant I had to make five choices for each of the twenty items, which equaled 100 choices!

Needless to say, my first several trips to the grocery store were exciting, but exhausting. Not only was I not used to buying certain products any more, I was also not used to having so much choice. The variety here is mind-boggling! Do I want brown eggs or white eggs, large or small, cardboard carton or styrofoam carton? Do I want one dozen or a half dozen? Do I want the store brand or the name brand, etc.? I went through this with every item. Someone who is used to shopping generally has buying patterns already established. They know what they like, how much to spend, what brands they prefer, and they know for the most part what they're looking for before they even get to the store. I had done plenty of grocery shopping before I went to Benin, but being away so long I had forgotten what I usually bought.

As time went on, certain things about the grocery store experience started to bother me. There was no mystery or adventure in shopping as there was in Benin. Here everything is organized, clearly labeled, sterile, and regulated to the n'th degree. It is quiet except for the musack playing and the only smells are the fish in the fish section and floor polish. It was also a very impersonal experience, as no one talked to me and I didn't have to talk to anyone. There is no need to speak to anyone because I cannot bargain and everything is clearly labeled. In a way shopping in the U.S. is too easy. If you don't know what something is, all you have to do is read the label. If that fails, you can easily ask someone who speaks English. You don't have to hassle over change, because the cashier always has it or you can just use a credit card. It is nice not having to worry about paying too much for something because everything has a price tag, and everyone pays the same price (even me!). On the flip side, I no longer felt a sense of heroism going to the supermarket as I did when I ventured into a Beninese market. I missed the feeling of accomplishment I got from adeptly navigating the Beninese markets by overcoming all of the inherent cultural and linguistic obstacles, the excitement of it being an important event, as well as the social aspect of it. The African market is intense, social, and stimulating. The American supermarket has the advantage of being fast, efficient and hygienic, but the experience is mundane, impersonal and dehumanizing. Going to the grocery store for most Americans is just a chore to get done in a busy week but the West African market experience is so much more.

For the first month or so, I was happy living at home with my parents, as I was catching up with family and friends and everyone was happy to see me. There were so many friends and family to visit or talk to on the phone. It felt so good to belong again, to fit in and no longer be the Yovo. Everything was easy because I understood how things work in the U.S. I enjoyed the efficiency and conveniences offered by technology and a developed economy. Speaking English was effortless, and it was no longer a struggle to communicate as it was in Benin. However, the first few weeks back, I had a tendency to want to speak French or Fon to people. A few times French or Fon words just slipped out, and I got blank stares from the person I was talking to.

### Reverse Culture Shock Sets in:

By the third month being home, I had caught up with everything I missed when I was gone. The euphoria was over and the reality of being home and getting back on my feet again started to set in. The flipside of no longer being different in the U.S. was that I felt anonymous and unimportant. In Benin I enjoyed being a celebrity, because I was one of five white people in a village of 10,000. I got a lot of attention and because the Beninese tend to give a lot of respect to white people and, I was often made to feel important even when I did not deserve it. Not being constantly hounded for money, and not being pestered by curious people who just wanted to talk to me was refreshing after arriving back in the U,S., but after a while I began to miss it.

The Beninese are extremely outgoing and uninhibited about talking to strangers. On the other hand, Americans are, at least in Connecticut, much more reserved and reticent to talk to strangers. I felt that here, people who do not know me do not want to talk to me. I wanted to shake everyone's hand I met, as is the custom in Benin, but people here are reluctant unless they want to sell you something, or if they know you well and haven't seen you in a long time. Handshaking in Benin is very important. They shake everyone's hand in a restaurant when they enter before they sit down. Most restaurants are small and there usually are no more than a handful of people. If they do not shake the other person's hand, they would be seen as aloof. If your hand is dirty in Benin when greeting someone, you have to offer your wrist to shake instead. Besides not getting special attention anymore, I had few opportunities to socialize with people in my community. I didn't get much respect from anyone either because I was unemployed. I did not have a clear career path cut out, I was living with my parents, and I didn't have my own car. In short, things were beginning to look dreary.

I no longer felt a sense of accomplishment just getting by as I did in Benin since even the smallest tasks took a monumental effort. Life in the U.S. felt too easy and comfortable because of all the conveniences and technology we have. For example, Peace Corps Volunteers see cooking a good American style meal in Benin as an act of heroism. It takes so much effort and creativity to procure the ingredients and cook with very limited utensils and appliances. As a new volunteer, it takes a lot of time just to figure out where you can get the different ingredients, when you can get them, how much you should pay for them, and also how to bargain for them. The time I made that awesome carrot cake, the new Benin Peace Corps director happened to stop by my house unexpectedly and I offered him a piece. He was clearly very surprised how good it was and that I could pull it off with such limiting conditions. A simple task such as this was a major accomplishment in Benin while in the U.S. it would not have been anything special. Here we have all the ingredients and appliances at our disposal, so cooking is nowhere near as difficult as it was in Benin.

I made new cultural discoveries on a daily basis in Benin, which was very rewarding. For example, the first time I heard someone ringing a bell and talking loudly outside, it seemed odd. I went outside to find out what it was. I was told that he was the public crier. He was paid by different people to walk around town to make official announcements, since most people are illiterate and there are no newspapers or other means of communication in town. He was announcing the Beninese Independence Day parade. I found such discoveries very stimulating and rewarding because little by little, I was gaining a greater understanding of a seemingly enigmatic culture. With each new discovery, I felt myself becoming more and more integrated into the culture, which was one of my goals in being there. Back in the U.S., I didn't have those daily discoveries because I had lived here all my life and I understood my culture well.

During my first month at home, the cultural differences I noticed didn't bother me because I was too distracted by the newness of it all. Now that I had an acute awareness of my own culture, I wondered if I should point out the differences to other people to share with them my newfound point of view. I tried not to because I knew I would come off sounding critical of the U.S. When I did speak up, it was to my friends and family, who luckily for me, were usually patient and humored my alternate point of view on many topics. I struggled with the question: should I assert my newfound Beninese values in this society, or should I cave in to societal pressures to be just like everyone else and "fit in" again?

## Mourning the Loss of my Overseas Experiences:

After the initial euphoria of being home wore off, I began to grieve the end of my experience in Benin for many months. Whenever I thought about Africa and Africans, I became very emotional and nostalgic. I wrote a lot of letters to my Beninese friends back in Allada, and I was very happy when I received a few replies. I felt a strong desire to seek out people who looked African because they reminded me of Benin, and I hoped that by chance they would be Beninese. I hoped they would be interested in discussing Africa, or at least be African born. Unfortunately, they usually were not. I quickly realized this created awkward situations when the person I approached was not from Africa, and I therefore abandoned this rather insensitive practice.

I wanted to share my experiences in Benin with everyone, but often people lost interest in what I had to say after a few minutes, whereas I could have gone on talking for hours. It was frustrating, as I wanted to share so much, but most people's level of interest and attention span for the topic was usually far less than mine. I had a strong desire to educate people about Africa's many positive attributes, which most people have rarely heard about due to the media that normally only reports Africa's negative stories. To help me in my "mourning" process, I volunteered at many locations and gave slide show presentations about my experiences. I did so at several schools, a homeless shelter and a retirement home. I was happy to teach others about Benin, and it helped me in many ways to feel less sad about being away from Benin.

## Idealizing Benin and Criticizing My Own Culture:

Missing Benin, I quickly became very critical of my own culture, and I idealized the Beninese culture. I somehow forgot how uncomfortable I was in Benin, and I focused only its positive aspects. While I was in Benin, I felt and thought the complete opposite. I often dwelled on the negative aspects of Beninese culture and I idealized the United States. After returning to the U.S., it was more than "the grass is always greener on the other side of the fence," because my emotions changed so quickly from euphoric to critical of my own culture.

I will describe how I was critical about American culture here, but please don't think I am unpatriotic. It was a natural state of re-entry shock that I went through for a few months. I love the United States and I am proud of its many positive aspects. Today I feel that our culture has many things it needs to improve, but those things don't bother me as much as when I was experiencing re-entry shock.

The one thing that bothered me the most about being back in the U.S. is how little meaningful personal contact we have with others on a regular basis. We have to work many hours per week, which only allows a limited amount of time for relaxed socializing with friends and family. In Benin there is ample time and opportunity to socialize, so people spend a lot of time hanging out and conversing. On average we have little social interaction because we're so busy, because we place a higher priority on efficiency, and because producing measurable results is more important than developing meaningful relationships. Our need for efficiency, made possible by technology, has also removed many opportunities for social interaction.

For example, we often communicate by phone and e-mail instead of face to face. Everything that can be automated is, and we rarely have time to engage in a relaxed conversation with the people we do have contact with. I noticed this when I went to see the doctor. He was rushed. He got right down to business, and I was on my way out the door in about five minutes. I felt like a unit of production in his medical factory. I found the process was cold, impersonal, and dehumanizing.

Westerners are often aloof and standoffish compared to the Beninese. Ignoring people is common here, usually by avoiding eye contact. In urban areas, eye contact can even be interpreted as an act of aggression. Few people have time to talk and get to know one another, so they seem cold and reserved. There is a high level of distrust of strangers because we live in such a large-scale mobile society. People often live in one location for only a short time, making long lasting relationships and involvement in the community difficult. When we do have free time, we often choose more solitary activities such as using computers, watching T.V., or reading. These are all positive things in moderation, but are not inherently social. In Benin few people have TV's or read books, and no one had a computer at home, so sitting around talking with friends and family is a very important part of life that I missed. Our obsession with acquiring, using, maintaining, discarding and replacing material objects is another large time consumer that allows us less time for friends and family.

In the West our families tend to be small and there are less people around to talk to and to help out in times of need. Our family structure is nuclear, and usually consists only of the mother, father, and children. The high divorce rate puts further strain on families. Once the children grow up, they leave, and that family as a cohesive unit ceases to exist leaving a weak support system for the elderly and parents with young children.

On the other hand, Beninese families are usually very large extended families. Children are seen as a source of wealth and status. Most Beninese are poor and cannot afford many material goods, so instead, they have a lot of children, even if they don't have the money to provide for them. In the extended family, only the daughters leave. When they get married, they go to live with their husband's family, which is usually not very far away. On the other hand, the sons of the extended family stay and have their wives come and live in their extended family compound. In Benin the whole family lives together in one compound which often includes the grandparents, their children, the grandchildren, their great-grandchildren, and all the nieces, aunts, uncles and nephews. These large families provide a more extensive support system for each other. They help each other with childcare and taking care of the elders. If someone falls ill, they have their relatives to take care of them and contribute for major medical expenses.

Today urbanization is affecting Benin somewhat. More and more people are leaving their traditional family compounds and are moving to the cities to find work. However, this has not yet affected my neighbors, aside from a few family members who have moved to cities. Because there is less economic opportunity in Benin, people rarely move out of town for jobs. The result is most of their friends and the family members who they grew up with are around them their entire lives, which serves to enhance their sense of community.

My neighbors' extended family compound is comprised of about 40 people, and more than half are children! They all live together and support each other in times of need. They bring up their children together, and the phrase "It takes a village to raise a child" is an every day practice, not just a fanciful ideal like it is here. They don't need to pay for daycare or babysitters because there are always family members around to lend a hand. When the elderly get old and frail, they don't need to be put in retirement homes because there are always family members around to take care of them. When there is a death or illness, and money is needed for the funeral or doctor bills, there are usually family members who can contribute. If one family member is having financial problems, he or she can also turn to his family for help.

The Beninese are so social that they don't even understand the concept of "privacy." Sometimes when I spent the entire day at home alone on the weekend doing things like reading, cooking, cleaning, listening to music and writing in my journal, my neighbors came to check on me and asked me why I hadn't come out to see them. I would tell them that I was fine, but that I wanted to be alone. I learned that the Beninese perceive spending time alone as being aloof and antisocial. They don't understand the concept of privacy because they are almost never alone. They are so used to being in a close-knit society, and live with so many people in small huts, that privacy is virtually impossible for them.

In the U.S. parents have less time at home to spend with their children. They have to work more to "get ahead." "Getting ahead" usually means having more money to buy things, going on vacations, sending their children to better schools, and having more job status. The inevitable result is spending less time at home. They commute longer hours to be able to afford larger houses in the suburbs. Children often move far away from their parents in order to chase their career aspirations and land their "dream job." In that case they may see their family only a few times a year, which further weakens the family structure. To solve our problems that are caused by having family and friends far away, we often resort to paying institutions to take their place, such as day care centers, retirement homes, psychologists, and medication. Symptoms of our weak social structure can be seen in part by our problems with depression, suicide, and drug abuse, all which are very rare in Benin.

An interesting example of how Benin is a much more social culture than ours is how the "work life" / "social life" separation does not exist there. We are forced to separate our lives into "work lives" and "social lives" in the U.S. because the expectation of efficiency at most workplaces leaves little time for being social. The Beninese would probably not understand this concept. For them life is social, period. They socialize all the time. Every morning when I went to the CARDER office, everyone spent at least 10 to 20 minutes chatting before anyone did anything. Once they started to work, their pace was slow, and they would always be willing to stop what they were doing in order to have a relaxed conversation if the opportunity arose. Of course they got work done, but not as quickly and efficiently as we do here. They are less efficient, but they develop stronger relationships with the people that that they work with.

In the U.S., on the other hand, we are more productive and efficient, but the cost is that we rarely get to know the people we work with well. If we do, it usually takes many years. Socializing on the job has to be kept to a minimum, because it is perceived as a waste of time. When I first started working at a regular job in the U.S., I was amazed at how people worked through lunch or ate at their desks and had very little time to socialize during the regular workday. The seemingly few people who did take lunch usually spent it alone doing errands or reading. Only a few people seemed to go to lunch with others on a regular basis. Benin taught me that the key to happiness is having close personal relationships, so the American workplace seems very antisocial. We instinctively know that relationships are important, but limited time and pressure to be productive allows us to maintain only a few key relationships such as those we maintain with our spouse, our children, and a couple of good friends. In Benin people form relationships with almost everyone that they see on a daily basis, and this helps to build a stronger community.

I noticed that Americans are often friendly in a superficial way, but are less likely to take the time to really get to know each other. Europeans often comment on how Americans are very friendly when they visit because we usually say "please," "thank you," and we sometimes say "hello" to strangers. We also initiate smalltalk sometimes. We wait in lines politely, and occasionally let others go in front of us. However, when it comes to being giving of ourselves and creating deeper and more meaningful relationships, we fall short.

One aspect of the U.S. that really bothered me is our lack of community. It's no secret that many Americans don't know their neighbors. If they do know anyone, it is usually only one or two families who live right next to them. In the U.S. our home is our castle, and our individualism and privacy is our moat. After arriving back from Benin, I laughed to myself every time I saw "Welcome" written on someone's doormat or on a plaque near their front door. I was sure I would be made to feel less than "welcome" if they didn't know me and I happened to knock on their door. The doormats should read "Welcome Invited Guests." I couldn't help thinking "Who are they trying to fool and why bother with these silly mats and plaques!?" The Beninese, however, truly know how to make you feel welcome, even if you are a stranger. Whenever I ended up at strangers' hut or house, no matter how poor they were, they would give me water, a seat, and occasionally they would offer me food, and they would always offer me their company. They often made me feel stingy with their extreme generosity and hospitality.

The sense of community is much stronger in Benin. They are not very mobile, and they do not have cars or money to move around, so generally families live in the same village for generations, if not centuries. This permanence allows them to form deep-rooted communities where everyone knows everyone, and they are there to support one another in times of need. However, this is not to say that they live in perfect harmony by any means. In the extended family compounds, there are personality conflicts, jealousy, and quarrels. There is also a great pressure to share resources, so it is difficult for one family member to have more than the others, even if he or she works harder than everyone else. The advantage is that they have a strong social net, the type we are so lacking in the U.S.

When I got home, I was living with my parents in a suburban neighborhood in Connecticut. Some new families had moved into the neighborhood while I was gone. I did not go over and introduce myself because I would have felt odd knocking on their door unannounced. I figured they would have thought I was odd and that I was being intrusive. Because it was winter, they would have had to invite me in if we were going to talk. I was worried that they would have been suspicious of my motives, and they would not have wanted to invite me in, creating an uncomfortable situation. Instead I waited several months until it got warmer out and I saw them outside. That was the only time I felt that I was not intruding on their privacy and could approach them.

In the winter it is easy to never see your neighbors, which I found outrageous. When I got back it was November and I was wondering where everyone was. I saw lots of houses with lights on and cars around town and in the neighborhood, but I saw very few people. It seemed desolate and reminded me of the market in Allada on an off day when it was deserted. Sometimes I had grimmer notions that reminded me of the end of a science fiction movie where everyone was killed by an epidemic or alien force. In Benin people live outside their houses because it is so hot, and they only go inside to retrieve belongings, to sleep, or to escape the rain. People in suburban America do just the opposite during the winter. They encapsulate themselves in their cars, houses, and workplaces.

I was also shocked at how you rarely see small children out in public. In Benin I was used to seeing children everywhere. They were always playing together outside and trying to chase me down. In the U.S. we have far fewer children in proportion to the number of adults, and they are always closely guarded. They are usually found only in specific locations that are appropriate for small children. As a result, people who do not have children (such as myself at that time) have little contact with children on a regular basis.

We have communities in the U.S., but they are usually centered around special interest groups whose members have something in common, such as parents who have children of the same age as other parents, athletic clubs, political organizations, religious groups, or hobby clubs. What it boils down to is that we don't have time to get to know our neighbors unless they share a common interest. Because of time constraints, we pick and choose carefully the people that we feel we have the most in common with and we often ignore everyone else, including people who live right across the street from us. We are also distrustful of people because we don't know them while in Benin everyone knows everyone within a given community.

People ask me what I miss most about Benin, or what was the most shocking thing about being back in the U.S., and my answer is how people interact. The most important factor that drives how we behave is the amount of free time we have. We have little time here in the U.S., but we have lots of money. On the other hand, the Beninese have plenty of time, but they have very little money. Time and money are both a function of opportunity. For example, the more opportunity you have, the more money and the less time you will have. The less opportunity you have, the less money and the more time you will have. Because Benin's economy is underdeveloped, there is little opportunity to work and earn money. The result is that they have a lot of free time allowing them to be relaxed and develop stronger relationships with family and friends. In the Western world, the economy is well developed, so there is plenty of opportunity to earn money, and the result is that we are always rushed because we are caught in a vicious cycle of earning and spending money. We suffer from stress because there is an overabundance of opportunity, and we feel as if we are wasting time if we let opportunities pass us by. Our natural tendency is to bite off more than we can chew, and stress is the inevitable result.

The importance of being productive seemed overwhelming to me when I got back. This was highlighted by the fact that I felt guilty if I was tired and ended up taking a nap during the day, or I felt guilty when I stayed around the house on the weekends and didn't change out of my pajamas until the afternoon. I had no guilt whatsoever doing this in Benin, as there is far less pressure to be productive there. In the U.S., we often place a higher importance on how much one produces than what kind of person he or she is. In Benin it is the opposite. By American standards, taking the time to develop personal relationships is unproductive from an economic standpoint, and is seen as a leisure activity. The exception is if you are in sales or politics. In that case, relationship building is a means to greater production, and is therefore very important.

Another example of how highly they value personal relationships was when I held a small business skills training class, and I was given permission to have it in the CARDER office. The class was successful because I was getting 8-12 people showing up every week for an hour-long class. The only problem was that I had to cancel the class on several occasions because when the other participants and I arrived, the doors to the office were locked! I had scheduled the class during the normal business hours after the lunch siesta when the office should have been open. The problem was that the secretary was not showing up to work and to unlock the door. All the other CARDER agents were not necessarily supposed to be there because they went out to the villages to work with the people in the field in the afternoons. After the second time that this happened, I went to see the head of the CARDER office to see what could be done. He admitted that the secretary was unreliable but could not give me the key. Later he said that he had reprimanded her but then she was angry with him. He said that he couldn't just fire her, as there was a long bureaucratic process that must be followed. He also said that everyone would criticize him and say that he was being mean and unfair. Not only his subordinates would have said this about him, but also his superiors! Knowing this was the case, she did little to change, so I was forced to move my training sessions elsewhere. Unfortunately this same attitude of lax work habits was prevalent in the whole office, so when I needed anyone's help, I was often frustrated.

In the U.S. the opposite is often true, companies could not care less about how good a person you are, how loyal you've been to the company, or how long you've worked for them. Generally, what they care about is what is in the best interest of productivity and sales, and keeping the stock price of the company high to satisfy the stockholders. I often wonder which system is better, and one can certainly argue either way.

In the U.S., ageism is also a result of the pressure to produce. We often look down upon senior citizens, and consider them second-class because they are no longer productive. Their wisdom from so many years of life experience is often overlooked, and because they are no longer working and up to date with current trends, we don't value their experience. In Benin the elderly are revered and the deceased ancestors are actually worshiped and deified. The elderly have the most power in families and are conservators of tradition. When there are problems, conflicts, and important decisions to be made by the family as a whole, the elders are consulted first, and their decision reigns.

When I first returned to the U.S., everyone I dealt with in large stores seemed so aloof. I felt like I was wasting the time of a cashier or clerk if I asked "how are you?" because sometimes they would not answer or even look at me because they were so focused on scanning the items. Sometimes if I was lucky, they would they would give me a quick "fine thanks," usually without even making eye contact. In Benin I would converse for at least a few minutes during most business transactions in places that I frequented and I got to know the vendors personally. Try asking, "How are you today?" to a department store cashier or to a post office clerk and see how long you will converse.

When I first returned, Americans seemed very superficial to me. For most life is so easy and cushy here. So many people are soft and spoiled, and they are unable to tolerate the slightest hardship or inconvenience without complaining. We are often preoccupied with money, status, clothing, beauty, and image, as well as entertaining ourselves with electronic devices, cars, TV, movies, music, and vacations. I couldn't help but feel that Americans are superficial and spoiled, as I had returned from a place where people had to struggle just to get enough to eat, or scrounge up enough money to see a doctor when they were sick. Despite all that we have, many people still complain, and want more. It is not enough to have the things we need, but the things we have must project a certain image through the brands and styles we choose. In Benin the people are lucky to have the bare minimum to survive. How could I help but feel that Americans are spoiled, soft and superficial? We're impatient and we constantly want instant gratification. Most Beninese live with no running water, electricity, or access to decent medical care. Children often die at a young age due to bad hygiene and lack of healthcare. Most people never have the opportunity to travel far or get much education. They work hard in their fields, and don't have anything that we would call a luxury or convenience, yet they seldom complain about their circumstances.

I was amazed at all the material objects that most Americans own, including myself. It seems like we not only have everything that we need, but we have at least two of each item: one or two old versions, and one new. My parents' house is modest by middle class American standards, but it felt like a palace to me. It had clean carpeting, nice furniture, tile floors, running water, a leak free roof, heating, appliances, and electricity. This perception was a reaction to living in my cinder block house with a leaky tin roof for two years. All cars on the road are so new here! In Benin

I was used to seeing old Peugeot cars that were too old and worn out to be used in France, so the French sold them to the Beninese. Here we often consider a car "old" after its fifth year, or when it is in need of more costly routine maintenance. Most cars on the road in Benin are at least 15-20 years old! As a response, when I returned I made sure I bought an inexpensive car that did not have air conditioning. I figured that if I lived for two years without it, I could easily survive the few weeks a year in the summer when it's really hot.

I was also shocked at how everything is so expensive in the U.S. because I was used to living off of $6 a day in Benin! I can't even get breakfast at a restaurant for that much in the U.S.! It seems like I cannot do anything here without spending a lot of money. People in the U.S. always talk about money, hinting at how much they earn and talking about the new job they are looking for, the stock market, and how much they paid for this, or what a deal they got on that. It seems like Americans obsess about money. Although the Beninese are very concerned with money as well, it does not define their culture to the extent it does ours.

We have a high standard of living, but in some respects, we have a low quality of life. I noticed how Americans often don't appreciate the art of conversation. We've always got to be doing something, or have the T.V. on in the background to fill all the silent gaps. I was appalled that most businesses in the U.S. give the majority of their employees only two weeks of vacation per year. We have so little free time to begin with! When I was in Benin, I had a lot of free time, and it was difficult for me to adapt to having so little once I started working in the U.S. What really surprised me was how some people aren't bothered by having so little free time, and they claim that they wouldn't know what to do with more than two weeks of vacation. It is sad that some people are so engrossed by work that they are missing what it means to live. Sadly, many people here place too high a value on their work lives, and not enough on personal growth and exploration.

I was amazed by our need to plan, predict, forecast, and analyze all aspects of our society, especially for the economy and the weather. Whenever I heard a report on the radio or TV giving the latest statistics on the economy or offering another weather forecast, it made me feel as if we are control freaks. We fear a drop in our standard of living as much as we fear death, and it is for this reason we are so uptight about the economy. To make an analogy, if the economy were a person, it would be hooked up to so many monitoring devices you would not see the body beneath the wires. Every gurgle of the stomach, every breath, heartbeat, brain wave, and minute movement would be studied, analyzed, talked about, and pored over every nanosecond. If we sensed one little hiccup or change in a measurement, we would rush the person off for further testing and evaluation. Benin on the other hand is in an information vacuum. To get economic data, you would have to go to a government center in the capital city to research it, and it would surely be either out of date, inaccurate, or unavailable.

I also couldn't believe how much time is dedicated on the news to the weather here. Why do we need to know about the weather in such detail? We have cars and houses, and most people work indoors, so why dedicate so much time to predicting the weather? Why not just wait and see? If the weather is bad, stay inside! In Benin, I lived for two years without weather reports, and I didn't miss them one bit. Can't we leave anything to chance? Must we predict everything? Determining the sex of unborn children is a perfect example of our need to control and predict our environment. I would certainly have a tough time explaining to someone in Allada the concept of analyzing DNA for genetic predispositions to certain diseases.

The wasteful practice of planned obsoletion really bugged me when I got back. In Benin they fix everything again and again until it can absolutely be fixed no more. They have no choice. They cannot afford to replace broken items and the price of labor to repair items is very inexpensive. In the U.S. the problem is of course, that labor here is too expensive to make fixing most things worthwhile. As a result Benin is a "fix it" culture while the U.S. is a "throw away" culture. If it's old and broken in the U.S., we throw it away and get a new one. Why not? It's actually patriotic in a way because consumerism drives our economy and creates jobs. Oftentimes we throw things that aren't even broken because they are outdated and need to be replaced by newer and "better" products. As a result, the amount of waste we create in this country is outrageous as evidenced by what people put out on their curbs for garbage collection every week. I felt a need to be very frugal, and make a strong effort to recycle as much as possible because I was not used to being wasteful. I did not want to throw things away that could easily be fixed after seeing children fight tooth and nail over my seemingly worthless garbage in Benin. I certainly refused to throw away anything that worked fine but was not the latest and greatest.

Why is it that what we have is never good enough? Why do things go in and out of style, driving and perpetuating the "out with the old and in with the new" attitude? Marketing and people's desire for new things certainly have a lot to do with it. We are too weak to stand up to corporate and societal pressure and say, "My old car, computer, stereo, and clothing are good enough. I like them, and I am not getting rid of them just to buy a new and improved one!" Sometimes when I said things like this, I almost felt as if I was being unpatriotic because it undermines our economic system and the sense of progress that defines our culture. If everyone felt as frugal as I did, our economy would slump into a depression for sure! Having been away for two years, all my "stuff" was old and many people pressured me by saying "That's a really old such and such you have, why don't you get the new such and such? It's ten times better!" I was also appalled by marketing's constant pleas for shoppers to spend more as demonstrated by the "the more you spend the more you save" paradox that is often touted by stores having "blow out sales." For me, the more you spend, the more you spend, period.

The difference in wealth between the U.S. and Benin was hard for me to deal with as well. After I got my first job, I moved to an apartment in Stamford, CT in the very wealthy Fairfield County. I saw many mansions and expensive cars in the north end of town. It bothered me when I contemplated how there were probably only three or four people living in ten room mansions, while there were four or five people living in one-room mud huts in Benin. If these wealthy people gave up the amount of money it cost to have one of those empty rooms in their houses, it would probably be enough for a Beninese family to live on for decades!

There were many other differences that I noticed when I arrived back in the U.S. For example, the sun never seemed to rise very high since I came back during the winter. It seemed gloomy, even on sunny days because the sun was so low on the horizon. I was used to living at only eight degrees north of the equator so the sun was always almost directly overhead like it is here in late June. The landscape was gray and barren, not lush and tropical like it was in Benin. American's clothing seemed too conservative, and nothing like the vibrant and brightly colored clothing that they wear in Benin. Also, when I returned from Benin, I was acutely aware of the racial tension that exists in the U.S. I was used to living among only black people. They respected me, and there was no animosity as there sometimes is between races in the U.S.

It was so damn cold here that I didn't sweat, and therefore I almost never felt dirty. It takes me a week to get as dirty here as it did in one day in Benin, so washing seemed almost unnecessary. I no longer had gastro-intestinal problems here which was a major relief. No more intestinal discomfort, running to the bathroom ten times a day and wondering if I would make it in time. When I got back, I found I had become sensitized to T.V. violence. It was very disturbing because I had not seen any murders, rapes, executions, shootings or stabbings in two years, and it made me wonder if T.V. was the cause or effect of our violent society.

I realized that the U.S. is a place of excess and extremes. We have so much choice for almost everything we need or want that it is overwhelming and mind-boggling at times. We suffer from information overload from an almost infinite supply of media sources such as print, radio, T.V., and of course the internet. Most people have much more than they really need. We are accustomed to having many luxuries and living in luxurious houses and having nice cars relative to Benin. I am not talking about Mercedes and mansions of course, but about the average middle class house and car.

One extreme that stood out to me upon my return was our level of cleanliness. When I was in a movie theatre with a fellow returned Peace Corps Volunteer, we saw a sticker on a urinal saying that they were sterilized by company X. We almost split our sides laughing because having clean urinals is not good enough here; they actually have to be "sterilized." They've got to be so clean you can eat off of them! This is a far cry from Benin where people always go to the bathroom in the bush, after which pigs come to dine on their excrement, or they go in putrid, fly and cockroach ridden pit latrines. The floors in most public buildings in the U.S. look so clean I could almost eat off them.

I noticed how America has shallow historical roots compared to Africa. Our ancestors have only been on this continent for slightly more than 500 years, while African's roots are thousands of years old and seem to reach the center of the earth. They have a strong sense of tradition and cultural identity, which we do not have. Our lack of tradition can make us seem lost as a society, as we don't have traditions to guide our decisions in many circumstances. The benefit of not having strong traditions is that it provides us more freedom and independence to do what we want. It allows us to be eccentric, dynamic, and prosperous economically because we embrace change while traditional societies such as Benin thwart and resist it.

## Reconciling my Beninese Values with American Values:

My readjustment process to living in the U.S. was very long. In fact, it took me even longer than the two years I had spent in Benin. I lived with my parents for the first few months, and then I traveled to Europe for a few months. When I came back, I lived with my parents for a few more months until I found a job a few months later. At that time I moved out and I was forced to re-adjust more quickly. I had to become re-habituated to and accept the way things are in the U.S. I also had to balance my newfound values that I learned in Benin with those of the American society and somehow find a compromise between the two. I had to leave my experiences in the past and begin moving on with my future.

As soon as I entered the workforce my pace of life quickly increased. I felt a great pressure to be productive, earn a decent salary, be independent and excel in a career which would earn me status. I had to get more done in less time. I became more Americanized again and my critical opinions of American society became weaker and weaker. I stopped feeling that "Welcome" on people's doormats were funny. I stopped drooling (figuratively) every time I passed a bakery, a pizza shop, or the food court in the mall. Going shopping in a large supermarket no longer fazed me, and I got used to having so many choices. I stopped hoping that cashiers and strangers would have a real conversation with me. I began losing the ideas, values, and habits that I gained in Benin, and I re-established habits, values, and ideas that were more or less in synch with the U.S. and the way I was before I left. I felt like a hypocrite because I began to adapt many of the values and behaviors that I criticized when I first got back. I realized that we are clay and culture is the sculptor. Culture is a powerful force that compels people to conform to it through societal pressure. You can swim upstream only so long before you get tired, and the current sweeps you along with it. This of course is not universally true, and people who are dedicated to certain values and behaviors that run counter to popular culture may choose to not allow societal pressures to change certain behaviors. However, I realized that in order to be a well-adjusted member of the society in which I lived, I had to give up many of my Beninese values, but not all of them. Ultimately, I had to decide which values I learned in Benin were worth the trouble of keeping.

Today I feel I have completely readjusted, but I am still not the same as I was before I went to Benin. Some of my behaviors are a mixture of my American and Beninese values. I am definitely more materialistic now than when I first got back from Benin, but I am certainly less materialistic than before I left. I try hard to keep my material wants and desires in check, and not be seduced by marketing and peer pressure to buy things that I don't really need. I try to live by the "less is more" principle because I know it simplifies my life and gives me more free time. I feel guilty at times when I indulge myself, especially when I remember how little my Beninese friends have, so I try to splurge less. I am not as social as I was in Benin because I have a full time job, a family and a house, so I have little free time. However, I am definitely more social than before I left, and I make an effort to see my friends and family on a regular basis. I don't try to strike up conversations with everyone I meet anymore, but I do try to get to know the people that I deal with every day. I am more opposed to waste. I am thriftier, and more likely to recycle than before I went to Benin. I try to place a higher value on the simple pleasures of life, and enjoy what I have and try to concentrate less on what I don't have. I am more appreciative of the efficiency, luxuries, opportunity, and wealth that we have in the U.S. I am more appreciative of the virtues of our society as well, such as healthcare and all the conveniences that our technologically advanced society has to offer.

My experiences also helped me grow personally. I feel now that I am more confident having lived on my own in such a different place. I am more open-minded, more likely to try new things, and more likely to speak to people who are different from me. I am more sensitive to the feelings of minorities or people who are seen as different for any reason, as I know very well now what it is like to be singled out for being different. I am more likely to see a situation from another person's point of view because I had to be very understanding in order to relate to people who were so different from me in Benin. I am much more flexible and patient, and I have a more "go with the flow" attitude once I realize that nothing can be done to change a particular situation at hand. I am more resourceful and creative, and I am more resilient in the face of adversity. I have gained a broader perspective on the world, and I am able to see past and think past the cultural boundaries of our society. I am also more aware of the faults of our society. I am more outgoing and assertive.

Re-entry shock is not easy, but no extended trip to another country would be complete without it. It is a process that forces you to analyze your experience, and shows you what you learned when you were gone. It also shows you how you changed, and as a result, it gives a lot more value to an extended overseas trip.

For me, re-adjustment was a multi-step process which lasted several years. At first I was both sad and happy to leave Benin. I was sad to leave my unique experience and friends behind. At the same time, I was elated to be returning to my own country where I would be much more comfortable and I was able to see my friends and family again. I feared returning to the U.S. because I was not sure how I had changed, and if I would still fit in. I feared getting on my feet again, finding a career and a place to live. I was euphoric to be back in the U.S., to experience all the things I missed and to be with all the people I had been away from so long. I went through a critical phase where I compared aspects of the American culture to aspects of the Beninese culture that I felt were superior to ours. During that time I was nostalgic for Benin, and I grieved my departure. I discovered that not much had changed in the U.S. during my absence. What had changed most was my perspective, and I began to reconcile my newfound values with the values of the American culture. It has been almost fourteen years now since I left Benin. It has been a long time since I felt the last effects of re-entry shock, but I know that many values I learned in Benin are still tightly woven into the fabric of my personality.

-------------------------------------------------------------------------------

During one of my bouts of nostalgia for Benin, I wrote this poem in response to the word "native" that I have heard people use to refer to the Beninese people. The word shows their biases or lack of knowledge about West Africans. When people use the word "native" it immediately evokes images of savages living in the "Dark Continent," wearing loincloths, and being portrayed as primitive as seen in old movies. The word connotes a large difference between us and them, when in reality the differences between us and them are minimal at a fundamental level.

## Living with the "Natives"

So what were the natives like?
People ask
Were the natives restless?

The "natives" are my friends.
The "natives" are just like you and me
But in some ways, we are more primitive
And they are simpler

We don't know our neighbors
We have little sense of community
We shoot and kill and
Suffer from many social ills

I've laughed with the "natives"
I learned, ate, shared, danced and cried with the "natives"
The "natives" have little technology and industry
But they know how to work and survive
And they provide for their very large families

They do not live in nice houses
And have few things
But they have roofs over their heads
Their huts are devoid of possessions
But are cluttered with love

We work from 9-5 in the office
They work in their fields in the hot sun
The "natives" are just like you and me
In so many ways.

# Seven Years Later

## Why I Had to Go Back:

Even before I left, I knew I had to return to Benin one day because Benin is an amazing country that puts a spell on anyone who visits. Most visitors develop a love/hate relationship with Benin. There are so many aspects to love, but there are also many aspects to hate. Whether you love it or hate it, one thing is for sure: once you visit, you will never forget it. Whether you live there for an extended period, or for a short period of time, it becomes part of you and begs you to return long after you have left. In the seven years that I was away from Benin, I thought about it constantly and I talked about it extensively with friends, family, students, strangers, and frankly, with anyone who would listen. After I left, I had a strong desire to reconnect with this significant period of my life. Luckily I was able to go back for two weeks in 2004 with my wife Cara, seven years after I left in 1997, and then again in 2009 for one week.

When I was a Peace Corps Volunteer, I was just out of college. I began my service in 1995 when I was only 22 years old. I was looking for adventure in a place where I could learn about an exotic culture and learn a new language. I was looking to challenge myself, do something meaningful, and meet people who were very different from myself, all while postponing other major life commitments such as establishing a career, buying a house, finding a wife, and having children. I made many Beninese friends and I was very sad to leave them behind. I knew that I had to go back to see them someday. I fell in love with the culture and language, and I needed to reconnect with them. During my Peace Corps service, I was often frustrated because I never knew if the small business skills I was teaching would be useful or would make a difference. I wanted to go back several years later to see if I had, indeed, made a lasting difference, and to see if the standard of living in Benin had improved much since I had left.

Since Benin had become part of my identity, it was important for me to share my experiences with my wife, Cara, to help her understand me better. I had told her countless stories about Benin, and I knew she would be able to appreciate them much better after having been there herself.

As I discussed in the previous chapter, adapting to life in Benin required me to change in many ways, so when I got home from the Peace Corps, I had a serious case of reverse culture shock. In order to readjust to American society upon my return, I had to change some aspects of my personality back to the way they were before I went to Benin. I hoped returning to Benin would help me realize which aspects of my "Beninese" personality I kept, and which aspects of my personality were only temporary adaptations to life in Benin. I hoped going back would help me compare my three personalities: the young college kid I was before Peace Corps, the "Gandaho" persona I assumed while in Benin, and the adult I had become in the seven years after I returned to the United States. My life had changed considerably since I returned because I was seven years older. I had established a career in teaching, earned a master's degree, married and bought a house. Returning to Benin allowed me to reevaluate my experiences from this new perspective.

## Visiting as a Tourist, not as a Volunteer:

As I suspected, my perspective as a tourist staying in Benin for two weeks was much different from my perspective as a Peace Corps Volunteer. As a volunteer my priorities, responsibilities, and dilemmas were quite different from those of a tourist. For example, as a volunteer, I had to live on a shoestring budget, and I dealt with both homesickness and culture shock. I tried hard to make Beninese friends, learn the language, understand the culture, and simply fit in. I had a lot of time on my hands and I had to work hard to keep busy.

One of my most challenging tasks as a volunteer was finding satisfying work. My job was to find and help those who wanted and needed assistance improving their small businesses. To me, "satisfying" meant that the recipients of my services were willing to implement skills that I taught them, and subsequently demonstrate positive results because of these new skills. I needed a small amount of appreciation from time to time to keep me motivated but I did not always get it. I hoped that I would make a long-term difference in the lives of these people; the type of difference that takes many years to see.

As tourists, my wife Cara and I came with plenty of money, and very little time. My only priority was to see people and places I missed, do things that I had not done in seven years, and initiate Cara to Benin and West African culture. In addition, I had to oversee the exportation of several local dogs to the U.S.

When I was a volunteer, I had a local dog as a pet. The local dogs are called Basenji's, which are breed dogs. The original foundation stock of Basenji's brought to Europe in the 1930's were taken from the Congo and the native dogs in Benin are also Basenji's. We were lucky to have part of our trip financed by Robert, a Basenji fancier who wanted to import several Basenji's to the U.S. He wanted to do this project because inbreeding Basenji's outside of Africa created health problems in the breed, and introducing new genetic diversity in the breed would help alleviate them. It was a very expensive and ambitious project for Robert. He had to pay for the dogs to be shipped via air cargo, pay the vet bills, pay my expenses, pay Nestor, my neighbor in Allada, as well as the dogs' care when they arrived in the U.S.

Nestor did most of the groundwork before we arrived. He scouted for dogs in remote villages and purchased them. His parents housed them in the vacant hut adjacent to theirs. Nestor had to arrange for the vaccinations and the doggie passports that the airline required. I had to make sure the dogs received all of their vaccinations and that they had all of the necessary papers. Nestor and I then brought the dogs to Cotonou. We picked up the doggie crates that Robert had shipped to the airport. We went through a very lengthy process to complete the customs paperwork by visiting the offices of many customs officials. We finally shipped them off to Washington, DC after forking over about $1700 in cash for the freight fees. Luckily, I was able to return to Benin again in 2009 when another Basenji fancier, Marie, replicated this project by importing five Basenjis to the U.S. with the help of Nestor and me.

Initially, I was afraid that being away from Benin for so long caused my memories of it to become biased towards its positive aspects. When I lived in Benin, I was often uncomfortable, jaded, frustrated, lonely, and sometimes depressed. Just as when a loved one dies, you often forget their negative qualities and you end up eulogizing them. I wanted to verify whether what I remembered about Benin was realistic, or if my memories inaccurately glamorized Benin. I wanted to see what I remembered about Benin and what I forgot. I had several questions I wanted answered such as how well would I be able to speak Fon? Would people remember me? Would I remember them? How had the people changed? How had the country changed? Would I be able to see results of my work seven years later? I knew so many children. Would I even recognize them now and remember their names? When I lived in Benin, I toughened up to the realities of life in a poor country. After living in the U.S. again for so long, would going back be as difficult as it was when I arrived in Benin the first time? Did I become soft after being spoiled by the comforts of the United States for seven years?

I was surprised at how much work it was to plan a trip to Benin, and how expensive it was to go there on my own. As a volunteer, Peace Corps took care of my visa, spending money, airline tickets, vaccinations, anti-malarial prophylaxis, and they provided my in-country healthcare through the American embassy. In addition to arranging for all of these things ourselves, we also needed to get medevac insurance in case we had an accident requiring hospitalization. Hospitals in Benin are extremely primitive, so we would need to be flown to Europe in case of a serious injury. The only flights we could get to Benin were through Paris, and because we went in July, the tickets were about $2,000 each. Because it was so expensive, we made two vacations out of one, and we spent two weeks in France before heading to Benin for two weeks. (See the appendix for more information regarding planning a trip to Benin).

## The Money Fiasco:

Our two weeks in France were fabulous but our trip to Benin started out with a problem. Initially, we had a major headache exchanging our money for CFA. Our problems began with our flight, which was delayed four hours in Paris. This meant that we arrived in Cotonou close to midnight and after the change office had closed. Luckily we had some Euro cash, which we used to take a taxi to the hotel. Credit cards are accepted in only a handful of places in Benin. Those places include a few banks where you can get a cash advance, and the most expensive hotels and restaurants in Cotonou. For everything else, you need cash in Benin. We arrived on a Friday night, and I was confident that we would be able to find an ATM, a bank, or change office that would be able to change our traveler's checks on Saturday.

On Saturday morning we set out to exchange money, a task that would be easy in any country that is used to having tourists, but we found this not to be the case. I heard that there was one ATM in Cotonou that took American ATM cards, but we could not find it, even after looking and asking people for almost an hour. I heard that Ecobank was open on Saturday, so we headed there. However, when we got to the main office, we found it was closed on Saturday. The guard informed me that several branch offices of Ecobank were open on Saturday, and he gave us directions. We found the branch office, and they told us that the only place where we could get traveler's checks cashed was at the main office, which we had just left, and it wouldn't be open until Monday!! Arrhhh! I had $160 in American cash, so I confidently approached the window expecting to be able to exchange it, just to tide us over until Monday. The woman quickly told me that they only accept $100 bills, and they could not accept my $20 bills! It was unbelievable that the bank had a rule like that considering how poor Benin is.

I knew we could easily get our twenties cashed on the black market in Jonquet, a neighborhood in Cotonou, or in Dantokpa, Cotonou's biggest market. There are always dozens of money changers there sitting on benches with stacks of cash and a calculator in their hand waiting to exchange money. On our way to Jonquet, we found a change office. In fact, they even had a sign that said they exchanged traveler's checks! However, the man said they would be exchanging traveler's checks soon, but not yet. At least we were able to cash the $160 we had.

Not being able to cash our traveler's checks was a big inconvenience, as we were planning to leave Cotonou and not return until at least a week later. We had to be in Allada for our welcoming party on Sunday, and now we had to come back to Cotonou on Monday to get money.

On Monday morning I planned on an hour and a half taxi ride to Cotonou, an hour or so to get our money, and I hoped we'd be back in Allada by about 1:00 PM . . . . Again, this was not the case. We got to Ecobank at 11:00 AM, and we were greeted by a line that went almost out the door. I found the window that said *"Change de Cheques de Voyage,"* and we waited, and waited, and waited (for at least an hour!). When we finally reached the cashier, I gave him my passport and the checks. He asked me if I had an account at the bank and I said "no." He said, "Sorry, we only exchange traveler's checks for people who have accounts here." I was dumbfounded and furious. I asked him how this could be.

Why would anyone who had an account here want to exchange traveler's checks? "People who need to exchange traveler's checks are from other countries and therefore would not have an account here!" He gave me a sorry look and could offer no explanation. I was so angry that I stormed out of the bank.

I knew there had to be banks that exchanged traveler's checks, so we headed to the Bank of Africa. I asked where we could exchange traveler's checks, and we were lead to the proper window. I handed the woman my passport and traveler's checks. She gave me a look, handed them back and pointed to the hours on the window. It was 12:10 and she closed at 12:00. You have to come back at 3:00 PM she told me. ARGGGHHH! Both Cara and I were furious and thoroughly disgusted at this point. As a volunteer I never had problems with money because Peace Corps always deposited my money in CFA into my bank account. Since nothing had to be converted, it was much easier. Cara and I were angry because what we had intended to take half a day would now take the entire day, and we had only a few thousand CFA (i.e. a few U.S. dollars) left. I knew that all the banks closed at 12:00 or 12:30 so we had no choice but wait until 3:00.

We killed some time at the Peace Corps office and got some lunch before arriving back at the bank at 2:55. We were down to only a few CFA so we were first in line as the doors opened. My frustration had increased to a dangerous level as well as my fear that we would be screwed if we could not cash our traveler's checks. I politely passed my passport and traveler's checks neatly tucked inside to the cashier. She looked at them and then said, "Where are the receipts? You can't cash traveler's checks without the receipts." My blood instantly began to boil. My temperature rose about 10 degrees and adrenaline raced through my veins. I was so angry because we were in Cotonou, and the receipts were in our hotel in Allada. "What!!," I said grabbing back my passport and traveler's checks, "You don't understand! You are supposed to carry your receipts separate from your traveler's checks because if they are stolen, you need the receipts to get the money back. That is the whole idea of carrying traveler's checks!! If I carry the receipts with my checks and they are stolen, my money is gone!" She repeated herself saying, "I cannot exchange your checks unless you have the receipts." I was so angry I yelled "*Vous êtes des imbéciles!*," and I stormed out of the bank with Cara.

We had no choice but to continue on to the next bank. It was 3:00 PM, and the banks didn't close for another two to three hours, and we were going to get money if was the last thing we did. Next we went to Financial Bank, and believe it or not, we were able to cash our traveler's checks with no problem, as no receipts were necessary. We were elated that this fiasco was finally over, and we could get on with our vacation.

In retrospect, I cannot blame myself for getting so angry but I felt badly about blowing up and insulting them. She and everyone else there probably thought I was acting like a jerk, but they had no idea what we had been through, and what she was doing to us. I felt as if our safety and our vacation were being threatened if we could not get money. I was also frustrated about not being able to do something as simple as cashing traveler's checks at a bank in a capital city. I think that every westerner who spends time in West Africa experiences similar situations, where he or she gets progressively more frustrated with a given West African inefficiency, until he or she blows up or breaks down. There is actually a name created by English speaking expats for infinitely frustrating situations like this. It's called "WAWA" (West Africa Wins Again). As a volunteer we frequently threw out this term in frustrating situations when we knew we were helplessly trapped by third world inefficiencies and bureaucracy.

As I mentioned before, cash rules in Benin, as credit cards are accepted almost nowhere. You realize this whenever you stand in line at a bank because you see business owners pull huge wads of cash out of briefcases stuffed with money to deposit, and you see the cashiers constantly doling out huge sums of cash to customers. I realize how much I have taken credit cards for granted. I have learned to appreciate how easy and safe they make life, which becomes clear when you travel to countries where they are not readily accepted.

When I was a Peace Corps Volunteer, I didn't have much money to spend, and since I was there by myself, I didn't have to carry much cash on me. However, while Cara and I were in Benin, we spent about $100 a day for all of our expenses, which included hotel, food, transportation, souvenirs, and gifts. Because it was so hard to get to a bank in Cotonou and exchange money, we had to carry $800 in cash on us at times. Carrying that much cash or leaving it in the hotel was unnerving to say the least.

Every night I had to count our cash to make sure we had enough, and I had to plan carefully for the next time we'd be able to get to Cotonou, Bohicon, or Parakou, where a bank would be open to cash our traveler's checks. Our cash ran low after the first week so I had to change more traveler's checks in Bohicon at the Bank of Africa. The bank was packed.

The teller told me to have a seat, and that he would call me when he could. Every half hour I went up to the window and said "*C'est bientôt, non?*" (You're coming soon, right?) He would usually shrug his shoulders and say, "*Ah, oui, je viens*" (Yea, I'm coming). After waiting more than an hour, I finally broke down and offered the man a bribe so we could get out of there before old age set in. He refused it politely, and again assured me that he would help me "soon." It was another maddening situation, as we had no idea how long it would take, and we were thoroughly disgusted with banks at that point. This time, at least we were sitting while we waited. When he finally called me to the office in the back, he had the teller make a phone call to Cotonou to get the exchange rate. Of course, the phone was busy so I had to wait even longer.

While I was waiting, I figured I would try to educate him about tourism. I explained in a friendly way that Benin needs tourism to help the economy, and that he could help Benin by exchanging money for tourists faster. I explained that tourists spend a lot of money to get here, and they usually don't have a lot of time because they come for only a week or two. For that reason, they don't want to spend several hours in a bank. If they do, they will tell their friends how difficult it was to get money, and their friends will not want to come to Benin. Despite my best efforts, the teller was impervious to my logic, and his response to me, which he repeated several times, was, "You're really in a hurry," and, "This takes time you know. I am very busy. Do you see how busy I am? You're lucky I made time to help you because with all the work I have here, someone else may have told you to come back after lunch."

Luckily this time I remembered to bring the receipts, and despite the bad exchange rate and high fees, we had cold hard CFA's in no less than two hours. Not so bad for Benin, I suppose, considering what we went through in Cotonou. Near the end of our trip, we ran out of traveler's checks when I had to pay to ship the dogs to the U.S., so I used our credit card to get a cash advance at Financial Bank. Luckily that was a relatively painless process. This was in 2004 and I hope by now the banks have made it easier for foreigners to change money. I have heard that the large expensive hotels like the Benin Marina and Novotel change money for tourists, but I'm sure they don't give as good a rate as the banks do.

The difficulty exchanging money, in addition to the expense of airfare, visas, vaccinations, anti-malarial medicine, and travel insurance creates a strong deterrent for Western tourists to travel to Benin. It is sad, as Benin has so much to offer tourists, and tourism would significantly help their economy. However, there is a positive side to there being so little tourism in that most things you see and do are authentically Beninese.

## Our Arrival in Allada:

Although it got off to a bad start, the rest of our trip was much more positive. The most memorable moment of our trip was when we arrived in Allada at my neighbor's housing compound, and we got out of the taxi. They had been waiting for hours for us since we were running late and they were anticipating impatiently our arrival. Almost all of my former neighbors, about 40 people, were waiting there to greet us, and they all went crazy! They came running as soon as they saw us drive up in the taxi. They yelled and screamed and jumped up and down. They hugged and kissed us and greeted us for at least 10 minutes before we could even sit down. When we finally sat down, they kept coming up to touch me to see that I was really there, making sure that they weren't dreaming. I too had to reassure myself that I was really there, and that I was indeed not dreaming. They frequently called out "Ohh Gandaho," or "Ohh Cala" ("Cara," as best they could pronounce it) as a way of continuing to greet us. They even gave Cara a beautiful bouquet of wild flowers. I had told them in letters several times that I was going to come back to Benin soon, but each time I had to change my plans, as major events in my life, such as changing jobs, getting married, and buying a house, prevented me from coming back sooner. Some people told me later that they did not believe that I would ever come back, and they would only believe it when they saw me there with their own eyes. One reason they didn't think they would ever see me again was because there had been at least three other PCV's who lived in my old house before and after me. None of them kept in touch with them very long, and I was the only one to come back.

Everyone was so excited, and I was glad to see so many familiar faces. Many faces looked different, as all of the children were now seven years older. Small children had become young adults, and the toddlers had become big children. Any child younger than seven I had never met before, and there were several. I had some catching up to do in order to find out their names and who their siblings and parents were. Later I found out that a few people moved away, and a few died. A few girls moved away to live with their husbands, as is tradition. A few women I knew who married into the family left because their polygamous husbands were neglecting them, which is effectively a divorce. Pierre died of a strange illness, and his brother Jean was nice enough to take care of his children, since his wife had left Pierre with the children before he died.

## Our Welcome Party:

They planned an elaborate welcoming party / ceremony to welcome us, which started as soon as we arrived. I had been in contact with my friend Nestor via letters since I left in 1997. We started communicating by e-mail a few years prior to our arrival shortly after Allada got e-mail access. When we bought our plane tickets, I informed Nestor we were coming, and he informed everyone else. We were grateful to him because he organized such an amazing party in our honor. He promised that it would be big, and big it was! I sent him a list of names of about a dozen Beninese friends of mine from town that I wanted him to invite, and he did.

Since my Beninese neighbors are very poor, I promised to bring most of the food and pay for the drinks. All told, we probably spent only $70 for the party, and we bought enough to feed 50 people, as the American dollar goes a long way in Benin. They offered to provide the fish, as no party in Benin is complete without meat or fish. The average Beninese person cannot afford to eat it every day so it is de rigueur at any celebration. To get the food, we went to Dantokpa, a gigantic outdoor market in Cotonou that covers 50 acres. There is a huge building in the center of the market, but more of the market sprawls out around the building that in it. When we went, it was only our first full day in Benin, and it was Cara's first African market experience. It was like taking someone who's never skied before to the top on an expert slope and saying, "Come on, follow me!" Nevertheless, she did a great job navigating through the swarms of vendors and market-goers.

Dantokpa is the epitome of chaos. It is enormous, and it is so crowded that you can barely move. People were constantly calling us to buy from them and occasionally tugged at our arms to try to make a sale. When I was a volunteer, I was used to it, but not anymore. It was a novel and overwhelming experience again, but I knew how to get around from my two years as a PCV. We hired a *pousse-pousse* man to pull a two-wheeled cart to carry all of our purchases, and then we found a taxi to take us to Allada.

We bought 25 kg of rice, onions, bread, cookies, beans, hot pepper, charcoal, and some other things we needed, like bottled water, towels, plates, spoons and forks. We bought towels for ourselves, as you are lucky to get one small, worn out towel in all but the most expensive hotels in Benin. We also bought plates and utensils to use when eating street food. If the food is kept covered and is hot, you are not in danger of getting sick, but often the plates and utensils are rinsed in the same cold, dirty dishwater for the entire day, and you can easily get stomach bugs from that. By having our own plates and utensils that we knew were clean and dry, we hoped to stay as healthy as possible.

It took some time to get all of these things because we had to walk quite a bit to find everything, with our *pousse-pousse* man's help of course. We had to bargain for most of the items and then wait for the *tanti* (woman) to find us *changie* (change). Dantokpa was even more busy and chaotic than I remembered seven years ago. It was so busy that we could barely cross the road without being killed! The only way to cross was to wait until several other people arrived to cross with us. Then we would stop traffic by slowly walking out in front of the cars and motorcycles basically daring them to run over the entire group.

When we arrived in Allada on Saturday night, it was only the pre-party. The real party wasn't until Sunday afternoon. Nevertheless, everyone was very excited and giddy. We were treated to a traditional Fon welcome ceremony, where roughly ten children had rehearsed and performed at least six different dances for us, accompanied by singing and drumming. They painted themselves and put on grass skirts that they made for the occasion. Everyone sang and danced to drum music until about 9 PM. They sang songs in which they welcomed us by name, and they even wrote a beautiful welcome speech for us. We ate dinner with them (*pâte* with sauce of course), and we went back to our hotel at 10:00 PM.

On Sunday many women in the compound worked together and cooked all afternoon. The children who weren't dancing helped serve people. The children repeated the same ceremony with just as much energy. They even added a few new things to their repertoire such as a magic trick. One of my Beninese friends from town tried to figure out how the magic trick worked, and when he couldn't reveal the secret, everyone went crazy. They did an interesting dance that was similar to a Conga line but more elaborate. I was surprised because I had never seen any of these dances during my Peace Corps service. When the kids were done with their dances, everyone else got up and danced too. The Beninese love it when the Yovos try to dance like them, so we did our best. All my friends from town were there, and we ate rice with sauce and fish. To drink, we had soda, Beninese beer and sodabi. During my seven-year absence, we sent toys to the children at Christmas, and we sent about $100 each year for their school supplies and school fees. I am sure they would have welcomed us warmly even if we had not sent gifts, but it certainly didn't hurt to help them remember me.

A group photo of Cara and me with some of my neighbors.

## "Discovering Benin" Documentary:

I was glad I brought a video camera to capture much of the festivities. Nestor was also excited because I asked him to be my cameraman, which he appeared to thoroughly enjoy. After we returned to the U.S., I made a three hour, five episode documentary of our trip. I have sold many copies of the DVD, and I have given all the profits to Nestor and his family. Along with donations from Basenji fanciers, friends and family, and my DVD profits, I was able to put Nestor through college. He recently received his four year degree in accounting. I also used the money to help pay for the school supplies and school fees for the younger children in his family. I also sent him money to pay for his family members' medical expenses, as they rarely can afford to go to a clinic when they are ill. You can purchase a copy of the DVD at my website where I teach people to speak Fon: www. fon-is-fun.org. Making the video was very enjoyable because it allowed me to show others what it is really like in Benin. Before this trip I only had photos to share with others, and photos do not give a good a feeling of what it is like there. Before I had the documentary, memories of my experiences in Benin seemed like a dream at times. Now, I can watch the video to remind myself that they are indeed real.

The party went on from about 4:00 PM until around 8:30 PM. We left with Patricia, the current Peace Corps Volunteer in Allada and her two friends who we invited. We debriefed at a local *buvette* over a few *Grande Beninoise* beers. It was great to talk to them and reconnect with Peace Corps life. It was interesting for me to hear their stories, and to hear about their problems, concerns and frustrations. They were all similar to the things I had gone through as a volunteer and it brought back many memories.

Later on Cara and I took Zemis back to our hotel, which was located just outside Allada on the road to Togudo (a small village). They actually started building the hotel before I left, and at the time, I was very cynical. It was very big, and I kept asking myself "Why would anyone want to come to Allada and stay in a hotel?" It is true that the king of Allada lives in Togudo and has elaborate ceremonies at least once a year that do attract visitors, but how could such a large hotel stay in business? I was sure it would not survive past a few years, but I was very happy to find out that it was still around.

The hotel had about 30 rooms and three floors. The rooms were clean, and the beds were comfortable. They had air conditioning, a TV, and bathrooms with running water, all for 11,000 CFA, or about $22 a night! They had a decent restaurant where we ate breakfast every day, and we had dinner there a few times as well. If it weren't for this hotel, we would have had to stay at a friend's house, and it would have been much less comfortable. I was told that the owner of the hotel often rented it out for large conferences, and they made most of their money that way, as there are very few tourists who stay there.

## Visiting Friends and Evaluating my Contribution:

We spent the next several days visiting my old friends, most of whom I had worked with. Cara and I kept a busy schedule, making rounds visiting my friends individually. As a volunteer, I gave classes on basic business management skills to small business owners. I then consulted with them one on one to encourage them to implement what I had taught them and discuss their concerns. My most serious students were Jean, the wood sculptor, René and Augustin, the pineapple producers, Alice the weaver, Solange, the seamstress, and Arthur, the carpenter. Cara and I went to their workshops and hung out with them individually, which took two days.

I was happy to see that most of them had improved their businesses somewhat. Some had improved more than others, but I can't say for sure how much of the improvement was due to what I had taught them. I asked them if what they learned from me was helpful, and they all said "yes," enthusiastically, which was encouraging. However, I can't help but wonder if they were just being nice. I had taught them how to do basic bookkeeping, and I asked them if they were still keeping books. They all said "yes," but I did not ask for proof. Ultimately, I still feel I received more than I gave, in non-monetary forms of course. In terms of the contribution I made, I feel the relationships I forged with them had a greater impact than the business kills I taught them. In my opinion, that is the true nature of Peace Corps.

Meeting with Rene and Augustin, I discovered that they had done exceptionally well. When I was working with them, they were only growing pineapples. I enjoyed working with them because they were very motivated, disciplined, and intelligent. They headed a cooperative that had several large pineapple fields. I helped them plan their production, and we worked on bookkeeping, marketing, and distribution. I also helped them estimate their yields by mapping their fields. Now they have a pineapple-drying factory where they produce and export dried pineapple and pineapple juice! I can claim little credit for their advances because they were made possible with funding from ADF, a quasi-non governmental American aid agency. ADF and another French aid organization gave them much of the money necessary to build several small buildings, to buy the drying machines, to buy other necessary equipment and to dig a cistern for water. They also helped them make connections to start exporting to Europe.

Their factory is very simple, with about 14 people working there. Everything is done by hand, and they have limited production, but it is still very impressive for a private industry in Benin. I was glad to hear them say my training helped them get started. More importantly, the fact that they received training from me looked good on paper when they applied for funding from ADF. It improved their chances in the competitive grant process because it showed that they were serious about their business.

I always wished I could have done more for them, and at times I felt guilty I had not. I wished I had been able to get them grants to fund their projects to compliment the small business training that I offered, but that is not a priority for Peace Corps. Some volunteers are able to get one or two funded projects for the most worthy people they work with, but we are not encouraged to do so and we are not given the resources to make it easy. As a result most volunteers feel getting funded projects is a very long and difficult process. Peace Corps puts more emphasis on being a cross-cultural organization and on creating good public relations for the U.S. than it does on improving the economies of the countries where volunteers serve. The fact that other development organizations in Benin offered training and capital, but we did not, was a constant source of frustration for PCV's. I was reminded of this as Jean, Alice, Arthur, and Solange were still asking me to help them obtain financing from an international aid agency on my return visit. After I returned home, I sent them some information on an aid agency that I knew of, and Jean was lucky enough to win a small grant to improve his sculpture business.

I had to remind myself that my making a difference in Benin was limited by many factors. All I had to offer the people I worked with was training and encouragement. My level of training and experience was very limited when I first arrived in Benin. I only received three months of training, and a few extra seminars during my two years as a PCV. I was accepted into the program because I ran a College Pro exterior house painting franchise during my summer breaks while I was in college, but I did not have a business degree. In fact, most volunteers are just out of college, and they have limited experience in the fields that they are assigned to work in. They usually have no experience working in the developing world either. For the most part, volunteers are on their own in figuring out how to help people when they are sent to their posts after their training is over. They must rely on their resourcefulness, resilience, persistence, flexibility, cross cultural interpersonal skills, and creativity in order to truly make a difference. For these reasons it was not surprising to me that the people I helped only made limited progress. Despite the fact that only Réné and Austin had made any significant advances in their business since I had left, I was happy to see that everyone I worked with remembered me and claimed that what I did for them was helpful.

Aside from the people I worked with, I was very flattered that so many other people in Allada remembered me after so many years. I was glad my favorite food sellers who sold on the side of the road in Allada were still there. It was great to see the surprised reaction of my *abobosato* (rice and beans lady) and that of Ali, my *Shwarma* (spiced mystery meat kabob) man when he recognized me. In fact, there was no one I remembered who did not remember me. Because I was one of three white people who lived in Allada at the time, everyone knew me, and I knew relatively few people. When I was in a supermarket in Cotonou, an employee walked up to me and asked, "Do you remember me?" And I did. It was someone I knew from Allada, and I was shocked that in a city as big as Cotonou, I would run into someone from Allada who I knew seven years ago.

## Speaking Fon Again:

On my trip back to Benin, I spoke Fon to everyone, and it was a lot of fun. Both they and I were surprised that I hadn't forgotten much of it. I forgot how crazy people go when the Yovo speaks Fon. I got the *"Ahh! Yovo se Fongbe"* (Ah, my God, he speaks Fon!) routine over and over. When I was waiting in line for an hour at Ecobank, I started speaking Fon to someone in line next to me to pass the time. I swear everyone waiting in line, which amounted to probably 50 people, were all staring at me and listening intently because I was speaking Fon. When I really wanted to impress people, I explained to them in Fon that I was initiated to several Vodun cults, which is true, and I showed them my magic gris-gris ring. When I told them that I know how to read Fah, a slight exaggeration, their jaws usually hit the ground. They would then shake my hand and say, *"Vraiment, tu es un vrai Beninois!"* (Wow, you are a true Beninese person!). After a few days, however, it got tiring speaking Fon, because of all the attention that it drew to me. Sometimes I would just speak in French when I wasn't in the mood to hear the "*Ah, Yovo se fongbe*" routine. I have to admit, most of the time, I did enjoy the attention it brought me.

Cara and I visited so many people that after a few days it got tiring. I had to say "hi" to my old landlord, to the old guy who always said "hi" to me on the road that lead to my house, to my old counterpart Clément (the Beninese person that Peace Corps arranged for me to work with), my elderly Italian friend who was still living in Allada, the veterinarian who took care of my dog, and my friend Korantin who helped me research Vodun. Cara and I felt rushed because along with visiting so many people, and arranging to export Basenjis, we wanted to see several of the interesting places in southern Benin. I also wanted her to see a few Vodun ceremonies.

## Sightseeing and Cultural Activities:

We had planned on going up north, but we had already lost a day in Cotonou trying to get money changed, and understandably Cara was very nervous about traveling in bush taxis. It takes a full day to get up to Natitingou, if all goes well, and a full day to get back. Because of the bush taxis, the long distance, and because we would have only two days time to stay up there, we decided not to go in order to have a more relaxed time in southern Benin. I knew that it would take at least two days to complete all the tasks related to exporting the puppies, and I didn't want to be too rushed. The farthest north we got was Abomey, the capital of the Dahomey kingdom, where we spent a day and a night. It's about an hour and a half bush taxi ride from Allada.

My Beninese friend Nestor, who was 21, had really grown up. When I left Benin in 1997, he was only 14. We had become even closer during the seven years when I was back in the U.S. because we wrote many letters to each other, and we also spoke on the phone a few times. Whenever I sent money or gifts to his family, I asked him to be in charge of distributing them because he was so trustworthy. I sent toys for the children at Christmas, and money for school supplies and school fees. I also sent money for medicine and doctor visits when his family members were sick.

Nestor had lived in Allada all his life, but had never been anywhere except the villages around Allada, Cotonou, and the village in the Mono where his family is from. Cara and I were blown away by the warmth and hospitality of the party he organized, and we wanted to thank him, so we invited him to travel with us. We invited him to come with us to Ganvié, the city built on stilts on a lagoon, Ouidah, the former Slave Port on the coast, Gran-Popo, a beautiful beach with a small hotel, and Cotonou on our last day. We wanted to spend more time with him, and it was a good opportunity for him to see more of his own country since he had had few opportunities to travel. He also accompanied us when we took Zemis in the bush out to Dekanmé and crossed lake Ahemé in pirogues to visit Bopa.

I wanted to reconnect with Vodun and expose Cara to it. I had my old Fah priest read our Fah. We asked if the Basenjis would have a safe journey back to the U.S., and luckily the answer was yes. My Bocono (Fah priest) also told us that we would be successful and so would our future children.

My Fah priest in the process of consulting Fah to tell our future. Notice the cult of twin dolls on each side. Twins are sacred and these dolls commemorate deceased twins in his family.

While in Benin, I was initiated into a Vodun cult called *Ja*. Since I had not been around for the annual ceremonies, Nestor's dad, who is the priest of this cult, suggested that I make an offering. I paid 5,000 CFA ($10) to have him do a small ceremony. With the money he bought sodabi, and a chicken, with a bit left over for his services. A few other Ja initiates and I drank some sodabi, and then sprayed some from our mouths on the bottles containing the powder and spirit of Ja. He then consulted Fah using cowry shells to determine whether or not my sacrifice was acceptable to Ja. Luckily it was, so it was time to kill the chicken. He slit its throat, as this is the way all animals are killed in Benin. That way it is easy for him to drip the blood on the bottles (the Ja altar) because animal blood is what all Vodun gods want. By making an offering of animal sacrifice, I appeased the god to ensure my good fortune. Ja's powers are specifically against witches and snakebites. Since I was initiated, I have never been bitten by a snake or attacked by a witch, so I know Ja has been protecting me.

Another day my friend Korantin took us to see the Gambara Vodun dancers perform a ceremony in a nearby village called Agongblamé. A few of the dancers fell into a trance, which was very interesting. We paid a visit to the King of Allada at his royal palace, which was within walking distance from our hotel. I was surprised that he remembered me from his Vodun ceremonies that I had attended many years ago.


## Time Versus Money Tradeoffs:

As I mentioned before, it was much different being a tourist in Benin for two weeks than it was living and working there for two years. As a volunteer I had very little money and an unlimited amount of time. Now we had as much money as we needed but we had very little time. As a volunteer I often bargained to the death over 50 CFA (10 cents). I had to do this as I was only paid 3,000 CFA ($6) per day. I also wanted to be treated like another Beninese person since I was living there and serving them. Now I didn't have the time or energy to bargain quite as hard.

Many times during my return trip, when someone tried to overcharge me 10 cents, I simply gave in. At times I did bargain hard, just to prove to myself that I hadn't lost my touch. I certainly bargained hard if I felt we were really getting ripped off. Sometimes I felt bad paying more than I should have because I knew it would make it harder for volunteers and other Yovos to get a reasonable price the next time, and I also felt like I was being a pushover. I rationalized this behavior by saying it is a built in charity tax that we could easily afford.

Having more money than I did as a volunteer meant that Cara and I could enjoy many luxuries that I could not afford as a volunteer. For example, we always bought an extra seat in the bush taxis so we wouldn't be jammed in and lose circulation in one cheek and leg. Sometimes we rented the entire taxi for short trips, so we wouldn't have to wait for it to fill up and then wait again for it to let out passengers. We could stay in hotels with air conditioning and eat hotel food.

I made the discovery that good health in Benin has a price. As a volunteer I probably had diarrhea at least once a month and when I didn't have it, I was always wondering when I would be suffering the next bout. However, if you have money, it can be avoided. On our trip Cara and I drank nothing but bottled water, and we did not eat street food very often. I am sure that using our own plates and utensils that we kept clean and dry when we did eat street food helped as well.

Having more money also meant we could be generous with my friends. One woman had a broken ankle that was very swollen from a Zemidjan accident, and it had been that way for seven months! We gave her 10,000 CFA (around $20) to go to the doctor. A few days later, she showed us an x-ray and said the doctor was going to reset it for her. Nestor's mother was not feeling well for a few months, so we gave her some money to go to the doctor as well. As we have done every year, we gave $100 for school supplies and school fees for all the children in the compound. There are about 20 of them, and $5 per child goes a long way to keep them in school.

## How I Changed:

When you live in Benin for two years, you have to get used to many discomforts and inconveniences. However, there are some things you can never get used to. When I returned to Benin after a seven year absence, I couldn't help being bothered by some things that did not bother me before I had left, as I had grown soft living with the conveniences of the United States for so long. For example, mildew in the hotel pillows from the extreme year-round humidity, the pollution and traffic in Cotonou, and the constant dirt and grime in the air grated on me. Most taxis had exhaust leaks, so we had to breathe exhaust fumes for most of the ride and we certainly did not enjoy that. In addition, because we were there for only two weeks, I noticed that I was less patient, especially in the banks, where we wound up spending so much time. It annoyed me that I always had to worry whether or not I'd be able to get change for a 5,000 CFA ($10) bill when buying an inexpensive item, and always having to plan ahead accordingly to avoid change crises. It bothered me that I had to pay for everything with cash, and subsequently having to go through the arduous task of getting money exchanged at a bank when it ran out. Aside from these aforementioned annoyances, I was fine with everything else I experienced on my return trip. I'm sure that using a latrine and being squeezed into an over-packed taxi would have bothered me more on my return visit than when I was a volunteer. Because I was able to afford hotels with a flush toilets and an extra seat in taxis, I gladly did not have to relive such arduous experiences.

As I stated earlier, there are practically no garbage cans anywhere, so people have no choice but to throw their garbage on the ground. When I was a volunteer, I got tired of carrying garbage in my pocket only to find out that I ultimately had no other choice but to throw it on the ground somewhere. However, on my return trip, I could not bring myself to throw garbage on the ground as I did when I was a volunteer. Whenever I had garbage, I asked a Beninese person what I should do with it knowing very well that the answer would be, "Throw it on the ground." I asked just to have justification and to not feel guilty doing so. When I was with Nestor, we had a prescribed routine where I would ask him, "Where should I put the garbage?" He would always say, "Throw it on the ground." Then I would hand it to him, and he would immediately drop it on the ground, allowing me to walk away guilt free.

Oddly enough, a few things that bothered me when I was a volunteer did not affect me on my return trip. The Yovo song drove every volunteer and me absolutely crazy because we heard the kids sing, "*Yovo, Yovo, bon soir, ca va bien? Merci!*" dozens of times per day. Since no one had sung that song to me in years, I somehow thought it was cute again when I heard it, and hearing it even made me feel somewhat nostalgic. The small children who were smiling and waving while singing it were especially cute, but the older children who sang it and pointed in a taunting manner would have gotten on my nerves had I stayed another week. As a volunteer I hated *akassa*. It's a flavorless, gelatinous ball of slightly fermented cornstarch that you dip into sauce and eat with your hands. However, on my return trip, I ate some and I somehow liked it. The *pâte* tasted good, and the rice and beans were scrumptious with a little *gari*. I figure I must have enjoyed these foods for purely nostalgic reasons, as I can think of no other explanation.

## The Positives and Negatives of Benin:

Returning to Benin made me recall both the positive and negative aspects of the country. In Benin most Western visitors love the people but hate the inefficiencies and discomforts associated with the low standard of living. When you visit a Western city, people often go to see the sights, but not so much to get to know the people. In Benin getting to know the people is as interesting, if not more so, than the sights. Because Benin is so poor, almost nothing works efficiently. A situation such as trying to get money exchanged is a perfect example of this. Luckily "WAWA" induced frustration is usually offset by the kindness of the Beninese people.

There were several examples where the kindness and friendliness of the Beninese people made unpleasant situations much more bearable. The Beninese are extremely outgoing and often initiated conversations with us. I'm sure one reason they did so is because we're foreigners and they were interested in talking to us. Regardless of us being foreigners I know they are genuinely friendly people because they readily make conversation with other Beninese people as well. They are not afraid to talk to strangers and they have time to have in-depth conversations such as when I was stuck in lines at the bank. When Cara and I were running all over Cotonou trying to get money exchanged, we needed to cross a busy road. I saw a police officer who just happened to be walking by and I asked her to help us cross. She took out her whistle and gladly stopped the traffic for us. That same day we needed a place to sit down after Cara got a "sewer sandwich," so called because they are sold by a woman who sells sandwiches near an open sewer. After looking around, we found a stoop to sit on. Some men who were working nearby stopped what they were doing to dust off the stoop, and found a wooden bench for the other PCV's we were with to sit on. Experiencing these acts of kindness that day reminded me how nice the Beninese people truly are, and I no longer felt so bad about the frustrations of the day. The little things the Beninese often do can really make up for the annoyances created by inefficiencies one must deal with while in Benin.

That same day we were supposed to go to one of my friend's house for lunch in the afternoon, but we were held up in Cotonou trying to get money. Luckily I was able to call one of the few people I knew in Allada with a phone, and I had someone deliver a message relaying that we would be very late. When we got there in the evening, our friend served us the food she had made us for lunch, and all of our friends who had intended to join us for lunch gathered again. Their wonderful hospitality made us forget about the terrible day we just had in Cotonou. To enjoy Benin one must focus on the positive aspects of the people and try to forget the discomforts and hassles.

When I returned to Benin, I felt almost as if I was coming home and I had never left. I remembered almost everything about it. I could still speak Fon and French well. I remembered most of the people, and I remembered how to get around. I did forget a few words in Fon and a few people's names. I forgot many of the roads in Cotonou, and some of the bush paths that I took when I was riding my bike out to the villages to work with cooperatives. However, these things were not significant.

## How Benin Changed:

Although I never felt completely at home while living in Benin, I had adapted to it fairly well. I had become familiar with the people, the language, and the culture. Despite the seven years I had been away, Benin was pretty much the same, and it still felt somewhat like home. Going back made me realize how much I had learned about Benin and how much I had adjusted to it. I was surprised that Benin felt like home again because it is so different from the U.S., and I had been away for so long. When I went back, I had feelings similar to those I have when I visit the town I grew up in after not having been there for a long time. I looked for changes since the last time I was there and recalled the many memories different places evoked. Since Benin is such a poor country, and I was there as a PCV to help it develop, I wanted to think that in seven years there would have been many improvements. At best I would say there were some modest improvements. Unfortunately, they were partially offset by an increase in population which resulted in more crowding and pollution.

Many businesses opened and closed in Allada. There was a new bakery and their baguettes were absolutely fantastic compared to what we get in the U.S. When I was a PCV, the bread was always day old in Allada because it came from Cotonou.

It appears that Christian evangelism is on the rise in Benin, as I saw a lot more Jehovah's Witness buildings, and I saw many new churches. In Allada there is a huge new church, and there is a very large radio antenna that broadcasts evangelical programs in Fon. I actually heard it on the internet in the U.S. before I left for Benin.

They have improved the roads and bridges somewhat, but unfortunately it seems that the increased traffic has offset any gains in that area. Cotonou seems much more crowded and polluted. The traffic is also a lot worse. I remember being able to get from Allada to Cotonou in about an hour to an hour and a half on a bad day. On the few trips I took during my return trip, it usually took almost two hours, as traffic came to a standstill frequently between Godomey and Abomey-Calavi. I heard that Abomey-Calavi had become an "upscale" bedroom community for all the professionals in Cotonou, so traffic was particularly bad. I remember being able to cross the street in Cotonou without fearing for my life, but not any more!

The pollution is also a lot worse from the many more cars and Zemis on the road. There was a constant traffic jam on the bridge in the downtown area. At one point, I was on a zemi and it took 10 minutes just to cross the bridge! After that experience we decided to cross the bridge by foot later that day. By that time, the traffic had worsened, and we had to dodge zemis riding on the sidewalk! Luckily they were building an adjacent bridge, which appeared to be almost finished. Cotonou is still very dirty and the sidewalks are crowded by vendors forcing you to walk in the busy streets. I saw garbage cans on the street in only one neighborhood for the first time, and guess where they were? In Haie Vive, the Yovo neighborhood, of course!

Access to modern technology has definitely improved in Benin. When I left in 1997, there were a few internet cafes in Cotonou, but there were none anywhere else. On my trip in 2004 Cotonou had dozens of internet cafes and Allada had three! It seems like most towns with electricity and phone service have at least one internet cafe, although connections are usually very slow and unreliable. I found that many cafés in Cotonou and Ouidah claimed to have internet, but it was not working when I asked to use a computer. Internet at these café's costs from 400 to 700 CFA (80 cents—$1.20) per hour depending on the time of day. Surprisingly, at some internet café's they hade quite modern computer equipment. When Beninese people began asking me for my e-mail address, and then giving me theirs, I realized just how widespread the internet had become in Benin.

By the time I went back to Benin in 2009, cell phones were everywhere, and many Beninese were using them. In Cotonou, Allada, and Ouidah, there were signs everywhere advertising boutiques that sold prepaid phone cards, as cell phones in Benin usually don't use monthly calling plans. Many of my friends who I thought would not be able to afford cell phones had them and used them. I saw DVD players and DVD's for sale in Cotonou, which I certainly had not seen when I lived there. I saw that Allada now has a photo-developing store that can develop pictures in 25 minutes. Western Union began a joint venture with the postal system, and you can now send and receive money from any post office in the country. I have sent Nestor money through Western Union many times and it has worked great. (See the preface for discussion about how technology has changed in Benin more recently and how it is changing current PCVs' experiences).

## Reverse Culture Shock Again:

After returning from my trip, I experienced many of the same feelings of culture shock that I did when I returned from Benin the first time. However, because I was only there two weeks this time, the feelings were not as strong. Having already experienced re-entry shock made it easier this time because I knew what to expect. Nonetheless, there were many things that bothered me when I returned from my two week trip. There were things that I missed about Benin, aspects of the U.S. that I appreciated more, as well as things about the U.S. that I couldn't help but criticize internally.

Again I missed being a celebrity and knowing so many people. It bothered me how little face to face social interaction one has with people in the U.S., and I thought back to how I would do almost nothing but talk to people all day in Benin. It bothered me how few people I know well in the town where I have lived in New York for several years, and how I only know a few neighbors well.

I also thought a lot about the huge discrepancy of wealth between the U.S. and Benin. A perfect example was the tomato can vs. the chrome air filter. I marveled at the ingenuity of the Beninese mechanics who keep their cars going with very few spare part and almost no money. On several occasions I saw them take a small tomato paste can, poke holes in it, and put it on top of the carburetor in place of an air filter! I don't know why they even bothered to do that, as it's useless to keep anything out of their engine except small stones. Considering all the dirt roads and dust, I can't believe their engines lasted more than a few thousand miles before needing to be rebuilt.

In contrast, shortly after returning to the U.S., Cara and I went to an antique car show. I was shocked at how meticulous, and perfect all the cars were. Every nut, bolt, screw and every square millimeter of the car was polished and waxed. They were so clean you could probably eat off them because the owner probably buffed it for an hour before the show. Most of those cars had air filter covers that were chrome, and polished so well you could easily mistake them for mirrors. The air filters alone probably cost what the average Beninese person earns in six months! I was sorry I didn't bring the picture of the tomato paste can air filter to show them. Something like this reminds me again that as a society we are spoiled, and our priorities are much different than those of most Beninese. They are mostly concerned with having enough food over the long dry season, or how to scrape up enough money to get a seriously sick child to a doctor. So indeed, I had a mild case of re-entry shock, even after a mere two-week trip to Benin.

## Closure:

Overall, I found going back was a great experience, and I recommend that everyone who visits or lives in Benin go back at some point. Returning allowed me to put closure on my Peace Corps service and reevaluate it from a new perspective. It allowed me to share an important part of my life with my wife Cara, who enjoyed it the first few days until culture shock set in for her. She then had some rough days due to the language barrier and many difficulties one encounters while staying in Benin. However, by the time we left, she was very sad to go. Today she still talks about our trip to Benin with enthusiasm and is intent on going back some day. It is nice to be able to talk to her about Benin, knowing that she understands what it's like there.

It was wonderful to see old friends and see familiar places. I was surprised at how many people remembered me and how happy everyone was to see me. It was reassuring to me that although I had been gone for seven years, I had not forgotten much Fon, or much about the culture. It was reassuring that I could get back into the groove of living there very quickly. It was very gratifying to hear people I worked with say that what I had done for them was useful, and that they were still appreciative of what I had done seven years later. Going back refreshed my impression of Benin, bringing both its positive and the negative aspects back into focus. I was reminded again how nice the people are, and how they make up for Benin's many inefficiencies and inconveniences. It was interesting to see how the country had changed over the years and how the children had grown up. As for me, I could see that some of the characteristics of my personality that I acquired in Benin had not changed since being away. For example, I still appreciate people more, I am still frugal, I hate waste, and I am more flexible, although I definitely still appreciate the efficiency and conveniences of living in U.S. Saying goodbye to Benin again was difficult, but it was not as difficult as the first time I left since I knew I will go back again someday. Most importantly from this trip I realized that Benin is in my blood, and it will always be a significant part of who I am no matter how far I am or how long I have been away.

# Appendix:

## Planning a Trip to Benin

Planning a trip to Benin turned out to be a daunting task compared to planning trips to more local and accessible locations that I've traveled to. In some ways I envy PCV's who served in nearby countries such as the Dominican Republic, as they can go back where they served very easily. It is much less expensive, there are much fewer formalities to deal with, and the flight is much shorter. The fact that Benin is so inaccessible makes it much more exotic. It is a place where you'll see almost no tourists unless you're at the most popular sights, and they are almost never crowded. Most of the tourists you see are visiting friends or relatives who are working in Benin.

## Airfare:

Our airfare was the most significant cost of the trip and it was pricey! We paid about $2,000 each to get there in 2004: $780 to get to Paris, and another $1200 to go from Paris to Cotonou (both round trip). Our trip was so expensive primarily because the U.S. dollar was very weak compared to the Euro, and because we went in July during peak flying season. Unfortunately flights are even more expensive today. In 2011, roundtrip prices in July have risen to roughly $3,000! Just a few years ago, Air Afrique, Sabena, and Air France had direct flights to Cotonou from Paris, Brussels, or other African Cities like Abidjan and Dakar. Today, Air Afrique and Sabena no longer exist, so Air France and Lufthansa are the only airlines with direct flights to Benin from Europe. They are charging exorbitant prices in my opinion.

Since we were paying a lot of money to get to Benin, and we had to pass through Paris, we made one vacation into two, and we spent two weeks in

France before going to Benin. The other less expensive possibility to get to Benin is to fly into Accra, Ghana on Air Ghana. It cost between $800 and $1000 for a direct flight from New York. The major disadvantage is that you will have to get visas for Ghana and Togo in addition to Benin. You will also have to suffer a full day bush taxi ride to get to Cotonou unless you break it up with a stop in Lomé, Togo.

## Vaccinations:

After we got our plane tickets, we had to get our vaccinations updated by a doctor who specialized in travel medicine. Usually only doctors who specialize in tropical medicine have vaccinations specific to tropical countries such as yellow fever and typhoid. It is better that you see a doctor who specializes in travel medicine because they keep up to date on what vaccinations are required for specific countries around the world. If you can't find a travel physician where you are, it's more likely you'll find one in a large city.

Some vaccinations like Yellow Fever, Hep A, and Hep B are good for 10 years or more, so I didn't need those shots. I needed only polio, meningitis, tetanus, and typhoid, which are only good for two years or so. We took an oral form of the typhoid vaccine, which my doctor said was more effective than the injectable version. Your doctor will also have to give you a prescription for your malaria prophylaxis.

When I asked my family doctor if most insurance companies pay for travel related vaccinations, he said "no." I called my insurance company, and they said the same thing. I was very worried that our vaccinations would cost us a fortune because Cara needed all the vaccinations. Luckily, my travel doctor informed me that insurance companies usually pay for all vaccinations except for those pertaining to diseases that do not exist in the U.S. The catch is that the doctor cannot say that the vaccinations are solely for travel purposes. He or she has to submit the claim without mentioning anything about needing them for a trip to Africa. I suggest checking whether your doctor is willing to do that before you go for an appointment, or you could end up paying a lot of money out of pocket. The vaccinations that you need for Benin that are not routinely given in the U.S. are Hep A, Hep B, polio, and meningitis but were covered by our insurance. We had to pay for yellow fever, typhoid, and the malaria prophylaxis vaccines, as those are never prescribed in the U.S., and our insurance would not cover them. Our doctor prescribed a relatively new anti-malarial drug called Malarone. It's supposed to have fewer side effects than Mefloquin, but the disadvantage is that you have to take it every day, so it's easier to forget than Mefloquin, which is taken only once a week. We took Malarone and we had no problems. We had to start taking it two days before we left and continued one week after we returned. Our doctor did not sell Malarone, or the oral typhoid vaccine, and our insurance didn't cover it. To save money we bought them online from a Canadian pharmacy through mail order.

## Visas:

Step three was getting our visas. I was appalled when I found out that the Beninese embassy increased its fee from $40 to $100 for a visa for Americans only, with no explanation. However, after doing some research, I found out that the American Embassy charges $100 for Beninese citizens to apply for a visa to enter the U.S. Not only is $100 a huge amount of money for most Beninese, but they are often denied a visa and their $100 is not refunded! I suspect the American Embassy increased its fee in order to lower the numbers of visa applicants. The Beninese Embassy was just catching up with us. After hearing this I was no longer so angry about the high visa fee we had to pay. The visa is good for 90 days, and is good for multiple entries.

In order to obtain a visa, you have to send your passport, a passport picture, and your WHO card to the Beninese embassy or consulate office. The WHO (or World Health Organization) card is a universal document that officially lists all of the vaccinations you have received, and it is signed and stamped by the medical practitioner who administered them. You have to send in your WHO card to the Beninese government because it requires visitors to have an updated yellow fever vaccination before entering the country. You also have to send an application, a money order, and a postage paid envelope so they can return your WHO card and passport with the VISA stamped in it. I got mine back a week after I sent it the first time I went back to Benin.

The second time I returned to Benin, I had a bad experience obtaining a visa. It was particularly unnerving mailing my passport when my travel date was only a month away, because if it happened to get lost in the mail, I would have had a big problem. To avoid worry I sent it overnight via United States Postal Service, and I included another postage paid overnight envelope for them to use to return it to me. Overnight packages are trackable, so they are almost impossible to lose. Unfortunately, someone at the Beninese consulate in New York City stole my eleven dollars of return postage, and resent my passport to me via untrackable first class mail! After two weeks I still had not received my passport, and I started to get worried. I looked up the tracking number, and I found that it was not entered as being shipped. The post office told me that it may not have been scanned when it was picked up. I called the Beninese consulate and they said they had mailed it a few days prior. I had a few sleepless nights thinking that it was lost, as I live only 30 miles from the consulate in New York City and it should have arrived one to two days later. I also thought a lot about what I would do if it was indeed lost in the mail. It wasn't until it arrived a few days later that I realized that they stole my postage, and mailed it first class instead of overnight! Nonetheless, I was very happy and relieved to have it in my hands.

### Travel and Medevac Insurance:

Another task we had to do before we left was to obtain travel and medevac insurance. Because we paid so much for the plane tickets, I wanted travel insurance that offered cancellation benefits. The insurance cost $200 for both of us for our one month trip. If we got sick, if a close relative died, if we lost our job, or if the state department issued a travel warning against traveling to Benin, our airfare would have been reimbursed. As a Peace Corps Volunteer, I was grateful for the medical care I had available to me. When you go back on your own and you get hurt, the embassy medical staff is not available to you. Healthcare in Benin is still very primitive, so it is important that you get medevac insurance. If you break a leg and you catch the next first class seat out to Paris, you will pay a lot but it won't bankrupt you. On the other hand, if you have a serious head injury, you will not want to have brain surgery in Benin. You will want a private plane to fly you to London or Paris with a doctor to accompany you, and it could cost well over $50,000. For that reason we got $100,000 per person medevac insurance, and a lot of peace of mind, which was included in the

$100 per person fee. The insurance also included other benefits such as reimbursement for emergency medical expenses, reimbursement for lost luggage, missed flight connections, and delays over six hours. Our total cost just to get to Benin was a whopping $2,520 per person: $2000 each for roundtrip airfare, $300 for vaccinations and Malarone, $120 each for the visa with postage and the photo, and $100 each for travel/medevac insurance. For more details related to planning a trip to Benin, see my travel page on my website, Fon is Fun (www.fon-is-fun.org).

As I mentioned before, one of the most popular means of transportation in Benin is the zemidjan or motorcycle taxi. Often it is the only way to get around unless you spend a lot of money to rent an automobile taxi for the entire day. In Cotonou you may have to wait a long time to find a regular taxi, so you will invariably end up taking a Zem at some point during your trip. Traffic in Cotonou is often chaotic so you will most definitely want to wear a helmet. The Peace Corps is so serious about this that they send volunteers home immediately if they are caught not wearing a helmet on a Zem. When you go to Benin, you should either bring a helmet with you, or arrange to borrow a helmet from Peace Corps. They often have extras, and if you know a volunteer, they may be able to get one for you.

Lastly, as I emphasized in the previous chapgter, getting money was a big problem for us on our trip. Make sure you bring American Express traveler's checks, a Visa Card, and American cash or Euro cash in case of emergencies. Luckily we had all three, which saved us some problems, despite the headaches we did endure.

# BIBLIOGRAPHY

*Bianco, David,* "Ahmed Mathieu Kérékou." *Answers.com* http://www. answers.com/topic/ahmed-mathieu-kerekou

"Benin" CIA Factbook, 2011, https://www.cia.gov/library/publications/ the-world-factbook/rankorder/2091rank.html

Briney, Amanda, "Environmental Determinism," About.com, http://geography.about.com/od/culturalgeography/a/envdeterminism. htm

Brown, Mike, "The Next Frontier," Parade, The Sunday Newspaper Magazine. July 17th, 2011.

Morrison, Jessica, "The Tuareg Rebellion in Niger and Mali," ZIF Berlin, September 2008, http://www.zif-berlin.org/fileadmin/uploads/analyse/ dokumente/veroeffentlichungen/Tuareg-PPT Mai. 09.pps

"Niger," CIA Factbook, 2011, https://www.cia.gov/library/publications/ the-world-factbook/rankorder/2091rank.html

"Stopping Guinea Worm Transmission: Benin." Carter Center.org. http:// www.cartercenter.org/health/guinea worm/benin.html